YOU, THE WARRIOR LEADER

BY BOBBY WELCH

PUBLISHED BY
BROADMAN & HOLMAN PUBLISHERS
NASHVILLE, TENNESSEE

YOU
THE WARRIOR
LEADER

APPLYING MILITARY STRATEGY
FOR VICTORIOUS SPIRITUAL WARFARE

BOBBY WELCH

BROADMAN
&HOLMAN
PUBLISHERS

NASHVILLE, TENNESSEE

Published by Broadman & Holman Publishers
Nashville, Tennessee

Dewey Decimal Classification: 235.4
Subject Heading: SPIRITUAL WARFARE

CONTENTS

III. ATTACK, ATTACK, ATTACK!
The Combat Infantryman Badge
The Warrior Leader's Mission ("Do")

IV. SOLDIERS NEVER DIE
The Purple Heart
The Warrior Leader's Maturity ("Die")

APPRECIATION

* TO OUR MILITARY FORCES

The following pages and I join multiplied millions of others around the world in expressing thanks and tribute to the United States of America's military forces that so courageously protect and defend us. The appearance in this book of the Medal of Honor, Silver Star, Combat Infantryman Badge, and Purple Heart—along with every other military expression and illustration used here—is to show these brave professional men and women the highest esteem and honor.

Further appreciation and acknowledgments are given for the public domain use of military manuals and publications, which are used throughout the book. Field Manual 22-100 is listed here because of its primary contribution. This acknowledgment prevents me from having to reference and footnote it continually throughout the book.

* TO OCF, CMF, AND CHAPLAINCY

Among dedicated soldiers there are no finer Christians than those found in the Officers' Christian Fellowship and the Christian Military Fellowship for noncommissioned officers and enlisted soldiers. These, along with other Christian soldiers, are united throughout the branches of the military for fellowship, outreach, equipping, and ministry. Their vision is to exercise biblical leadership that will be used of God to bring about a spiritually transformed military. To them and especially the Christian Chaplaincy Corps, which is unsurpassed throughout the world, I wish to dedicate this book.

* TO THE FAITH FORCE AND OTHERS

There is another band of brothers—another army that has risen in past years—to which I express my thanks. The FAITH Sunday School Strategy has been seized by hundreds of thousands of Christians all across America and in numerous other countries. FAITH has become a fellowship and a family, as well as a powerful force for intentional evangelism and discipleship.

To those FAITH churches, their pastors, and people and especially the originator churches, pastors, and people—I wholeheartedly dedicate this book. You, along with many other relentless hot-hearted soul winners, have shown us how to be Warrior Leaders for the twenty-first century.

* TO THE SOLDIERS OF CHRIST AND HIS CROSS

Most important of all, there is no way to properly give thanks, appreciation, tribute, and honor to all the millions of Christ's soldiers who have so gloriously given their lives for our Savior and His kingdom's cause.

Even the Book of Hebrews, chapter 11, is a mere sentence among the roll call roster of millions upon millions of unnamed and unknown soldiers who have given their all in faithful and victorious war fighting against Satan—the enemy of souls. These are the original Warrior Leaders and to them, above all others, this book is dedicated.

* TO OUR FAMILIES AND THEIR FUTURE

The purpose of this book is to mobilize the masses of Christians to be victorious spiritual-war fighters and keep souls out of hell and get them into heaven. Also my hope and prayer is that our families who come after us will find themselves in a country where Christianity flourishes and that our nation will remain "one nation under God."

To that end, for your families and for the four grandchildren of my wife Maudellen and me—Madison, Zachary, Peyton, and Bo— I earnestly dedicate this book and its purpose.

INTRODUCTION:
OUR CALL TO WAR

*T*he church is not a passive, milquetoast organization to be tossed about by the whims of a pagan world. But the church is a militant, aggressive army, marching against the enemy. . . . The battle is won. The victory is ours. . . . That is the church. Militant! Aggressive! Victorious!"[1]

The Bible often uses parables and metaphors to describe the Christian's earthly life.[2] But in this matter of warfare, the Bible does not use a parable or metaphor. It says what it means and means what it says. It speaks of the real thing. The Christian life is not compared to a war; it *is* a war! Therefore we will learn through this book how to be more effective and victorious combatants in our spiritual-war fighting by understanding the application of military strategy and leadership. This will be true for both individuals and groups. To serve as a constant and consistent reminder of the connection between physical and spiritual warfare, I will use military terms, language, and jargon throughout this book.

I have kept my old pocket-size combat leader's field guide all these years, and I wish you could see it. The pages are yellow, marked, and dog-eared. The paperback is torn, bent, and taped together. It is wrinkled and twisted from being repeatedly soaked in water and sweat. But that little book has been a lifesaver for me and others, time and time again. Its opening line reads, "This material is designed to assist leaders or prospective leaders of combat units which must fight."

The following pages are offered with that same desire—to assist those leaders or prospective spiritual leaders of combat units that must fight. Many find themselves in spiritual combat leadership positions, which they were not expecting, and they do not feel prepared. However, we are in a war and we must lead and fight or be defeated. Every Christian man, woman, girl, and boy can become a victorious, spiritual-war-fighting leader. We should! We must! We can!

General Edward C. Meyer, former U.S. Army chief of staff, said:

Just as the diamond requires three properties for its formation—carbon, heat and pressure—successful leaders require
interaction of three properties—character, knowledge, and
application. Like carbon to the diamond, character is the
basic quality of the leader. But as carbon alone does not create a diamond, neither can character alone create a leader.
The diamond needs heat. Man needs knowledge, study and
preparation. The third property, pressure—reacting in con-
junction with carbon and heat—forms the diamond. Similarly,
one's character, attended by knowledge, blooms through
application to produce a leader."[3]

Like the diamond, there are properties that are required to forge
you, me, and others into the Warrior Leaders whom God wants us to
become. In the following pages you will discover what those are and
how they are used to build the Warrior Leader.

The United States Army is the world's premiere land combat force.
All army leaders are aware that leadership training is conducted on a
threefold framework: Be, Know, Do.[4] Leadership training for the
Warrior Leader of Christ is based on a fourfold framework: Be, Know,
Do, Die.

| Motivation: | *Be* | Mind: | *Know* |
| Mission: | *Do* | Maturity: | *Die* |

At a number of places throughout these pages it will be easy and
helpful to associate the military framework with the Warrior Leader's
task, and I will attempt to make that connection each time it is of
benefit.

Some people might wonder if these associations of military fighting with spiritual-war fighting are appropriate. Scripture makes it clear
that the two are definitely connected. In fact, physical war is a result of
being defeated in spiritual war. James 4:1 underscores the fact that all
physical-war fighting is actually part of a spiritual war: "From whence
come wars and fightings among you? come they not hence, even of
your lust that war in your members?"

On September 2, 1945, at the surrender of Japan, General Douglas MacArthur proved he understood this fact. Here's what he said on that occasion:

> It is my earnest hope and indeed the hope of all mankind that from this solemn occasion a better world shall emerge out of the blood and carnage of the past—a world founded upon faith and understanding—a world dedicated to the dignity of man and the fulfillment of his most cherished wish for freedom, tolerance, and justice. . . . We have had our last chance. If we do not devise some greater and more equitable system, Armageddon will be at our door. The problem basically is theological, and involves a spiritual recrudescence and improvement of human character that will synchronize with our almost matchless advances in science, art, and literature and all material and cultural development in the past 2,000 years. It must be of the spirit if we are to save the flesh.[5]

Ours is most certainly a spiritual war, but it is fought by flesh-and-blood Warrior Leaders.

Tom Clancy, a best-selling author, asked about the Green Berets,[6] "How do they build these unique warriors?" Clancy discovered that unique warriors are not born or mass-produced: "Each one has to be hand-crafted, one at a time, by time-tested process."[7]

Recently in the middle of the night during a Special Forces, Green Beret leadership training exercise, a senior combat veteran instructor handed me a worn 3" x 5" note card from his personal papers that issued this challenge:

> ## LEADERSHIP
> *The so-called "born leader" is fiction invented by "born followers"! Leadership is not a gift at birth; it is an award for growing up to full moral stature. It is the only award a person must win every day. The prize is the respect of others earned by the disciplines that generate self-respect.*

Although the origin of the above quote is unknown, the truth of it is well known to the military and any other organization whose success depends on strong leaders. Further, it must be remembered that leaders can always be improved. This is biblical and foundational to discipleship and equipping the saints. To not understand this and to fail to invest heavily in equipping the people will destine a "could be/should be" leader to the frustration and defeat of mediocrity. The Warrior Leader is determined to rise above such and is worth whatever effort it takes to develop and train him to reach his highest potential.

In this book you are about to come face to face with disciplines that most people have never heard about—the disciplines that develop an ordinary soldier into a Warrior Leader.

I.

FIX BAYONETS

The Warrior Leader's Motivation ("Be")

THE MEDAL OF HONOR

This medal is presented for fearless gallantry and courage at the risk of one's own life, above and beyond the call of duty while in armed conflict against the enemy.

YOUR MEDAL OF HONOR

As the Warrior Leader, the highest honor you can be given is to hear the Lord, your Commander-in-Chief, declare of you, "Well done, good and faithful servant." That commendation is not only your Medal of Honor; it is to be your driving motivation which determines your character and who you are to *be*.

THE WARRIOR LEADER'S MOTIVATION ("BE")

This is what the Warrior Leader is to *be*, and it is what forms and defines his character.

THE ORDER TO "FIX BAYONETS"

ix bayonets!" That is the most chilling command a combat soldier can receive. Your heart seems to stop at the sound of the unmistakable metallic click of the bayonet locking into the muzzle end of your rifle barrel. This dagger-like steel blade is designed for stabbing and slashing the enemy in close combat. The following observation about combat comes from the book *Black Hawk Down:*

> Every battle is a drama played out apart from broader issues. Soldiers cannot concern themselves with forces that bring them to a fight, or its aftermath. They trust their leaders not to risk their lives for too little. Once the battle is joined, they fight to survive as much as to win, to kill before they are killed. The story of combat is timeless. It is about the same thing whether in Troy or Gettysburg, Normandy or the la-Drang. It is about soldiers, most of them young, trapped in a fight to the death. The extreme and terrible nature of war touches something essential about being human, and soldiers do not always like what they learn. For those who survive, the victors and the defeated, the battle lives on in their memories and nightmares and in the dull ache of old wounds. It survives as hundreds of searing private memories, memories of loss and triumph, shame and pride, struggles each veteran must re-fight every day of his life.[8]

This is an accurate account of real fighting in war, and nothing sears it into a soul more deeply than bayonet fighting. This spells the end of the line for someone's life! Such personal warring is known as "final-phase fighting." Final-phase fighting means there is nothing left for you to do but go face-to-face and hand-to-hand with your enemy with a fixed bayonet, which serves as an extended knife blade. It is your last resort and final means of defeating your would-be killer in an assault.

The latest weapons, improved equipment, modern technology, and the newest tactics are all useless now. The soldier is reduced to the most primitive and barbaric knife-fighting techniques. Full body mass, motion, physical fitness, and mental attitude to survive this savage fight are all that can help. Final-phase fighting must be executed aggressively; hesitation will result in your sudden and horrible death.

Yes, *fix bayonets!* means the end of the line for someone. Every soldier does two things when he is ordered to fix his bayonet. First he prays, and then he asks himself, "Why in the world am I doing this?"

The Warrior Leader understands what compels him to the forefront of the spiritual battle being fought in the twenty-first century. His motivation is to be a warrior of character. This establishes him as a good and faithful servant-soldier for his Commander and His kingdom's cause. He must be on the front line of spiritual-war fighting.

⚜ ⚜ ⚜

SCRATCHING, BITING, EAR-RIPPING-OFF WAR FIGHTING

"Greater love hath no man than this,
that a man lay down his life for his friends."
JOHN 15:13

During a raid in Mogadishu in October 1993, Master Sergeant Gary Gordon and Specialist First Class Randall Sughart, leader and member of a sniper team with Task Force Ranger in Somalia, were providing precision and suppressive fire from helicopters overhead to helicopter crash sites on the ground. They learned that no ground forces were available to rescue any of the downed air crews. They became aware that enemy soldiers were closing in on the site. Gordon and Sughart volunteered to go in to protect their critically wounded comrades. Their first request was turned down because of the danger of the situation. They asked a second time, and permission was denied. Only after their third request were they allowed to land to help the fallen soldiers.

Gordon and Sughart were inserted about one hundred meters south of the downed chopper. Armed only with their personal weapons, they fought their way to the downed flyers through the intense small arms fire and a maze of shanties and shacks as the enemy converged on the site. After they pulled the wounded from the wreckage, they established a perimeter, put themselves in the most dangerous position, and fought off a series of attacks. The two soldiers continued to protect their comrades until they ran out of ammunition and were killed. Their actions saved the life of an army pilot.

No one will ever know what was running through the minds of Gordon and Sughart as they left the safety of their helicopter to go to the aid of the downed air crew. The two soldiers knew no ground rescue force was available, and they certainly knew there was no going back. They may have suspected that things would turn out as they did. But they still did what they believed was essential and right for the cause of the mission. Soldiers of the highest honor are willing to die in order to accomplish their mission.

These two soldiers acted based on army values, which they had clearly made their own: loyalty to their fellow soldiers; the duty to stand by them, regardless of the circumstances; the courage to act, even in the face of danger; and the willingness to give their lives to save others. They were posthumously awarded the Medal of Honor.

When we talk about living up to something, we mean being worthy of it. We must make choices, decisions, and actions based on our core values. Nowhere in our values training does it become more important to emphasize the difference between "knowing" the values and "living" them than when we discuss the value of honor. Honor is a matter of carrying out, acting, and living the values of respect, duty, loyalty, service, integrity, and personal courage in everything we do. Noticing a situation that will require action to assist another involves respect, duty, and honor.

It was a matter of honor that soldiers, at great risk to themselves, distributed food in Somalia and kept the peace in Bosnia while managing to protect the communities. There are hundreds of examples of soldiers who have distinguished themselves with honorable and sacrificial actions.

The nation's highest award is the Medal of Honor. It goes to soldiers who make honor a matter of daily living—those who develop a habit of being honorable and who solidify that habit with the value choices they make.

The Christian's Commander-in-Chief, the Lord God Almighty, also awards His followers who distinguish themselves in order to glorify Him and to accomplish the Great Mission, our Great Commission. The Savior's highest award goes to His soldiers who end their earthly service by distinguishing themselves as servant soldiers in the likeness of their leader. At the awards ceremony, the Lord Jesus Himself will declare His highest award by saying, "Well done, good and faithful servant; you were faithful over a few things, I will make you ruler over many things. Enter into the joy of your lord" (Matt. 25:21 NKJV).

A SOBERING ACCUSATION

"Decisions we make change our lives and impact our histories," said James T. Draper, Jr., president of LifeWay Christian Resources of the Southern Baptist Convention. "Robert Frost captured the magnitude of our choices in his poem, 'The Road Less Traveled.' He chose one way and realized, 'knowing how way leads on to way, I doubt it if I should ever come back to the crossroads of the original choice.'" Draper goes on to say, "My question is: will Western Christianity, essentially Christians in the United States, shape history, or miss an opportunity by our level of commitment to Jesus Christ?"

David Watson, an Anglican priest, wrote two sentences that have haunted me for twenty-one years: "It is widely held that the battle of the century will be between Marxism, Islam, and Third World Christianity. Western Christianity is considered too weak and ineffective to contribute anything significant to this universal struggle."[9]

That's a sobering accusation I've been unable to discredit. I fear that the church in America has wandered down one path when we should have taken the other. The path exactly opposite our current direction is the path of a disciple.

I believe that Jesus is in search of disciples, but He is having a hard time finding many in the evangelical churches of America. We've turned our churches into comfortable country clubs for members when, in fact, the church is designed for those who are not members. People shop for churches like they shop for automobiles or groceries. People want something that fills their needs. We have missed the boat because we think Christianity is about us. It is not about us. It is about God and His kingdom on earth as it is in heaven. He has chosen Christians to play a significant role in showing the world what His kingdom looks like.

Western Christianity has retreated from the battle for the souls of people into the pursuit of personal comfort. *"It is widely held that the battle of the century will be between Marxism, Islam, and Third World Christianity. Western Christianity is considered too weak and ineffective to contribute anything significant to this universal struggle."* These words *still* haunt me. Do they haunt you? These words should drive the spiritual-war fighter of the twenty-first century forward with the determination to be faithful servant soldiers.

To become a victorious spiritual-war fighter in the days and years ahead, each Christian must *be* a soldier of character as the result of pursuing the believer's highest motivation. Receiving the Lord's highest award is not without risk, danger, and sometimes death. Christians of the current century are forced to face this reality because there is no doubt that *we are in a war.* This war is against our enemy Satan, and it is being fought for souls.

How intense, violent, and furious can face-to-face fighting in a battle against an enemy become? Army Master Sergeant Tony Pryor graphically answers that question: "Whatever digging, scratching, biting, hair pulling, ear-ripping-off—whatever you've got to do to get the job done—that's what you do." Pryor's blow-by-blow account of such a battle has been recorded for us to ponder.

For a few seconds on a frigid Afghan night, Army Master Sgt. Tony Pryor fought America's war on terror with only his bare hands.

One of 26 Special Forces soldiers raiding an al-Qaeda compound in mountains north of Kandahar last year, Pryor found himself alone in a room with three enemy fighters. He shot two of them dead in the first few seconds. The third he would have to fight—and kill—hand to hand, so close he could smell the man's sour breath.

War creates widows, orphans, disabled Purple Heart veterans—and soldiers such as Pryor, proficient in the dark art of killing. All of the nation's nearly 30,000 special operations soldiers, sailors and airmen are skilled at close combat. But Pryor was specially trained. He was one of more than 80 Army Special Forces troops who drilled relentlessly in close-quarter fighting—a combination of martial arts and street fighting—to prepare for a series of raids in Afghanistan.

"Whatever digging, scratching, biting, hair pulling, ear-ripping-off—whatever you've got to do to get the job done—that's what you do," Pryor says, explaining actions that night that won him the Silver Star for heroism and saved the lives of other team members in the compound. "Because, bottom line, I got a life at home. They (his comrades) got a life at home. And we're coming home."

That kind of close-up killing, though rare in Afghanistan, has become more common in the broader fighting in Iraq. In several fights, including the attack on the 507th Maintenance Company in which

PFC Jessica Lynch was captured, American soldiers have been required to fight and kill Iraqi insurgents face-to-face.

It is killing, not from the more sterile distance of a cruise missile or rocket launcher or tank turret, but so close to the enemy that the soldiers sometimes hear the rattle of a dying man's last breath.

"Not nice business," Pryor says.

The specific reason for the assault that night remains a secret. The soldiers say only that they were after intelligence on al-Qaeda and that the raid was a success. The fight for the compound lasted twenty minutes. But it was the most intense clash any of the Green Beret soldiers had ever experienced.

In a recent interview at 5th Special Forces group headquarters at Fort Campbell, Kentucky, Pryor describes fighting and dying that was nothing like the slick Hollywood portrayal in action films.

A forty-year-old father, Pryor asked this reporter to turn off the tape recorder before he recounted the most graphic details of his hand-to-hand struggle. "Would you want your kid to know that about you?" he asked this reporter.

This is his story.

EPITOME OF A WARRIOR

On January 22, 2002, as Pryor and the other Special Forces soldiers prepared to helicopter into the mountains north of Kandahar, they paused for a prayer at base camp. Sergeant First Class James Hogg asked God to fill their hearts with courage. Pryor wore a medallion of St. Michael, the patron saint of soldiers, duct-taped to his dog tag.

The men were "direct action" A-Team members, also known as assaulters, door-kickers, or "five-minute wonders." They are the first to enter buildings, and they use SWAT-team-like tactics. Close-in combat skills are crucial.

Pryor, the senior enlisted officer that night, is a bull of a man. Only five feet, eleven inches tall, he weighs 235 pounds. At the time, he could bench-press almost twice that. Team members call him a ferocious competitor, the epitome of a warrior.

"He makes you a better soldier just being around him," says Sergeant First Class Steve Ourada, a team member. "He built that assault force into what it was. We were on top of our game."

From aerial photos, their target looked like a U-shaped building within a walled compound. But on the ground that night, they found it was actually three buildings separated by covered breezeways.

The team charged into one breezeway and lobbed a flash-bang grenade, designed to disorient enemy troops, into the central courtyard. The area was filled with shiny new Toyota pickups and a trailer carrying a double-barreled anti-aircraft weapon. Al-Qaeda fighters fired back, and the bullets raised clouds of dust and rock from walls of the alleyway.

The troops had to push through the gunfire and cut left and right to clear the rooms. Pryor, whose giant head has earned him the nickname "Bucket," led the way. He stepped around a corner and shot a man coming at him with an AK-47 a few feet away.

Night-vision goggles cast everything in a greenish hue and gave the Special Forces troops an advantage. Al-Qaeda fighters, most of them bearded men wearing long *dishdashas,* or floor-length shirts, had only the starlight for illumination.

Even so, the al-Qaeda soldiers appeared well-trained and disciplined. Twenty-one of them would fight to the death.

CLOSE-QUARTERS BATTLE

As Pryor entered the first room to his right, he came face-to-face with a second fighter emerging from the doorway. Unable to see a weapon in that split second, Pryor slugged the man and knocked him down, blowing past him into the room. But the fighter got up with an AK-47. Another American soldier, still in the courtyard, fired a single round from his M-4 carbine and killed the man.

Other team members had gone on to clear the rest of the buildings, and Pryor faced the fighters in the room alone. If any got past him—or worse, killed Pryor—they could shoot other GIs in the back.

It was Pryor's fight now to win. As he entered the 25-by-25-foot room, his eyes swept from left to right. Bedrolls littered the floor, and two fighters at the rear of the room took aim through windows at other Americans entering the compound. Both swung toward Pryor with Kalashnikov weapons in their hands. Pryor fired, the rounds striking so dead-center that the men's beards fluttered.

As he reloaded, Pryor felt a foot brush up against his boot. At first, he thought it was another American. It wasn't. An al-Qaeda fighter struck Pryor hard from behind. The blow, possibly from a wooden board, dislocated Pryor's shoulder and broke his collarbone.

The fighter, bearded with his hair in a ponytail, jumped on Pryor's back and clawed at his face, tearing off his night-vision goggles.

"He started sticking his stinking little fingers into my eyeballs," Pryor remembers.

His left shoulder felt like it was on fire. He was winded and weary from fighting at an altitude of eight thousand feet. Without his night-vision goggles, everything was black.

The battle outside raged on, punctuated by AK-47 and rifle fire and the steady boom of a forty-millimeter grenade launcher from a Special Forces Humvee. The air reeked of gunpowder and the smell of blood. Inside that first room, the two fighters—one an al-Qaeda terrorist and the other an American soldier—were fighting to the death.

Pryor had only a single thought: *You're not going to kill me.*

"That's how I attack things," he said later.

With his one good arm, Pryor grabbed his enemy by the hair. But the man's weight, combined with the eighty pounds of Army gear that Pryor was wearing, caused the two to fall. Pryor landed on his left elbow, and the impact jammed his shoulder back into the socket. In spite of his injuries, Pryor broke the man's neck and finished him off with a nine-millimeter pistol.

Miraculously, not another American was injured in the fighting that night.

"There aren't any widows or orphans because of him," a fellow soldier says of Pryor.

"THEY ALL LOOKED LIKE THEY'D AGED ABOUT TEN YEARS"

In his fourteen years in the Special Forces, Pryor has killed before, but never in hand-to-hand fighting. That night he worried first, however, about his soldiers who had shot it out with al-Qaeda terrorists inside other rooms.

Around a wood fire at base camp several hours later, Pryor offered solace. "I went around and touched every one of those guys," he says. "They all looked like they'd aged about ten years."

For him, sleepless nights followed.

He dispelled the demons with cathartic heart-to-heart talks with his tent mate Hogg, replaying details of the fighting and dying. "A little bit of defragging of your hard drive," Pryor calls it.

Three articles of faith got him through, he says.

First was pride in a successful mission. Their training had paid off.

Second was seeing the war as righteous. "We didn't start it," Pryor says. "They started this fight. We're in the right."

Third was his children and the future. "I remember Pryor saying," his buddy Hogg recalls, "You know, it's an ugly business; it's a terrible thing for us to do. But hopefully our kids won't have to cope with it.'"

In addition to Pryor's Silver Star, seven Green Berets in the unit received Bronze Stars for valor in that fight. Pryor sent letters to their fathers. "I would like to thank you for raising a fine young man," he wrote. Many of the letters wound up framed and hung in living rooms.

Including Pryor, nineteen soldiers have received the nation's third-highest decoration for fighting in Afghanistan. One soldier received the second-highest award, the Distinguished Service Cross.

This year, eighty-six additional Silver Stars were awarded by the U.S. Army for fighting in Operation Iraqi Freedom. One Army engineer, Sergeant First Class Paul Ray Smith, made a last stand with a fifty-caliber machine gun against dozens of attacking Iraqi soldiers during fighting in April at the international airport outside Baghdad. He is being considered, posthumously, for the Medal of Honor, the military's highest decoration.

"NO IDEA OF THE TOLL IT TAKES"

"The thing that kind of boggles my mind," says James Bradley, author of *Flags of Our Fathers*—the story of the fighting and flag-raising on Iwo Jima during World War II—"is that (the nation is) sending out these guys who would rather be whittling and spending time with their kids. And they're sending them out to kill. They have no idea of the toll it takes on humans to do something like that."

Major General Geoff Lambert, a former Special Forces commander, agrees.

"In all wars, there are certain circumstances like this that happen to good men," Lambert says. "We try to train them the best we can to have them ready for these moments. We hope that they are few."

To cope with the fighting and killing brought on by war, Pryor says he lives two lives—one consumed with training for and fighting war, the other immersed in family.

"Two different lifestyles, two different on-and-off switches," he says. "If you're Johnny-on-the-spot, focused on destruction all the time, where do you have time for compassion in a relationship with your wife? We're dedicated to our job. But there has to be a time to turn that off."

It is not easy for him to explain how he flips this switch, though he says that one way is to simply not discuss work and war when he leaves the base.

It bothers him that civilians might see him and his troops as Rambo-like soldiers.

"People look at people who do this stuff and it's always, 'They're killers, and that's what they live for,' Pryor says. "That is so far from the reality."

Certainly, soldiers like Pryor don't shrink from the task of taking life if necessary. Pryor is a student of Sun Tzu's classic *The Art of War.* One of his favorite topics is the legend of the Mongoday, the elite warriors of Genghis Khan. Pryor and his troops train exhaustively in the art of spotting the enemy and withholding fire.

The night of the assault recounted above, members of a farming family, armed with a rifle in a building that was searched nearby, were left untouched because they offered no resistance. And at the height of the action, with adrenaline running high, an al-Qaeda fighter chose to surrender and was captured unharmed.

The control seems as ingrained as the reaction.

The other GIs tell of a firefight weeks earlier during which Pryor entered a room that was ablaze and spotted movement under a blanket. He didn't shoot. Pausing to search, he found a baby girl, pulled her free, and passed her to a team member.

Off the battlefield, Pryor has a gentle reputation. For security reasons, he declines to discuss his immediate family, but he says he forbids toy guns in his home.

Pryor's buddy remembers finding "Bucket" in his garage one day nursing a newborn raccoon with an eye dropper. "The wives just think he's a big old teddy bear," Hogg says.

"IT NEVER GOES AWAY"

Raised in the logging town of Toledo, Oregon, Pryor grew up admiring perseverance and hard work. A strong influence was his father, Jerry Pryor, who started out as a timber man and became the town's chief of police.

The first movie Pryor saw in a theater was *The Green Berets* starring John Wayne. He says the image of these soldiers stayed with him when he enlisted in the Army fresh out of high school in 1981.

Though he was earning straight A's by the end of high school, college held no appeal. Like many other young men from rural towns, he longed to get away. In 1988, he was accepted into the Green Berets, one of 79 chosen from 429 applicants.

He has been on missions in Haiti, Somalia, Kuwait, and other locations that remain classified. Early this year, he attended the Army's Sergeant Major Academy at Fort Bliss, Texas, on track to attain the highest enlisted rank.

He has also started working toward a business degree. After retiring from the Army, he hopes one day to manage a sawmill.

Pryor has had two reconstructive surgeries to repair damage from that battle in Afghanistan. He keeps a chunk of his collarbone, removed during an operation, in a jar as a souvenir. That, and the violent images is what he has left.

"It never goes away," Pryor says. "It just gets put further back in your mind."

His buddy Hogg, who helped Pryor exorcise his demons from that night, says this is the price that soldiers pay for their lethal work.

"I wouldn't wish it on anybody," Hogg says. "But there are a few of us who are called to it. So that's what we do. Maybe people should at least keep us in their prayers."[10]

Is spiritual-war fighting against Satan for souls just as brutal and vicious as what Sergeant Pryor and other military warriors experience? Absolutely!

Hogg and Pryor said there are some "who are called to it. So that's what we do." All Christians are "called" to wage war against Satan in order to rescue lost souls. Jesus understood that better than anyone. He knew that the clash of two strategies for souls—one from hell and one from heaven—is no game. This is an all-out war from beneath and above. People of all kinds—even good, sweet, kind people, even children and infants—will be marred and mauled, thrown into fires, turned inside out and upside down by demons. The devils will come and live in them if they can. The ungodly enemy is set on total destruction.

This sort of war fighting has no safe harbor. It will scream out in the marriage bed. It will abandon babies crying in the streets. Such warring wheel spikes will grind up old and young alike and then blow all their hopes and dreams and lives out like so many millions of burning wood chips. This close-combat confrontation will blow diseases into your body, tear out your lungs, brains, and heart. This is a real war that is ugly, bloody, mean, and gory. It is about murder, rape, and mayhem perpetrated upon men, women, boys, girls, and infants.

But that is not the worst. What is a million times worse than the unthinkable and unspeakable torment of the body is Satan's savaging of man's eternal soul. This hellion out of the pit has plans and preparations to cook every soul possible in fire and brimstone without any end—ever! Don't turn away; this is a real war going on all around us right now. This is not a game. This is a war, a real war, a spiritual war. It's our war—your war. All believers are "chosen soldiers" to serve as the war fighters whom our families and friends depend on to lead them safely and victoriously.

❧ ❧ ❧

WE CAN WIN THIS WAR

Victories in war are not won by parlor games in board rooms. They are not won by those who remain well-dressed and manicured. This is blood-and-guts, dirt-and-mud warfare—low-crawling from trench to trench, house-to-house, person-to-person—all for the purpose of rescuing the perishing and caring for the dying. If Christians refuse to equip and train to be victorious war fighters, their friends, family members, and the world around them will continue to be dragged off to hell by the enemy.

The Warrior Leader is never satisfied by the victory of those few who can make it into the church fortress. He is overwhelmed and obsessed with the eternal lostness, confusion, and defeat of the masses of millions upon millions who are already ensnared. They are out beyond the forts, walls, and perimeters—in the highways and byways of life.

This warrior's spirit is burning within him because Jesus is living within this soldier—the same Jesus who went about the cities and villages with the gospel. He saw the multitudes and was moved with

20

compassion for them because they were harassed and faint and were scattered abroad like sheep without a shepherd (Matt. 9:35–36).

This same Jesus indwells and fills this ordinary, rank-and-file soldier who rises to be the courageous and victorious Warrior Leader he was saved to be. He knows he was born and reborn to live in victory: "For whatsoever is born of God overcometh the world: and this is the victory that overcometh the world, even our faith" (1 John 5:4). The Warrior Leader knows that we are in a war.

Our war and our enemy are every bit as real as the war those brave soldiers—Gordon, Sughart, and Pryor and others—were fighting. But we are not winning our war. The most cursory review of the facts leaves no doubt that our circumstances in this country are desperate. This is how McDow and Reid summarize the situation in their book on the history of revivals: "Civilization, as we know it, totters on the brink of self destruction. One does not have to be a prophet to foresee the disintegration of our society, unless revival comes."[11]

Volumes of facts, statistics, and trends could be amassed to document such clear conclusions. The urgent question to every Christian is, What are you who are chosen to be a soldier going to do to change things and win this war?

There is only one way to win this war—and that is by God working through you, the Warrior Leader.

William Barclay, renowned Bible scholar, is emphatic that Christians must, according to Scripture, regard themselves as soldiers who are under orders with a definite commission and mission. Each Christian should understand himself not as a person in the world to do as he likes, but as a vital soldier in the Lord's army and a part of a combat task force that must follow the orders of his Commander.

I was on a plane between Salt Lake City and Kansas City when a handsome and winsome middle-aged man, a Mormon or disciple of Latter Day Saints—as they seem to prefer these days—sat down beside me. He was a successful businessman and a proud husband and father of two children. The two girls were ten and thirteen years old.

Of course I was very interested in the Mormon Church's approach to getting their youth out on mission for two years, full time, after high school. Those are the ones who travel in twos and are often identified by their bicycles. This man emphasized how high the expectations of Mormon parents and their churches are for everyone to go on mission. He went on to say, "I met my wife on mission." He said that when Mormons gather in any setting—business, social, or otherwise—they always discuss "where were you on mission?" It is like a fraternity and rite of passage.

Then he concluded that their family was already discussing with their two girls the expectations for them to go on mission. "Both girls at ten and thirteen are already saving toward the $7,000 each it will take for them to go out and spread the word as Latter Day Saints," he said. And of course he, his wife, and two daughters were not waiting until then to continue to spread "the gospel of Mormonism."

This is exactly why the Mormons and the Jehovah's Witnesses and Muslims are growing and the so-called "evangelical" Christian church of North America is in decline. They go out—and we stay inside!

Implosion is when, instead of exploding out and impacting our sur-roundings, there is "cave-in," where things just fall in on those inside until there is nothing left but a heap of the past that has no ability to impact anything.

That imploding is happening in a big way in churches everywhere. Members of these churches are wrapped up with one another in a holy hug singing "Kum Ba Ya" or the equivalent while the world is going to hell all around them. They have the false impression that they are actually growing and making an impact with this inward approach. Such an impact, if any, is always tiny as compared to what they could do if they equipped the people and took the gospel into the streets. But worse, while such groups have a few years of inward enjoyment, in time—just like all those of the past—they will fall victim to the enemy by implosion.

"It's all about Him and not about me." I hear that all the time. Every Christian has to agree with that statement. It is "all about Him

and not about me." If the church says and sings that phrase, it should prove its belief with its actions. We should trust God enough and be unselfish enough to get equipped and trained so we can go into the highways and byways to witness effectively for Christ. We need to stop and examine the message of the songs we sing, the sermons we hear, and the books we read. So often, these things are turning us inward.

It sometimes may seem as if "it's all about Him and not about us." But upon closer examination of our actions, the truth is otherwise. It appears to be all about getting more of Him into us with little or no thought about getting Him to those who are lost and without Christ. A preacher who preaches only about salvation is depriving his hearers of other essential and powerful parts of the gospel. His message is incomplete. On the other hand, if he preaches only on the so-called "deeper life" and leaves out the salvation message, his message is incomplete.

The same is true with music. For the music message of our church to be complete, it must have praise and adoration, but it must also have outreach and evangelism. Otherwise, the music deprives the hearers of the whole truth of the gospel message.

Inside the church we have preaching, music, Sunday School, training, and equipping. All of these elements must have evangelism in them, or the church starts down a slippery slope of implosion as it turns inward more than outward. This is without a doubt the greatest danger to the church, and it is already having devastating results across North America.

Explosion, on the other hand, is the greatest need in the church today. With explosion, it is impossible not to affect everyone around you. That has always been the intent of the gospel.

The Jesus church, the New Testament church, was one of explosion—turning the world upside down—for the sake of saving lost souls. Our churches today should be exactly the same. Explosion should happen in every church in North America, but it must happen immediately. Every hour that goes by without this nationwide explosion, we move closer to the point of no return. The Warrior Leader is committed to the multiplying of forces as the only way that such a do-or-die explosion of intentional evangelism will occur.

"Be one, win one, bring one" is a slogan and an idea that is outdated. It is too little, too late to turn back the tide. The Warrior Leader, doing force multiplying, is an absolute must for this time. There is a way to win this war, but it will never happen without you, the Warrior Leader.

❖ ❖ ❖

JESUS, THE WARRIOR LEADER

What motivates the spiritual-war fighter to be a "good faithful soldier" is the commission, command, and example of Jesus. God so loved the souls of this world that He sent His one and only Son off to war against Satan and hell for the sake of His kingdom. Jesus brought together a happy band of warriors, ordinary people who were used in an extraordinary way because of the grace of God. They multiplied their forces over and over while under attack from ambushes, clashes, and battles with the enemy. Satan's terrorists roamed the land like savage, demonic animals on seek-and-devour operations.

In the most courageous action ever demonstrated, Jesus stormed the stronghold of Satan, armed only with the truth, the love of God, and an overwhelming compassion for the souls of all mankind. He made His way to the hilltop where the climactic battle would take place.

During this assault all the firepower of hell and the demon world was concentrated on this one lone war fighter. In spite of devastating wounds to His head, back, side, feet, hands, and legs—and even though bleeding from His upper abdomen—He pressed on. With

24

almost no strength remaining, He called out instructions to His fellow soldiers. One of His last actions was to muster enough strength to rescue the soul of the person nearest to Him from the jaws of hell. Finally, completely and physically devastated from fatal wounds all over His body, He gasped and called out to everyone, "It is finished!" Then He died.

Three days later it was verified that this one solitary action had crushed the enemy forever from this point on. Although other battles would be fought, captives would be set free, souls would be saved, and victories would be declared. Jesus, the Warrior Leader, had demonstrated fearless leadership, tenacious devotion to His duty, and courageous actions in the face of what appeared to be overwhelming odds—all in order to accomplish His mission: "to seek and to save the lost." Before Jesus made His victorious assault on the enemy, He issued these commands to His growing army of servant soldiers—the Warrior Leaders:

- "The Son of man is come to seek and to save that which was lost" (Luke 19:10).
- "As my Father hath sent me, even so send I you" (John 20:21).
- "Follow me, and I will make you fishers of men" (Matt. 4:19).
- "Go ye into all the world, and preach the gospel to every creature" (Mark 16:15).

This Great Commission is unmistakably the Great Mission for every follower of Christ today. The driving motivation of the Warrior Leader is to stand before the Lord one day and hear Him say about us and our obedience to His commission, "Well done, thou good and faithful servant" (Matt. 25:21).

There He is—arriving at a commanding summit that provides a long strategic view across countless towns, people, and time. His silhouette is practically statuesque, except for the humanizing sweat soaking through His clothing. It makes an expanding contrast to the layers of sand and dust on the rough outer garments over His shoulders. His hand and arm are already outstretched toward the future. These are hands and arms that have been forged strong, thick, and wide by laboring with wood, struggling after wandering lost sheep, and in most recent years from driving Himself obsessively across this harsh land day and night to town after town and person after person.

His hands and forearms have scars, scrapes, and wounds received as a shepherd facing down bears and lions in close combat—pulling legs and ears from their teeth and claws while jabbing, stabbing, and flailing them with His rod in the other hand. Little wonder that those following after Him have no doubt that His feet, ankles, legs, and body are up to the challenge to move across such rough terrain to this hillside vantage point. They have marveled at His courage to always keep advancing toward His mission. Do we follow a centurion or Christ? We follow Christ—the Christ who presses His offensive against the enemy like a centurion. Yes, Christ, the Warrior Leader!

His face, like all else exposed—feet, legs, hands, and arms—has become burned, blistered, and bronzed by the sun, sand, and wind. His lips are chapped and his hair is tangled by these same elements that cause Him to squint his eyes as He peers into enemy territory. This sentinel of the summit is looking for people who are scattered, harassed, and tormented. He and those following Him are committed to the mission—to rescue those captives from their devouring enemy.

On His outstretched hand there is a dirty, swollen index finger with a fresh cut, from the nail past the first joint. This extended pointer jabs urgently into the future. At the same time His other hand is stretched in the opposite direction, back toward all of His followers—seen and unseen. Back a bit, never losing sight of Him, they are advancing, following Him faithfully. More and more people appear in a long, unbroken line, each demonstrating his unique spirit of servant leadership as exemplifed by the Warrior Leader, who is now just ahead of them. They also have the dust, sweat, and scars of conflict from along the highways, byways, and waterways where ordinary folks are hungering, thirsting, and searching.

In spite of all outward conditions and appearances, they are happy warriors, just like Him. Indeed, these followers are freed captives. He is overjoyed to have freed them. He has taught them and equipped them in the ways of victorious spiritual-war fighting. Theirs is no longer a spirit of fear. They are now more than conquerors themselves. He and His followers are now joined in an all-out, do-or-die assault into enemy territory to liberate other captives—some of whom are their own relatives and loved ones. They are happy, joy-filled warriors on the way to victory. This is only the beginning of His force-multiplying army.

His palm is open and facing upward on the hand that extends toward those who are following Him. His fingers are waving a signal to pick up the pace—to follow Him quickly. His face is now turned back toward them. There is that sparkle in His eyes and the trace of a smile as He starts to speak. The call back is loud, clear, commanding. He flashes them back to the day when they were recruited. It was the day He had that same sparkle, smile, and call—the day He personally chose and enlisted each of them as a soldier for His cause and kingdom.

Through the years—no matter how tired, hurt, frustrated, discouraged, hungry, misunderstood, unappreciated, or ready to quit they were—His voice has always filled them with renewed passion and compassion to get up again and go on . . . always advancing toward the Great Mission. The followers who are close at hand heard first His familiar, commanding call. It had become His army's battle cry, "Follow Me." All soldiers know Who this command had originated from and that they were only relays between one another, linking an eternal echo for the sake of souls to all soldiers who would come after them

This one leading is the good shepherd.

He is the suffering servant.

But make no mistake about it—this Jesus is supremely the Warrior Leader. Yes, the Warrior Leader on an intentional, aggressive offensive to accomplish the Great Commission—the Great Mission. He is calling each of us, "Follow Me, and I will make you fishers of men" (Matt. 4:19 NKJV).

You are chosen to be a soldier. Come now and be that—the Warrior Leader.

❖ ❖ ❖

YOU'RE A WARRIOR, NOT A CEO

I overheard an officer being asked by his commander, "What's wrong with those soldiers in that headquarters unit? They have stopped accomplishing their mission!"

The officer to whom he was speaking replied, "Sir, they have stopped being warriors and have become bureaucratic chief executive officers." That commander, who was also over the headquarters unit in question, acknowledged that he had come to that same conclusion and was about to "shake up that outfit so they could get on with accomplishing their mission, as soldiers should."

Of course, a warrior may sometimes function as a CEO (chief executive officer), and a CEO may be a warrior at heart. But every soldier knows that ultimately the mission will be accomplished not by the CEO but by the warriors.

What about the secular CEO model of leadership when it comes to the church accomplishing its mission? Jesus had a conflict with the secular model of leadership when it came to accomplishing His kingdom mission. There is no intent in these pages to struggle against the secular model of leadership adopted by the business world. Nor is there any effort here to have them change their leadership style.

The CEO approach has worked well for many corporations and businesses. Many fine Christian business people lead their businesses well with this approach. The church has actually benefited from a few of the time-proven practices adopted by the business world. These practices include team building, chain of command, leadership,

28

accountability, and such. But the CEO approach is not Christ's leadership model for the church.

Someone may ask, Why does the business world's approach seem to work well sometimes in the church? Many things are given a spiritual "makeover" in order to become more appealing and acceptable to the Christian church. Answers to this question include the following observations.

There is a great need for leadership help in the church. Not much else in the way of leadership for the church was offered or promoted until the secular model was popularized. Also, this approach is easily understood by most people because they make their living in the secular world. Business people inside and outside the church will usually commend the success achieved by secular approaches because they understand these methods. Laypersons will quickly recognize and find their place within this familiar secular system. Some results can be achieved by following this method, so church leaders often buy into the idea of the secular model for the church.

After listening to hundreds of frustrated and confused pastors, staff, and laypersons, I suspect that some of our church leadership struggles arise from the wrong choice of leadership models. Laypeople can detect the secular leadership model, once the pastor attempts to promote and follow it in the church. What is a fresh new idea to a church leader, with his limited business background, is the same old stuff to the typical church member, who senses where this leadership approach is headed.

While some laypeople will do their best to adjust to this leadership approach, others will reject it outright because they are subjected to this same approach every day in their jobs. They are aware it does not have a biblical basis nor is it the approach that Christ exemplified and exhorted His disciples to follow. They long to join with the servant soldier leader for the cause of Christ, but they have little interest in being just another "worker bee" for another executive at another business operation.

These good laypeople deserve better. The Warrior Leader should be committed to train, equip, and care for them as they become the victorious war-fighting leaders they long to be, for the sake of themselves, their friends, and their families.

Pastor and church staff person, if you have ever been caught in a secular leadership struggle, please be encouraged and don't lose heart. Don't throw in the towel but pick up the mantel of the Warrior Leader. The Warrior Leader approach to leadership does not guarantee that you will never have another problem, but it does assure you that you will face circumstances in the spirit and likeness of Christ's leadership.

Again, remember that I am not belittling the CEO style for secular business organizations. However, the fact that cannot be escaped is that Jesus calls and commands His followers not to take the secular approach to leadership, but to live and fight victoriously in accordance with His model of leadership. Frankly, it does not seem possible that secular leadership practices could ever lead the believer and the church to where Jesus, Peter, Paul, the apostles, and the early church went for the glory of God and the saving of souls.

Jesus explained His approach to leadership in Matthew 20:20–28, and He made clear that He wanted all His disciples to follow this same path. Jesus' aim was to cause His disciples then, as well as us now, to deal with the issue of what should motivate us. In verses 20–23 of Matthew 20, Jesus told the mother of Zebedee's children that the Father, not Himself, was the one who would give out the right-hand and left-hand seats in the coming kingdom. Then the remaining disciples became agitated because these two were attempting to jump ahead to what seemed to be the best position in the kingdom (v. 24).

Jesus called all His disciples together (v. 25) and gave them a verbal view of a secular ruler who had power over many people who were under Him. This was a picture, Jesus said, of how the world works—the secular leader at the top over a large pyramid of workers underneath his authority. But Jesus went on to make this observation: "It shall not be this way among you." Christ was saying that kingdom leadership is not to use the same approach as the secular world's leadership.

So how does the Lord expect us to carry out kingdom work? He left no doubt about it. He inverted the pyramid model (vv. 26–28). He turned it upside down and told His followers to get under the load as servants if they wanted to be used in His kingdom. The way up is down.

To end this discussion once and for all, Jesus illustrated the correct kingdom model and His choice for His disciples by telling us to follow His own leadership example: "Even as the Son of man came not to be ministered unto, but to minister, and to give his life a ransom for many" (v. 28).

There is a great difference between the ruler and the servant models of leadership. Remember, the aim of Jesus here was to cause us to deal with the issue of what should motivate us. The incentives for most secular leadership are pay, promotions, perks, pensions, and platinum parachutes. But this must not be the motivation of the Christian.

I couldn't resist picking up a new book on the topic of how to be a CEO. The very first chapter exhorted, "Take the job that pays the most." It continued with a similar focus on moving up the corporate ladder. At the heart and soul of what motivates the secular model leader is almost always *self*. Some people might be motivated differently, but most are not.

The Warrior Leader life is not the "self life" but the "servant soldier life" that is characterized by surrender, self-denial, suffering, sacrifice, and even death for the cause of the kingdom of Christ. Not only are we to live our lives this way, but it is Christ's will that we end our lives with such a crowning epitaph as, "Well done, thou good and faithful servant" (Matt. 25:21).

Here then is the motivation for the Warrior Leader. The ultimate issue and highest award is to hear his Lord say, "Well done, good and faithful servant." Any believer can have that award—and the Warrior Leader's life is the way to do so.

While Jesus has a conflict with the secular model of leadership, He seems to commend the Warrior Leader approach. This should come as no surprise, considering how mightily He used those people in the Bible whom He blessed with a warrior spirit.

Jesus commends the servant life that is yielded completely to higher authority and that follows orders and commands, even to the extent of denying self and experiencing suffering, sacrifice, and death. This approach is the essential foundation not only for the Jesus style but also for the victorious spiritual-war fighter's life. This must be why Jesus and a Roman military officer, a centurion, made such a favorable connection: "When Jesus heard these things, he marvelled at him, and turned him about, and said unto the people that followed him, I say unto you, I have not found so great faith, no, not in Israel" (Luke 7:9).

Instantly Jesus' mind, heart, and spirit resonated with the confession of this centurion servant soldier:

> Then Jesus went with them. And when He was already not
> far from the house, the centurion sent friends to Him, saying
> to Him, "Lord, do not trouble Yourself, for I am not worthy
> that You should enter under my roof. Therefore I did not even
> think myself worthy to come to You. But say the word, and
> my servant will be healed. For I also am a man placed under
> authority, having soldiers under me. And I say to one, 'Go,'
> and he goes; and to another, 'Come,' and he comes; and to
> my servant, 'Do this,' and he does it" (Luke 7:6–8 NKJV).

Jesus as the Warrior Leader knew He was the one under authority who took orders from His Commander-in-Chief so He could engage in victorious war fighting against the enemy, Satan. Centurions were warriors, and warriors were servants. These warrior servants expressed unwavering confidence and faith in battle against the enemy to accomplish the mission that had been given to them by their superiors.

Christ was thrilled at this Warrior Leader centurion example, so much so that He "marveled" at him. Then Jesus actually turned His military example around to face the crowd so He could press His point more forcefully. His point was that this servant soldier had characteristics that He could commend to His disciples.

The crowd had before them a heavenly and an earthly example. Both Jesus and the centurion were the opposite of a comfortable, passive, self-centered life. Before them was the Warrior Leader with a service-motivated life committed to accomplishing the mission that had been assigned by His Commander-in-Chief. This is exactly what the twenty-first-century leadership model must be for the sake of God's kingdom and the saving of souls.

A Christian is to be a Warrior Leader—not a CEO.

THE HAPPY WARRIOR

Jesus' life and death reminds us that there is a price to be paid for living the Christian life as Warrior Leaders. However, in the midst of hardships, disappointments, and troubles, you always know that Jesus is not only the Warrior Leader but also He is a *happy warrior* as well. Christ had so many reasons to be the happy warrior and so do we.

When I read Guy H. King's book, *Brought In,*[12] I started thinking about some of the things on the following list. King did not mention all of these; his emphasis was otherwise. Nor did he term them as I have, but he started me thinking. May these joyous things remind everyone who is a Warrior Leader that he should be like Jesus, the happy warrior.

1. *The Recruitment.* "Chosen . . . to be a soldier" (2 Tim. 2:4). We as Warrior Leaders are to be happy warriors because the Lord has hand-picked us to serve in His army. "Uncle Sam" points his finger

toward the world from a post office poster and declares, "I want you!" God Almighty not only wanted you and me; He sent His Son to get us. When we said *yes* to His call, we joined His army. Once in His army, as Hebrews 6:1 says, "Let us go on." It has been said that "we recruit what we are." The Lord recruits those whom He desires to inhabit and develop as Warrior Leaders. If you are saved, you're it—and that should make you a happy warrior.

2. *The Commander.* His name is Jesus. "We are in him" (1 John 5:20), and He is "the captain of [our] salvation" (Heb. 2:10). As the prophet Isaiah said, "Behold, I have given him for . . . a leader and commander to the people" (Isa. 55:4). The Savior is not only our supreme Commander, but He is also our supreme example of the Warrior Leader. The Warrior Leader is the happy warrior because He is our Commander-in-Chief. We will obey His orders, carry out His mission, and rejoice at His commendation. He has saved us, and we happily serve Him.

What a mixed crowd it was that made up David's army: "Every one that was in distress, and every one that was in debt, and every one that was discontented, gathered themselves unto him; and he became a captain over them" (1 Sam. 22:2). What an army of misfits we are, but by the grace of God and the command of Christ, we are happy warriors in His army.

3. *The Mission.* The Warrior Leader is a happy warrior because his mission is clearly defined. It is the Great Commission: "Go ye therefore, and teach all nations, baptizing them in the name of the Father, and of the Son, and of the Holy Ghost: Teaching them to observe all things whatsoever I have commanded you: and, lo, I am with you alway, even unto the end of the world" (Matt. 28:19–20). That is the mission of the Warrior Leader. Everything else is just an intermediate objective that must contribute to accomplishing the Great Mission. This Great Mission makes us happy warriors because we are prepared and willing to "die on this hill" and will be happy warriors if allowed to do just that.

4. *The Target.* God has clearly "painted the target." In military terms, He has unmistakably marked our enemy. It is Satan. The Warrior Leader is a happy warrior because he understands no human being or group is the true enemy but rather the devil over whom the victory has already been won. As Isaac Watts expressed it in one of his hymns, it is "His powerful blood." Jesus' blood has already won the ultimate victory over Satan and sin.

It is a glorious thought that one day Satan will be dragged off and thrown into his own pit of hell. That will be a happy day for the Warrior Leader.

5. *The Uniform.* The uniform tells the world who we fight for. "Now are we the sons of God" (1 John 3:2). Let that insignia be on our banner, body, and uniform. Jesus has made clear that He fully expects us to not "be ashamed of [Him] . . . in this adulterous and sinful generation" (Mark 8:38). Make much of Jesus! "Neither is there salvation in any other: for there is none other name under heaven given among men, whereby we must be saved" (Acts 4:12).

Jesus' name is the master key to the powerhouse of God for victorious war fighting. "Whatsoever ye shall ask in my name, that will I do, that the Father may be glorified in the Son" (John 14:13). Christ reminds us of how we got into His army and what uniform we should proudly wear: "Ye have not chosen me, but I have chosen you, and ordained you, that ye should go and bring forth fruit, and that your fruit should remain: that whatsoever ye shall ask of the Father in my name, he may give it you" (John 15:16). Always be grateful and proud to wear the uniform and name of Christ's cause, country, and kingdom.

6. *The Chow.* It is said that "an army goes forward on its stomach." Military food has always been the recipient of the worst criticism of soldiers—combat chow even more so. (Usually the criticism is unwarranted, given the situations.) However, the Warrior Leader will be a happy warrior when it comes to food provisions. The Commander always provides abundantly for His troops. Sometimes it comes by air (in the beak of birds). Sometimes it comes in the cover of darkness, only to be found in the morning (as with manna), and hundreds of

other ways. But He always provides the food, including the banquet and feast arrangements. "He brought me to the banqueting house, and his banner over me was love" (Song 2:4).

7. *The Training.* This is the part that so many pastors, parents, church leaders, and leaders in the home don't get. They believe that all the training anyone needs is a few hours each week. No sales force, no sports team, and certainly no army could survive on that strategy. No, it takes more. Dedicated, regimented class and on-the-job training time must be given to the troops. If this training doesn't happen in classes at church, they and their families will get "knocked off," and the church will lose impact and victory. The Warrior Leader is a happy warrior because he understands and is committed to the biblical model of training. "Thou therefore, my son, be strong in the grace that is in Christ Jesus. And the things that thou hast heard of me among many witnesses, the same commit thou to faithful men, who shall be able to teach others also" (2 Tim. 2:12).

The model of training Jesus gave us was *follow, learn, teach.* This was to be an unending cycle with Christ's unmistakable subject matter for training—soul-winning evangelism. He actually took His followers with Him so they could be trained in how to follow, learn, and teach. They did it, as Jesus told them to do it, "as you go" or "on the go" (Matt. 28:19). An army that will not train in this manner is destined to lose the battle.

8. *The Manual.* In such a long, furious, deadly war lasting over thousands of years, what will sustain our training, supply our tactics, and keep adding a surge to our morale throughout this vast and scattered army? The Warrior Leader is a happy warrior because he has in his possession the training manual that is the Book of all books. It is timeless and infallible with guaranteed victory for those who will follow it.

The Bible, the Warrior Leader's training manual, was compiled by God: "Holy men of God spake as they were moved by the Holy Ghost" (2 Pet. 1:21). "All scripture is given by inspiration of God, and is profitable for doctrine, for reproof, for correction, for instruction in righteousness" (2 Tim. 3:16). The more the Warrior Leader knows about this manual, the more confidence and courage he has to train others. Their training will get them ready for victorious war fighting against Satan.

9. *The MOS (Military Occupation Specialty).* The Warrior Leader is a happy warrior about his military occupation specialty. Every soldier has a specialty in which he is equipped and trained to excel. The entire combat team and unit are assembled around this fact. Every one must not do the same thing, and each one must perform his assigned responsibility. Otherwise the enemy will overrun your position, killing or capturing everyone. It is a team responsibility and effort.

First Corinthians 12:8–10, 28–30 and Romans 12:6–8 declare the spiritual gifts that the Commander-in-Chief has placed in individual soldiers. Everyone has at least one gift, and some people have several. The military would call those with more than one specialty "cross-trained." No matter how few or how many gifts we have, the Commander knows exactly where to assign us. With Him the people with few gifts are no less than those with many gifts.

Although most Christians have heard about the promotion of the "spiritual gift of evangelism," that term cannot be found anywhere in the Bible. What Ephesians 4:11 refers to are leadership positions and offices of the church for the purpose of training members for service and ministry. There is the office in the church of *evangelist* but there is no spiritual gift of *evangelism*. Evangelism is every believer's responsibility and privilege. All our spiritual gifts should enable us to do evangelism more effectively.

10. *The Security.* The Warrior Leader is a happy warrior because no one has ever been more secure in any type of personal combat than believers are in the spiritual war for Christ. "They shall never perish, neither shall any man pluck them out of my hand" (John 10:28). See where your security lies—in His hands. Consider how long your security lasts—forever. The Happy Warrior can rejoice with the psalmist's sense of security by saying, "My times are in thy hand" (Ps. 31:15).

Fight on, Warrior Leader, because you are invincible in the hands and under the command of our Lord.

11. *The Weapons.* "Put on the whole armour of God, that ye may be able to stand against the wiles of the devil" (Eph. 6:11). The Warrior Leader is a happy warrior because he is equipped with the necessary "body armor" not only to defend himself in a fight but to destroy his spiritual enemy.

No wonder the Warrior Leader has confidence that even the "gates of hell" (Matt. 16:18) will not be able to stand against such firepower and fighting. All captives could be set free if only Christians would become warriors and pick up their weapons and go to war for souls.

12. *The Fight Song.* Two Warrior Leaders had put in many days battling in an urban warfare setting, going from a riverside, to house to house, and then into the open marketplace. They stayed on the Great Mission and showed many people "the way of salvation" (Acts 16:17). Then they were captured. The local crowd tore off their clothes, and they were beaten "with many stripes." Bleeding and battered, they were thrown into a filthy prison cell. At midnight Paul and Silas began to sing. These Warrior Leaders in that hard time had not lost their fight. Years before, the psalmist had declared, "He hath put a new song in my mouth" (Ps. 40:3). I don't know if that had been their "fight song" before that glorious night, but I believe it probably moved to the top of the fight song charts the next day. Maybe what started them singing was quoting Isaiah 40:9: "Lift up thy voice with strength; lift it up, be not afraid."

One thing I do know: As soon as they started singing, the Lord started sending. The tide of the battle started to turn. Earthquakes shook the prison, the doors flew open, their hands and ankles were loosened, the keeper and his family rolled out of bed preparing to commit suicide. Then God poured out grace on the place, and the jailer and his entire family were saved and baptized. That's some fight song! Sing it again! Sing it again and again! The Warrior Leader is a happy warrior with a song like that.

13. ***The Supplies.*** In World War II General George Patton was always calling for more gasoline so his tanks could stay on the offensive. He once said, "If Ike . . . gives me the supplies, I'll go through the Siegfried Line!"[13]

The Warrior Leader will never have General Patton's problem and will be a Happy Warrior because the day he was recruited into the Lord's army he was given a promise. His lifetime enlistment bonus was, "God shall supply all your need according to his riches in glory by Christ Jesus" (Phil. 4:19). If you go to war with Jesus, you'll always enjoy His adequate supplies.

14. ***The Axis of Advance.*** The term "axis of advance" is how the military generally describes the direction the troops are moving forward. The Warrior Leader is a happy warrior to be headed in the way he is going. Early in Christianity, believers became known as those of "the way" (see Acts 24:14). That descriptive phrase is used in many places in the New Testament. The Warrior Leader is on the way that runs from here to hereafter, and he is obsessed with getting other people started on the way. They are not yet on the way because Christ is not yet their Savior—and He is "the way."

The Warrior Leader is always going in the correct direction if he is headed toward lost souls with the gospel. It is impossible to take the gospel to the wrong person.

15. ***The Reinforcements.*** Somewhere, sometime, every person needs some help. The Warrior Leader is a happy warrior because he knows that reinforcements are always available. The Commander has gone on record as promising, "I will never leave you nor forsake you" (Heb. 13:5 NKJV). Over and over the Warrior Leader has found that promise to be true. "We perish" (Mark 4:38) was the desperate cry of Jesus' disciples in their panic-stricken fear on the sea. "Your vessel may flounder but it will never founder"[14] because our Commander has already ordered, "They shall never perish" (John 10:28).

Elisha's servant saw the entire city of Dothan surrounded, and he exclaimed, "How shall we do?" (2 Kings 6:15). Elisha prayed, and the

Lord opened the servant's eyes to see the Lord sending a mountain full of horses and chariots of fire as reinforcements to defeat the enemy.

Reinforcements from the Lord also showed up when the three young Hebrew men were thrown into the fiery furnace (Dan. 18:12–15). A fourth person came to their aid inside the fire and brought them out untouched. Two depressed and dejected villagers going to Emmaus after the resurrection were blessed and encouraged by the resurrected Christ. They ran seven miles back to Jerusalem, filled with joy and optimism (Luke 24:13–35). Yes, the Warrior Leader can depend on help from heaven.

16. *The Victory.* The Warrior Leader is a happy warrior because of the great joy in knowing that he is on the winning side. The Warrior Leader may see some battles and efforts lost, but his happiness is in the fact that the war is already won.

17. *The Return Home.* The Warrior Leader is a happy warrior because he has a prophecy of his conquering Commander's return: "Behold, the Lord cometh with ten thousands of his saints" (Jude 14). Further, he has a preview of His return in Acts 1:11: "This same Jesus" will come again "in like manner." "Watch therefore . . . for in such an hour as ye think not the Son of man cometh" (Matt. 24:42, 44).

The Happy Warrior Leader continues to drive on relentlessly, accomplishing the Great Mission so he will be found faithful on his Lord's return. Warrior Leader, get happy!

18. *The Retirement.* There is a day coming when all spiritual-war fighters will study war no more and say farewell to their arms. The Warrior Leader who is found on that day to be a good and faithful servant will have a retirement benefits package out of this world: God has "raised us up together, and made us sit together in heavenly places in Christ Jesus" (Eph. 2:6). It is the Lord "who hath blessed us with all spiritual blessings in heavenly places in Christ" (Eph. 1:3).

Never believe that the Warrior Leader's life produces a person who is hard, rough, ill-tempered, stern, and unhappy. Nothing could be further from the truth. No one has more to be happy about than the Warrior Leader because he is on his way to accomplishing the Great

Mission and then he will be heading home to heaven to enter into the joy of the Lord.

Jesus said to His followers, "These things have I spoken unto you, that my joy might remain in you, and that your joy might be full" (John 15:11).

✠ ✠ ✠

YOU MUST GET TOUGH

*T*he drive deep down at the bottom of your heart and soul is your personal motivation. Most Christians agree that their deep and personal motivation is to hear our Lord say to them one day, "Well done, good and faithful servant" (Matt. 25:23). Every Christian should hear Christ say these words because it is within our reach. Each of us by the grace of God can be "good," we can be "faithful," and we can be His "servant."

Is that not a glorious thought? Our dear Lord has made His highest commendation available to every believer. No matter what insignificant place you may have arrived at in your Christian journey, you can receive the Warrior Leader's "Medal of Honor"—our Lord's "well done, good and faithful servant." Doesn't that touch your spirit and put fire in your heart? Doesn't that motivate you? This is what should motivate the servant soldier to be a Warrior Leader and receive his Lord's Medal of Honor.

"Finally, brethren, whatsoever things are true, whatsoever things are honest, whatsoever things are just, whatsoever things are pure, whatsoever things are lovely, whatsoever things are of good report; if there be any virtue, and if there be any praise, think on these things" (Phil. 4:8).

Stephen Ambrose observed about the Civil War, "At the pivotal point in the war it was always the character of individuals that made the difference."[15]

Some people believe that leaders are born. However, most leaders do not believe this because they know what it takes to become a leader, especially a spiritual Warrior Leader. Of course, some persons have natural skills and God-given gifts that help them, but all true leaders realize it takes effort to maintain longevity of leadership. Nothing is more important than Christ-centered character that is at the bottom of a servant's being "good."

A spiritual Warrior Leader must have good character. Developing character is a lifelong process. The Warrior Leader guards the development of character in himself and is committed to developing it in those whom he leads. Character helps us decide what is right and motivates us to do the right thing. The Warrior Leader always seeks to do what is right. Even when faced with the toughest choices, he is determined to inspire others to do the same.

Have you ever wondered what you would do if you found a million dollars on the side of the road and no other human being knew about it but you? There is no doubt about what the Warrior Leader's character would lead him to do.

An acquaintance of mine was leaving his church late one night when he found a wallet with some cash. There was no one else around. He found a phone, and with that wad of cash staring him in the eye, he called the phone number in the wallet. He discovered that the billfold had not been accidentally dropped but had been placed there by a local television station that was watching it with a hidden camera. The station had done this same thing at a number of locations around the city.

There was never a doubt about what my friend should do because he is a person of character. But don't you know he was glad he called that number! Of course, every Christian is aware that we live our lives and make every decision before the eyes of our Lord. This man not only had the character to do the right thing, but when he told about this, he taught and reinforced character in me and many others who heard the story.

Leaders are to live by the highest biblical standards. They should also spread character to others, especially their team, their people, their army of force multipliers who will in turn do the same with those whom they lead.

ETHICS

While they acknowledge it intellectually, too many leaders do not understand the importance of ethics in victorious spiritual-war fighting. The Warrior Leader radiates a certainty that motivates those whom he leads to conquer fear, withstand hardships, and make extreme sacrifices. Such moral toughness that is required to win is connected to the ethics and values that leaders exemplify.

Margaret Chase Smith said, "Just as fire tempers iron into fine steel, so does adversity temper one's character into firmness, tolerance, and determination."[16]

We are not ethical just to be nice Christian guys and gals, but to be "good" servant soldiers who are tough enough to win spiritual wars and press on in our Great Mission objective. The results of ethical moral toughness are spiritual strength, confidence, boldness, decisiveness, and initiative. When the Warrior Leader exhibits such moral toughness, it becomes another positive reference point for those who follow his leadership.

Several church leaders were reminiscing about the strengths they saw in their pastor. One paid the pastor a great compliment by confessing, "When I am faced with spiritual decisions, I always ask myself, 'What would Jesus do?' But I also ask, 'What would my pastor do?'"

That church leader was not minimizing our Lord's impact on his decision making. He was acknowledging that the Lord had provided for him and their congregation a powerful and positive reference point through the leadership of their pastor. The deacon was reflecting moral toughness through Christ as reinforced by a pastor as the Warrior

Leader. This happens a million times over as teens depend on the moral toughness of their parents, teachers, peers, and others who reflect moral toughness as Warrior Leaders.

The Warrior Leader is helpless to sustain spiritual victories long enough to accomplish the Great Mission unless he has moral toughness in the face of combat against Satan and hell on a daily basis.

Please read that statement above again, because our mission is not accomplished in a few years, in several battles, or in a handful of victories. It takes sustained offensive war fighting over a lifetime. This requires the moral toughness of ethical character for the long haul.

The Warrior Leader has at least three obligations when it comes to spiritual leadership in discharging ethical responsibility.

1. Live as an example worthy of emulation.
2. Encourage ethical development in others.
3. Maintain an ethical environment.

Ethical example, encouragement, and environment give the visibility that is a powerful weapon in victorious war fighting. It is one of the distinctives of the Warrior Leader as a conquering champion over the enemy. The Warrior Leader will want those whom he leads to learn and practice moral toughness in this way and pass it on to the force multipliers whom they are developing.

ETHICAL EXAMPLE

The ethical example of the leader will be shown by his actions. This is why the Warrior Leader must take seriously the Bible's instructions to "abstain from all appearance of evil" (1 Thess. 5:22).

As an illustration, a man or woman should not have a meal alone with someone of the opposite sex, other than his or her mate. Someone will protest that this is prudish and old-fashioned in our modern society. However, it is a bad practice that will be used by the enemy to undermine your positive role model as an ethical example.

ETHICAL ENCOURAGEMENT

At every opportunity the spiritual leader—whether a father, mother, pastor, FAITH team leader, Sunday School teacher, or deacon—must urge everyone to maintain the ethical high ground, at all costs. The Warrior Leader should speak, teach, train, coach, and encourage at all times and places with ethical sensitivity. This is a condition for clean, clear, ethical reasoning and decision making, which is then translated into victorious spiritual-war fighting by way of moral toughness. The Warrior Leader who does this will not get undercut by the enemy, and those whom he leads will continue to rally and follow his example.

ETHICAL ENVIRONMENT

Ethics is about the climate of the workplace and the ministry place as well as how we live. It is important for the Warrior Leader to be aware that most difficulties and problems about trust and confidence are the results of a poor ethical environment. If the environment is characterized by incompetence, policy conflict, jealousy, threats, fear, and unclear signals, moral toughness will erode and problems will come up. This is why unethical behavior cannot be tolerated; it undermines the character and motivation of a good and faithful servant soldier.

To create and maintain a high ethical environment, the Warrior Leader must reach out to the organization—trust it, stand up for it, listen to it, and support it. The Warrior Leader must even be willing to listen to constructive criticism and to tolerate honest mistakes by sincere people who are in the learning process.

Such an environment validates the Warrior Leader's character and assures those who are being led that they are also persons of character. This approach to ethics builds morale, trust, confidence, and moral toughness for mission accomplishment. This inward character of the Warrior Leader's spiritual life can never be separated from his courage to continue in daily war fighting.

Consider this comment about Corporal Alvin York, the World War I hero: "8 October, 1918—Argonne H. Forest, France. It was 0610 and Corporal Alvin York wondered why there was no artillery attack ahead of his unit's impending assault. Nevertheless, the 328th Infantry Regiment 'went over the top' of their entrenchments at the designated time to attack German positions and seize the Decauville Railroad."

Major Douglas V. Mastriano, U.S. Army, gives this account and commentary on Alvin York that appeared in *COMMAND* Magazine of Officers Christian Fellowship. This legendary example should drive into the heart of the Warrior Leader how connected his spiritual life is to his physical courage on the battlefield.

Taking the railroad was vital since it would sever lateral support and communications behind the German lines and open the way for a broader Allied attack. The assault took the 328th up a funnel-shaped valley, which became narrower as they advanced. Ahead and on each side were steep ridges, occupied by German machine gun emplacements. About half-way up the valley, the 328th encountered intense German machine gun fire from the left and right flanks. Soon, heavy artillery poured in upon the beleaguered regiment, compelling the American attack to waver and stall.

The blistering German fire took a heavy toll, with survivors seeking cover wherever they could find it. The German guns had to be silenced. Sergeant Bernard Early was ordered to take three squads of men and attack the machine guns. They successfully worked their way behind the German positions and overran the headquarters of a German machine gun battalion, capturing three officers, and 15 enlisted.[17]

Early's men were marshaling the prisoners when machine gun fire suddenly peppered the area, killing six Americans and wounding three others. German machine guns had turned to fire on the U.S. soldiers. Corporal York was the senior of the eight remaining U.S. soldiers. Leaving his men under cover, guarding the nineteen prisoners, York worked his way into position to silence the German machine guns.

York later recalled this event in his diary:

And those machine guns were spitting fire and cutting down the undergrowth all around me something awful. And the Germans were yelling orders. You never heard such a racket in all of your life. I didn't have time to dodge behind a tree or dive into the brush. . . . As soon as the machine guns opened fire on me, I began to exchange shots with them. There were over thirty of them in continuous action, and all I could do was touch the Germans off, just as fast as I could. I was sharp-shooting. I don't think I missed a shot. I didn't want to kill any more than I had to. But it was they or I. And I was giving them the best I had.[18]

Finally, a German major, already in custody, offered to surrender the entire unit to York, and his surrender was gladly accepted. At the end of the engagement, York and his seven men marched 132 German prisoners back to the American lines. His actions silenced the German machine guns and enabled the 328th Infantry Regiment to renew the offensive. Subsequently, York was promoted to Sergeant and awarded the Medal of Honor, Distinguished Service Cross, Italian Croce di Guerra, the Montenegrin War Medal, and the French Croix de Guerre for his action.

Sergeant Alvin York's life is relevant for us since it is an example for leaders to follow. His physical courage on the battlefield was a reflection of his moral courage and spiritual life.

A Lost Soul

Alvin York was born in the backwoods of Tennessee in 1887, the third of eleven children in a poor farming and blacksmith family. When Alvin's father died in 1911, York rebelled.

"I got in bad company and I broke off from my mother's and father's advice and got to drinking and gambling and playing up right smart," he recalled. "I used to drink a lot of moonshine. I used to gamble my wages away week after week. I used to stay out late at nights. I had a powerful lot of fistfights."[19]

CHRISTIANITY, CHARACTER, AND COURAGE

York's grandson recalled in an interview that "Alvin soon achieved local renown as a sharp-shooter. On 1 January, 1915, Alvin attended a revival meeting. During the sermon, York felt as if lightning hit his soul."[20] "He was moved to accept Jesus Christ as Lord and Savior. From this point on, his life was changed forever. He immediately abandoned smoking, drinking, gambling, cussing, and brawling. York took this commitment seriously, grew in his faith, taught Sunday school, led the choir and became an elder in his church."[21]

York's old friends tried to persuade him to go drinking, but he continually refused. It took a lot of moral courage for York to remain firmly committed to his Lord. But with the strength of the Holy Spirit and his personal resolve, York remained on the Lord's side. This temptation, and his resistance, sharpened York's character and moral courage, and this contributed to his heroic deeds three years later.

THOU SHALT NOT KILL

"For my thoughts are not your thoughts, neither are your ways my ways, saith the LORD. For as the heavens are higher than the earth, so are my ways higher than your ways, and my thoughts than your thoughts" (Isa. 55:8–9).

As Alvin grew in his faith, the U.S. entered World War I. In June 1917 he received a draft notice. When he read, "Thou shalt not kill" (Exod. 20:13) in the Bible, he believed a Christian could not kill a human. However, he also believed that God had ordained governments as instruments to be obeyed. York summed up this dilemma when he said, "I wanted to follow both (the Bible and the U.S.), but I couldn't. I wanted to do what was right. . . . If I went away to war and fought and killed, according to the reading of my Bible, I weren't a good Christian."

Alvin York applied for exemption from the draft as a conscientious objector, but his request was denied. This put York into doubt and confusion. He trusted God to get him out of doing what he perceived as contrary to the Bible. As he said, "I was sorter mussed up inside

48

worser'n ever. I thought that the Word of God would prevail against the laws of men."[22]

THE LASING IMPACT OF CHRISTIAN LEADERS

York did not understand what was ahead, but he trusted God and reported for duty to Camp Gordon, Georgia. Providentially, York's company commander, Captain Danforth, and his battalion commander, Major Buxton, were committed Christians. Alvin shared his concerns with them. Both Danforth and Buxton treated York respectfully and took the time to discuss this matter fully.

Buxton and Danforth knew their Bible well, and they dedicated hours of their time to contend with York's doubts. They literally walked through the Bible together to debate the issue. For every verse the commanders used to support their position on warfare, York countered. Finally, one night, Captain Danforth read a verse from Ezekiel, "But if the watchman sees the sword coming and does not blow the trumpet, and the people are not warned, and a sword comes and takes a person from them, he is taken away in his iniquity; but his blood I will require from the watchman's hand" (Ezek. 33:6 NASB).

At this, York stood up and said, "All right, I'm satisfied."[23] He resolved to serve his country and his God as a soldier. Armed with this assurance, he sought to excel in all that was entrusted to him.

TAKE TIME TO LISTEN AND TALK TO THE TROOPS

There are several lessons from the life of Sergeant York that reach across the generations and speak to us today. The primary one is that without the intervention of Danforth and Buxton, things almost certainly would have turned out differently. Both York's company and battalion commanders took time to listen to the concerns of this soldier.

"We talked along these lines for over an hour," York recalled. "We did not get angry or even raise our voice. We jes examined the old Bible and whenever I would bring up a passage opposed to war, Major Buxton would bring up another which sorter favored war. I believed that the Lord was in that room. I seemed to somehow feel His presence there."[24]

The article in *COMMAND* Magazine pointed out some lessons we can learn from the example of Alvin York.

Buxton and Danforth were courageous enough to share their own testimonies and biblical knowledge with him. In our days of political correctness, this is quite a challenge. Surely, we must endeavor to speak the truth boldly when called upon to do so. Because of Danforth and Buxton, York went on to save his regiment from annihilation only months later. What a difference a Christian commander can make in the lives of his soldiers.

God used Sergeant Alvin York to save the lives of hundreds of Germans and Americans on October 8, 1918. In the decades since his heroic deed, the testimony of Sergeant York echoes across the ages to remind those who have inherited his legacy to live up to God's calling. Like Alvin York, we must take our faith seriously, endeavoring to build our character and moral courage "muscles" by choosing to do the right thing in every situation. York was physically courageous on the battlefield because he was morally courageous in his spiritual life.

God has endowed each of us with distinct talents and gifts to fulfill His purpose for our lives. In the case of Alvin York, his ability as a sharpshooter made the difference during the fierce battle for the Decauville Railroad in October 1918. God has similarly equipped us to fulfill His plan.

Finally, the leadership examples of Major Buxton and Captain Danforth speak to us today. These men gave hours of their precious time to help Private York work through his spiritual doubts. Because of their boldness, patience, and understanding, York was able to fully commit himself and ultimately save his regiment from defeat, and many lives in the process. Although few of us can expect to be a Sergeant

York, surely we can live up to the examples in the bold tradition of Captain Danforth and Major Buxton.[25]

The heroism of an ordinary front-line field soldier named Alvin
York was the outworking of at least two relatively unknown Warrior
Leaders who were committed to force multiplying. The Warrior Leader
will execute a strategy to be certain that he and those around him are
deeply committed to a force-multiplying army. Is that happening
around you? When it does there will be a fresh and victorious spirit in
your actions as a Warrior Leader.

❖ ❖ ❖

MAKING HELL GUN-SHY

E *thos* refers to the attitudes, beliefs, and traditions that charac-
terize the spirit of a person or a group. The Warrior Leader's
ethos refers to attitudes and beliefs of a fraternity of warriors
who refuse to accept failure in spiritual-war fighting.

General George S. Patton said, "Wars may be fought by weapons,
but they are won by men. It is the spirit of the men who follow and the
man who leads that gains victory."[26]

Like any military that is victorious, spiritual-war fighters will win
because they fight hard; they fight hard because they train hard; and
they train hard because they know that is the only way to win. This
ethos is about more than forging victory out of chaos in battles and
overcoming fears, deprivation, and fatigue. The Warrior Leader's spirit
actually fuels the fire to train hard, fight hard, and win victoriously!

Far too many Christians are losing their spiritual battles because
they are not rigorously trained and equipped. They seem to feel that if
something has a high standard, requires deep commitment, or can
become testing and tiring, it must not be of God. Usually this attitude

prevails in the absence of the Warrior Leader's ethos. Churches are promising more and more to attendees while calling for less and less commitment. No army could be victorious in war by fighting with that philosophy—and that is exactly why we are losing the battle for souls and the soul of America. It is the reason why we must hear the Warrior Leader call and get up off our good intentions, stop whining, and go to war for God and souls.

Can you imagine a football team where the coach meets with the team a couple of hours each week, giving them a few plays and a pep talk and then telling them he hopes they do well at their games this week? No, everyone knows that it takes hard training through weeks, months, and years to build a winning team.

The training of too many churches is soft, sporadic, unintentional, disconnected, and intermittent. Most of what it takes to win in spiritual-war fighting comes the hard way. The Warrior Leader understands that the warrior spirit is essential if we are to overcome and win the victory.

Remember that in this section on the Warrior Leader's motivation, we are concentrating upon what we are to *be*. Our warrior ethos deals with who we are and what we do. Therefore, ethos has a direct link to the Warrior Leader's core values and such things as courage, loyalty, duty, and selfless service. All these have a part in the Warrior Leader's ethos.

This is what enables you and others to put your life on the line. You will be able to do this for the cause that is greater than yourself—that of souls and our dear Lord's kingdom. Pity the person who does not realize that the cause of God's kingdom—winning souls—is greater than he is.

Experienced military fighters will convince you that the warrior spirit is what spurs the lead tank driver into uncertainty. It drives the bone-tired medic to put others before himself. It pushes the sweat-soaked gunner to keep up the assault. It drives the heavily loaded foot soldier into an icy wind as he moves steadily to the objective. It compels the truck driver across frozen roads riddled by minefields because he knows his fellow soldiers at an isolated outpost must have the supplies he carries.

This warrior ethos of risky and tireless motivation is evident in many personalities throughout the Bible. They were propelled by the attitudes and beliefs that refused to accept failure in their battles to accomplish the Great Mission.

Such examples, both biblical and military, come as a part of the fraternity and comradeship that flows out of the Warrior Leader's ethos. This is what energizes warriors to fight for one another. They would rather die than let their buddies down or leave them behind. Marshall Maurice de Saxe said, "The human heart is the starting point in all matters pertaining to war."[27]

When the Warrior Leader allows the Holy Spirit to develop within him these attitudes and beliefs that refuse to accept failure and defeat in spiritual-war fighting, he will generate a band of warriors who will multiply that same ethos in others. This is when all of hell starts getting gun-shy.

⚜ ⚜ ⚜

WHAT WILL YOU DIE FOR?

Not only does moral toughness make hell gun-shy; so does commitment to core values. The Warrior Leader has some non-negotiable values. What is he willing to die for? What is he willing to live for? What is worth the best of the rest of his life? These are the things that will cause him to be found faithful.

These key elements are not just biblical truths that form high-minded sayings for us to pass on to others. These are core values that tell the Warrior Leader what he needs to *be* every day and in everything he does. These are non-negotiable, fundamental building blocks upon which all other things will rest. These include the ability to perform successful spiritual leadership and war fighting personally in the home, church, and throughout God's kingdom. These values declare to friends, enemies, and the world just who we are and what we stand for, even to the point of death. They are the glue that binds us together with other Warrior Leaders to form an army of force multipliers who are driven to accomplish the Great Mission.

These core values apply to everyone in every situation throughout the entire army of Warrior Leaders. These values are interlocked; you cannot follow one and disregard the others. The trust and confidence of those whom you lead are dependent upon your living out these values before them. These core values are the unshakable and unbreakable solid bedrock upon which all else stands, especially in times of spiritual-war fighting.

It is obvious then that the Warrior Leader must not only model these values but must teach and train others to do likewise. They become the essence of force multiplying. Following are the core values that are essential for Warrior Leaders.

THE TRUTH

The truth is the Word of God. The Warrior Leader believes the Bible is the inerrant, infallible truth that is God's written document in which the Warrior Leader's principle mission—the Great Commission—is declared. The Word also clearly identifies our enemy, Satan. It outlines the way to be victorious war fighters against the enemy and how to accomplish the Great Mission. The Word is an absolute core value to the Warrior Leader because all other values issue from the truth. Truth is the one thing that defeats the devil. It is our inerrant order.

THE WAY

The way and the only way is Jesus Christ. The Warrior Leader is dogmatically and immovably committed to the fact that Jesus Christ, as a personal Savior, is the only way to be delivered from the enemy and eternal hell. Further, the Warrior Leader is committed to the truth that Jesus living in us and filling us is the only way that spiritual combat is won and souls are rescued. Jesus said, "I am the way, the truth, and the life: no man cometh unto the Father, but by me" (John 14:6).

THE QUEST

The quest is for souls. The Warrior Leader's heart is preoccupied with souls. He believes that God's focus is on souls, that God views all of humanity as souls—either lost souls or saved souls. He believes that God's passion is for all lost souls to become saved souls and for all saved souls to win lost souls to Him. The Warrior Leader believes that he and others are to be consumed with fulfilling their mission. They are to equip a force-multiplying army to achieve this objective.

THE DESTINY

The destiny of souls for all eternity is either heaven or hell. The Warrior Leader is driven by this core value because he believes that a soul must be saved before his earthly life is over and that every Christian has been assigned the mission to lead people to be saved. Therefore, the Warrior Leader is filled with urgency because he is convinced he must do everything possible, as soon as possible, to reach all the souls possible for Christ.

THE APPROACH

Intentionality is the New Testament approach for Christian witnessing. It is a distinguishing mark of the Warrior Leader's life, ministry, and witness. This is a core value because it is the model of Jesus, the Bible, and the early church. Intentionality in witnessing is not to be confrontational but rather is directed by the Holy Spirit. It is essential because it is the active ingredient in offensive war fighting and opposite to other passive approaches that accommodate the enemy. Jesus declared, "You will be His witness to all men of what you have seen and heard" (Acts 22:15 NKJV).

THE WITNESS

The witness is the Christian who shares the saving gospel in an effective presentation empowered by the Holy Spirit. The Warrior Leader understands that the Spirit of God does all soul saving, but he also understands that God uses people as the human instruments. This is why the witness is often referred to as a "soul winner." Hear these words of our Lord, "Ye shall be witnesses unto me both in Jerusalem, and in all Judaea, and in Samaria, and unto the uttermost part of the earth" (Acts 1:8b).

THE MISSION

The mission that is top priority is the Great Commission. All other missions are focused to accomplish the Great Commission. The Warrior Leader believes that if he fails at this primary mission he has failed God, souls, and eternity. Jesus commanded us to go, teach, and baptize (Matt. 28:19).

THE CHURCH

The church is the forward operation base (FOB). God has established the church as a place and a people to be the base of operations in the forward combat zone upon earth. The church place (building) is to be the area for celebration and praise of victories won, for training and equipping for ongoing victorious combat, and for inspiring confidence and the will to return to the front lines of the battle, to attend wounds, and to fight and win.

What happens at the church building is not the accomplishment of the mission but the means to accomplish the mission. While they are important for the overall mission, you cannot determine the effectiveness of your FOB by the gusto of its barracks songs, its display of new equipment, its impressive defensive walls, and its technological fireworks. Rather, you can gauge its effectiveness by the church people's willingness to return to their battle stations and to advance in the Great Commission—the Great Mission.

THE NECESSITY

The necessity that is most basic is personal purity. The Warrior Leader must be under authority that is reflected in a Spirit-filled life of holiness and godliness. Such a spiritual warrior is controlled by the person of Jesus and the power of the Holy Spirit. He is unstoppable in his efforts to inspire confidence, trust, and will within those whom he leads as well as other leaders. If the leader is not pure and holy, he and all those whom he leads are in peril of chaos and defeat.

THE POWER

The power is the Holy Spirit. This power is given to the Warrior Leader in direct proportion to his yielding to the lordship of Christ. Without this constant filling power, no amount of leadership training or efforts to be victorious in spiritual-war fighting will be successful. One of the enemy's most deadly ambush tactics is to lure Christians into believing they can be victorious without the Spirit's power. Jesus assured us, "But ye shall receive power, after that the Holy Ghost is come upon you; and ye shall be witnesses" (Acts 1:8).

THE COMMUNICATION

The communication line for the Warrior Leader is prayer. The Bible gives God's verbal word to us, and prayer allows us to interact with Him. As a military combat leader, during close combat, I tried never to be anywhere near the radio operator. Why? The enemy knew to knock out the communication man first and then to kill the soldier nearest him because he was likely the leader who depended on communication for victorious war fighting. As the Warrior Leader, you should protect and preserve communication at all costs, or you will pay the supreme price.

THE CAUSE

The kingdom of God is the cause for which the Warrior Leader gives everything, including his life. The kingdom is the reign, rule, and lordship of Jesus in us by the power of the Holy Spirit.

The earthly cause of the kingdom will always be the same as the cause of Christ when He lived on the earth in His own skin. When Jesus is Lord, ruler, and reigner over your body and skin, His cause will continue to be seeking and saving the lost. That is Christ's cause, God's cause, the kingdom's cause, and it must be the Warrior Leader's cause. There is no other cause on earth worth the best of the rest of your life.

Adrian Rodgers told of a picture he saw in the newspaper. "A grown woman had her ear on the chest of a grown man. The man was not a relative of this woman's but he had received a heart transplant from the woman's son. She was listening to the heartbeat of her own son. Would to God that He could put His ear upon our chest and hear the heartbeat of His Son, which is world evangelization."[28] Yes, that is the heartbeat and cause of Christ and the kingdom.

CORE VALUE ASSOCIATION

Below are word associations that may help in connecting the essential values of the Warrior Leader's core commitments. The linkage of these core values to one another and how they are connected by mutual support should be understood and appreciated.

Value	Title	Application
The Truth	Bible	Inerrant Orders
The Way	Jesus	Only Savior
The Quest	Souls	All Saved
The Destiny	Eternity	Decide Now
The Approach	Intentionality	Essential Offense
The Witness	Christian	Human Instrument
The Mission	Great Commission	Top Priority
The Church	FOB	Equipping Center
The Necessity	Purity	Be Clean
The Power	Holy Spirit	Be Filled
The Communication	Prayer	Life Line
The Cause	Kingdom	No Other

Much more could be added to each of these, and you may even feel a need to add something to the list. However, it is unlikely that the Warrior Leader will have a list without the values indicated here.

Most Christians will agree intellectually and theologically with the majority of these core values. But the key to our victory over the enemy is for these truths to become our own core values. Then, because these values have an interlocking and overlapping connection to one another, an extraordinary Christlike focus causes the Warrior Leader to be a "faithful servant" who wins at spiritual-war fighting. In short—*be* these values and *be* the victor.

II.

THE QUICK AND THE DEAD

The Warrior Leader's Mind ("Know")

THE SILVER STAR

This medal is awarded for heroism and gallantry while in combat action against the opposing enemy.

YOUR SILVER STAR

As the Warrior Leader you receive your Silver Star from the Lord because your mind knows what it takes to accomplish the Great Mission He has assigned you. Intellect on fire for the sake of His kingdom and souls will lead to the most courageous acts of bravery. "Whosoever loses his life for my sake will find it." That will be your commendation from Christ.

THE WARRIOR LEADER'S MIND ("KNOW")

This is what the Warrior Leader is to *know,* and it is what forms and defines his competency.

"BE QUICK—OR YOU'RE DEAD"

*T*he scene has forever been branded into my heart and head. Up ahead just beyond the huge corral-looking gate was a clearing. Soldiers training for war had to pass this way. It was obvious that those before us had been in intense struggles at this site. All the grass had been killed and worn down into this gray, fuzzy layer over the hard, red clay. This terrain had been sand-papered smooth by the hides, heads, and hands of kicking, screaming, slapping, poking, choking, stabbing, fighting soldiers who for days on end had been perfecting the fine art of staying alive in close combat.

My group was next. As we unsheathed our knives and brought our bodies and weapons to a fighting position, the instructor's declaration turned our blood to ice water. Although we were not looking him in the face, due to a distraction above his head, we still heard him clearly: "You will this day *learn,* here and now, or die in combat later!" Almost gritting his teeth, he continued, "Soldiers, you must remember this one thing about combat!" Instantly he thrust his finger upward toward the sign over his head.

Skulls and crossbones were painted at each end of this principle that we war fighters were never to forget. The warning read: *"Under This Sign Pass the Quick and the Dead."*

The point of this sign and the training which we were about to undergo was that in our war fighting we must know so well what we were supposed to do that our actions would be instinctive and automatic. We must become that competent, as war fighters, or we would die! In combat I saw the truth of this sign more times than I care to remember. It is the same way in spiritual combat.

You're quick because you know what to do. You know because your mind has been trained over and over. You're quick—or you're dead!

❖ ❖ ❖

IF YOU KNOW

"If you know the enemy and know yourself,
You need not fear the result of a hundred battles.
If you know yourself but not the enemy,
For every victory gained you will also suffer a defeat.
If you know neither the enemy nor yourself,
You will succumb in every battle."[29]
SUN TZU (2,500 YEARS AGO)

All of us were about to kiss America good-bye. We soldiers had been assembled in the large aircraft hangar at Oakland, California, awaiting our aircraft to swing its tail around toward us for loading. All were destined for combat in Southeast Asia. Just about everyone's jungle fatigues were well-worn, and the soldiers looked like season-trained troops. Many of the uniforms had insignias and patches indicating special preparation and equipping for the type of war fighting we were headed into.

The uniform was one of the things that made the young baby-faced soldier stick out from the rest. His looked as if it had just been issued and did not have a single insignia on it. He was not yet even a PFC. It appeared he was a basic recruit, and yet here he was, headed for a fighting, cutting, blasting, shooting, killing war.

Our plane's engines were roaring as its rear ramp slowly opened as if preparing to suck us up into its belly. There was no one joking around now; days before we had kissed our loved ones good-bye. All that was left now was to shoulder our equipment and go. The line had formed automatically and slowly moved out of the hangar into the plane.

That was when this one lone soldier caught my eye. Still inside the hangar on the left-hand side, he faced in the opposite direction of our moving line that passed by him with hardly any notice. His equipment was not in hand. His shoulders drooped with his arms hanging limply down to his sides. His head was bowed, and his eyes seemed to be looking straight through the concrete floor.

"Soldier, is there something wrong?" I asked, stepping in front of him. There was no snap or salute in this recruit as he was questioned by an officer. He just slowly lifted his head and said with the same hopeless and defeated tone his entire body was projecting, "Sir, I'm not trained for war."

As I tried to encourage him, he found his way into the line with us and was engulfed by the plane as all of us went to war.

I saw some soldiers killed by the first bullet they ever heard fired. I have always wondered about what happened to the soldier who went to war saying, "Sir, I'm not trained for war." Victory is practically impossible for the war fighter who is untrained, unequipped, and unprepared.

If you *know,* as the spiritual-war fighter, it will make all the difference in the world and eternity!

- "My people are destroyed for lack of knowledge" (Hos. 4:6).
- "Let this mind be in you, which was also in Christ Jesus" (Phil. 2:5).
- "A wise man is strong; yea, a man of knowledge increaseth strength. For by wise counsel thou shalt make thy war" (Prov. 24:5–6).
- "Wisdom is better than weapons of war" (Eccl. 9:18).

Because Christ's mind was filled with what it took to accomplish His mission, He exhibited the most courageous acts. Our supreme Warrior Leader fights His way to His final objective victoriously. The unsurpassed act of bravery and the crowning sacrifice of heroism consisted of our Lord throwing Himself on the cross to die so others might live forever. As a Warrior Leader, what fills your mind not only influences your accomplishment of your Mission-Vision but also the manner in which you live and die as a soldier of His cross.

Daniel Webster said, "If we work on marble, it will perish; if on brass, time will efface it; if we rear up temples, they will crumble into dust; but if we work upon immortal minds and imbue them with principles, with the just fear of God and the love of our fellow men, we engrave on those tablets something that will brighten to all eternity."

There are Christians with wonderful character who are consistently defeated in spiritual warfare because of their lack of knowledge and competency. Usually their view is, *Let a sleeping mad dog lie.* The error of such a passive approach is that the devil, our enemy, is not a sleeping dog but "a roaring lion . . . seeking whom he shall devour" (1 Pet. 5:8). You must combat the enemy in order to advance the Great Mission.

Attempts to tiptoe around the devil, while ignoring our Commander's orders, seems to be the action of those who are centered on self-preservation rather than on the servant soldier life of Christ. This is also the path to personal spiritual defeat. Knowledge in the Warrior Leader's mind is essential if he is to wage victorious war fighting.

You may be mumbling, "Really, must I learn new skills?" I pray we will all be encouraged by the following account to go on and achieve maturity as the Warrior Leader.

As he was approaching sixty years of age, George C. Marshall was selected General of the U.S. Army. He realized his old ways of doing things were destined for change or he would experience failure. *I must become an expert in a whole new set of skills,* he decided. Marshall did just as he said he would and became one of the greatest strategic leaders in America's history. As General of the Army, Marshall served with vision and guided the greatest military victory in our nation's history—World War II.

Marshall provides an extraordinary encouragement for all who are willing to take on new leadership tasks and become Warrior Leaders, regardless of age. An unknown school teacher said it exactly right:

"If you think education is expensive, try ignorance." The Warrior Leader has calculated the worth of souls and has determined to pay the price of educating himself in order to be competent to accomplish the Great Commission, his Great Mission.

INTELLECT UNDER FIRE

Master Sergeant (then Staff Sergeant) Roy P. Benavidez, U.S. Army, distinguished himself by a series of daring and courageous actions while assigned to Detachment B-56, 5th Special Forces Group (Airborne), 1st Special Forces, Republic of Vietnam to gather intelligence information about large-scale enemy activity. This area was controlled and routinely patrolled by the North Vietnamese Army. After a short period of time on the ground, the team met heavy enemy resistance and requested emergency extraction. Three helicopters attempted extraction, but they were unable to land because of intense enemy fire.

Sergeant Benavidez was at the Forward Operating Base in Loc Ninh monitoring the operation by radio when these helicopters returned to off-load wounded crew members and to assess aircraft damage. Sergeant Benavidez voluntarily boarded a returning aircraft to assist in another extraction attempt. Realizing that all the team members were either dead or wounded and unable to be moved to the pick-up zone, he directed the aircraft to a nearby clearing. He jumped from the hovering helicopter and ran approximately seventy-five meters under withering small arms fire to the crippled team.

Before reaching the team's position, he was wounded in the leg, face, and head. Despite these painful injuries, he took charge, repositioning the team members and directing their fire to facilitate the landing of an extraction aircraft and the loading of wounded and dead team members. He then threw smoke canisters to direct the aircraft to the team's position. Despite his severe wounds and under intense enemy fire, he carried and dragged half of the wounded team members to the waiting aircraft. He then provided protective fire by running alongside the aircraft as it moved to pick up the remaining team members.

As the enemy's fire intensified, he hurried to recover the body and classified documents on the dead team leader. When he reached the leader's body, Sergeant Benavidez was severely wounded by small arms fire in the abdomen and by grenade fragments in his back. At nearly the same moment the aircraft pilot was mortally wounded, and his helicopter crashed. Although he was in extremely critical condition because of his multiple wounds, Sergeant Benavidez secured the classified documents and made his way back to the overturned aircraft. He gathered the stunned survivors into a defensive perimeter. Then he moved around the perimeter distributing water and ammunition to the weary men, instilling in them a will to live and fight.

Facing a buildup of enemy opposition with a beleaguered team, Sergeant Benavidez mustered his strength, began calling in tactical air strikes, and directed the fire from supporting gun ships to suppress the enemy's fire so another extraction helicopter could land. His indomitable spirit kept him going as he began to ferry his comrades to the craft. On his second trip with the wounded, he received additional wounds to his head and arms. He continued under devastating fire to carry wounded soldiers to the helicopter.

Upon reaching the aircraft, he spotted and killed two enemy soldiers who were rushing the craft from an angle that prevented the aircraft door gunner from firing upon them. With little strength left, he made one last trip to the perimeter to ensure that all classified material had been collected or destroyed and to bring in the remaining wounded. Only then did he allow himself to be pulled into the extraction aircraft.

Sergeant Benavidez chose to voluntarily join his comrades who were in critical status and to expose himself to withering enemy fire. He refused to be stopped in spite of numerous severe wounds. His actions saved the lives of at least eight men. His fearless personal leadership, tenacious devotion to duty, and courageous actions in the face of overwhelming odds were in keeping with the highest traditions of the military service, and reflect the utmost credit on him and the United States Army.[30]

Just like Sergeant Benavidez, you as the Warrior Leader must know some things if you are to be effective at rescuing the perishing and caring for the dying, as well as helping yourself, family, and friends. The motivation of a hot heart is critical, but our minds must be trained and equipped as well. Those whom we influence and lead must also receive training. Sergeant Benavidez was not able to accomplish such astounding life-saving feats only because of his brave heart. There was something else at work. Throughout his heroic actions his knowledge, training, and competency came into play. Intellect on fire is almost impossible to stop.

The pages of this book are designed to fill our minds with what will be required for us to move quickly, stay alive, defeat the enemy, and accomplish our Great Mission.

✤ ✤ ✤

UNCONVENTIONAL WARFARE

*T*he Warrior Leader is victorious in spiritual-war fighting and accomplishing the mission because he knows and practices a unique leadership focus. He does not perform leadership in the way most people define and envision leadership. Hence, to that degree, how the Warrior Leader thinks and leads is "unconventional."

The most basic definition of leadership is "getting people to willingly do something." This seems simple. But it has been observed that "leadership is like the Abominable Snowman, whose footprints are everywhere but it is nowhere to be seen."[31] Someone else added, "Leadership is the most observed and least understood phenomenon on earth."[32] Again, how can something so simple be so complex? What really causes the difference in leadership is the path it follows after leaving its basic definition stage.

The following is not a "vision statement." It is the Warrior Leader's unique and uncommon leadership focus. It is what he will *know* in order to fulfill his Mission-Vision. Consider the following definition of Warrior Leader leadership.

DEFINITION OF LEADERSHIP
The Warrior Leader's leadership is influencing people by:
- **Providing** purpose, direction, and motivation to . . .
- **Accomplishing** the mission vision while . . .
- **Caring** for the people and . . .
- **Expanding** a force-multiplying army for the kingdom of God and winning lost souls.

You've read the definition. Now apply the following explanation of this approach to leadership.

Influence: Get people to do. Influence is the ability to get people to do what is needed. This is more than just communicating the need. Your leadership example is just as critical as your communication—often even more critical. Every day and everywhere you are communicating to people the purpose, direction, and motivation by your personal example.

Purpose: Give people a reason. Purpose gives your people a reason for them to do what is needed. Every person will not understand or agree with every purpose for every mission. This is why trust in the leader is essential to accomplishing the mission. People must be assured from experience and your example that you will care for them and you will stand with them. The more challenging and threatening the mission, the more valuable this trust is. Trust is a basic bonding agent for leaders and must be earned and should be protected. Trust is essential for people to fully embrace purpose.

Direction: Mission accomplished. Direction is the way the mission is to be accomplished. People want and need direction. Train them, challenge them, resource them, give them direction, and then turn them loose and let them perform the Great Mission.

Motivation: Give people the will. Motivation gives people the will to do whatever must be done to accomplish the Great Mission. When the people do well, the Warrior Leader should commend them privately and publicly. If they fall short of the goal, give them commendation and credit for what was achieved. Help them to learn from their experience; coach and encourage them on how to do better next time.

Accomplish: Achieve the mission. A special mission comes from our Commander-in-Chief, the Lord Jesus, our highest authority. He has assigned us the primary mission of accomplishing the Great Commission. That is the mission for the Warrior Leader. He will organize, equip, train, and resource to his full capacity to accomplish the Great Mission. There can be an "implied mission" required to accomplish the primary mission. The FAITH Sunday School Evangelism Strategy[33] can be seen as an "implied mission" that results in achieving the primary mission.

Care: Take care of the people. Take steps to respect, love, praise, protect, and invest in your people. You cannot fake this. If you are a user and an abuser of people, your days as a leader are numbered. Even Attila the Hun understood this. "Chieftains should never misuse power. Such action causes great friction and leads to rebellion in the tribe!"[34]

Expand: Increase the force-multiplying army. The goal is for each person to become an individual force multiplier.[35] This will significantly increase the war fighting potential in the home, class, and army. This also increases the likelihood of the mission being accomplished. Force multiplying is the vehicle upon which fresh reinforcements will arrive. If the Warrior Leader will develop and equip force multipliers, he will always be victorious in advancing the Great Mission. The Mission-Vision gives us the focus to do just that.

⚜ ⚜ ⚜

THE MISSION-VISION

*T*he Warrior Leader's Mission-Vision has been verbalized through inerrant orders given to us from our Commander-in-Chief: "Go ye therefore, and teach all nations, baptizing them in the name of the Father, and of the Son, and of the Holy Ghost: teaching them to observe all things whatsoever I have commanded you: and, lo, I am with you alway, even unto the end of the world" (Matt. 28:19–20).

Our Lord's orders for each of us and His biblical strategy to fulfill these orders are capsulated for the Warrior Leader in what is termed the Mission-Vision.

THE MISSION VISION

- To develop victorious spiritual-war fighters
- who form a force multiplying army
- that accomplishes the great commission.

The Mission-Vision is what the Warrior Leader must know how to accomplish. An army of war fighters accomplishing their mission is the essence of this Mission-Vision. However, to help us understand this more fully, it is expanded in the following way.

Develop. To bring Christians to a state of trained and equipped preparedness.

Victorious. Effectively defeating their common enemy, Satan.

War Fighters. Those in spiritual combat.

Force Multiplying. Enabling believers to expand their group (force) to a far greater number.

Army. A group of spiritual warriors that is unified, focused, and mobilized in an intentional offensive campaign.

Accomplish. Succeeding at the mission.

Great Commission. To win and disciple their world locally, nationally, and internationally in their own lifetime, which is the Great Mission.

Here is the Mission Vision as an expanded statement:

To bring Christians to a state of trained and equipped preparedness, effectively defeating their common enemy, Satan,
in spiritual combat. Enabling them to expand their group
(force) to a far greater number that is unified, focused, and
mobilized in an intentional offensive campaign which succeeds at their mission to win and disciple their world locally,
nationally, and internationally in their own lifetime.

The Mission-Vision is the most dominating feature of the Warrior Leader. It becomes his target, goal, road map, compass, reference point, North Star, chart, bridge, and navigational instrument. It is the Warrior Leader's obsessive passion. Without a vision, leaders and those who are led become pointless mechanics and impotent dreamers. This truth further emphasizes our Commander-in-Chief's point, "Where there is no vision, the people perish" (Prov. 29:18).

For the Warrior Leader the Mission-Vision is more than a state-ment; it is his life. The Warrior Leader possesses a clear view of where he, Christians, and the church must go. He not only communicates this vision through example and on-the-job training, but he is focused enough to ensure the realization of the Mission-Vision. He has the character, competence, and commitment to be morally tough enough to stand against the enemy while generating the organizational leadership that is required to be victorious in achieving the Great Mission.

For the Mission-Vision to become a reality, the Warrior Leader must know a number of things. One of the most important things is to know how vital it is to "Raise the Bar."

RAISING THE BAR

One of the most distinguishing characteristics of the Marine Corps officer is his physical fitness. One can see at a glance that he is in the best shape of his life. And this is true pretty much across the board. Marine Corps officers of all ranks have the same flat-bellied "runner's" look—as if the Corps were trying to save money by issuing only one size uniform. Officers are not excused from the rigorous physical fitness test taken by non-commissioned officers, and they must test biannually.

But this is not their only motivation; being in shape is a matter of manhood. On a ten-mile, hilly, cross-country run, the Marine Corps officer must "lead" his troops in the literal sense of the word; he must be in front of the column. The troops behind him, gasping for oxygen, see only his back. And they think, *If he can do it, I can.* An officer who cannot stay in front of his men will never have their respect.

There is also an unspoken competition between the non-commissioned officers and the officers. A ten-mile run is gruelingly equitable; either you can do it, or you can't. There is no possibility of faking it. Rank doesn't help; it only allows you to publicly raise your hand and surrender, calling the run to a halt. An officer and his sergeant will eye each other during these endurance tests, each reluctant to be the first to show signs of exhaustion. The following anecdote is typical of this friendly competition.

Top Sergeant Andy Brown, arguably the most successful Marine Corps recruiter on the planet, remembers his first meeting with the newly assigned commanding officer, Lieutenant Colonel William Leek. "He came up here on a day when we were going to run the 'poolees' [recruits on a delayed entry program] up Heartbreak Hill. It was a real hot day. I wanted to see what the Colonel was made of, so I pointed out the mountaintop that was our goal and asked him if he'd like to come along."

Top Sergeant Brown, who himself looks as fit as a fiddle, laughs. "All we saw was the Colonel's dust. He beat us all to the top and was doing knuckle push-ups on the rocks when the rest of us staggered up." Brown was so impressed with his new C.O. that he signed up for another tour of duty, even though he had been considering retiring.[36]

This military example reinforces the fact that leaders must be actively engaged, personally, in order to bring the best out of those whom they lead. When those around you are making such evaluations as "if he can do it, I can" and "he never asks us to do what he won't do himself," you are in a leadership position that can begin to raise the bar and bring the best out of those around you. Those who are dependent on your leadership must be inspired by you and your efforts. Sometimes what you actually do may not seem so significant, but the fact that you are there and out front does have an impact.

General George Patton had one of those experiences in the United States landing at North Africa.

On the morning of November 9, 1942, I went to the beach at Fedhala accompanied by Lieutenant Stiller, my aide. The situation we found was very bad. Boats were coming in and not being pushed off after unloading. There was shell fire, and French aviators were strafing the beach. Although they missed it by a considerable distance, whenever they strafed, our men would take cover and delay unloading operations and particularly the unloading of ammunition, which was vitally necessary, as we were fighting a major engagement not more than 1,500 yards to the south.

By remaining on the beach and personally helping to push off boats and by not taking shelter when the enemy planes flew over, I believe I had considerable influence in quieting the nerves of the troops and making the initial landing a success. I stayed on the beach for nearly eighteen hours and was wet all over, all of that time. People say that army commanders should not indulge in such practices. My theory is that an army commander does what is necessary to accomplish his mission, and that nearly 80% of his mission is to arouse morale in his men.[37]

One of the most important places for the Warrior Leader to arouse morale and determination within those whom he leads is at the point of raising the bar. Mothers, fathers, teachers, and preachers must know how to raise the bar if they expect victory.

PEOPLE

Carrying out the Warrior Leader's Mission-Vision will require interpersonal skills—stretching the people whom he leads to rise to their full God-given potential; to bring out of them their very best for Jesus.

One of the worst tragedies of malfunctioning leadership is to say *no* to those who depend on you to train, equip, and lead them. My bonsai trees make this clear. I cultivate bonsai trees as a hobby. When you intentionally dwarf the trees, they live their entire lives in a reduced condition. The caretaker repeatedly says *no* to the trees. When the roots, leaves, and branches want to extend, I simply say *no* to them. Then I take subtle, non-combatic action to back up my *no* answer. The trees are slowly, surely, and painlessly denied their full potential.

One of my little trees is over eighty years of age with a natural potential of being forty to fifty feet in height. The tree, however, is only twenty-eight inches high and is confined to a small pot, only five inches deep. Its growth potential is denied because I am saying *no* to the tree. You may say, "How sad and cruel for the trees." Actually, the trees are pampered. They live in beautiful, expensive containers filled with specially prepared soil. They receive measured amounts of water and special foods. So these trees actually are blessed in an unusual way.

Tragically, this illustration from plant life is perpetrated upon the Christian people in our churches all the time with unspeakable damage and loss. Churches fail to reach their God-given design and potential because someone keeps saying *no* for them. It is possible for such

Christians and churches to feel happy, cared for, pampered, and satisfied. God has so much more planned for them, and they are denied the opportunity to discover it.

During a break at one of our international evangelism training clinics at First Baptist Church of Daytona, Florida, Doug Williams and I were having a casual conversation with several staff members from a well-known church. They had been there as part of a three-person training team, doing on-the-job visitation. After they were exposed to our laypeople's excitement, ability, and commitment, they said to me and Doug, "This is what we are missing back home in our church. We need people with the kind of commitment we see here among these laypeople!"

Two more days of clinic training passed, and the same staff members had another conversation. After inquiring about our week-by-week ministry in training, they declared, "We do not believe that such a level of commitment is possible among the busy laypeople in our church."

Those good men did not hear what they were saying and conveying. Their people did need a deeper commitment, but the staff members were not willing to believe in them enough to issue a challenge for deeper commitment. Some staff persons and volunteer church leaders are not willing to pay the price for a deeper commitment from their people, since it will require at least the same level of commitment from them. Leaders must not say *no* for the laypeople of their fellowship. We should believe in them, give them a chance, encourage them, call on them to try, exemplify commitment before them, and think *yes* on their behalf. Don't say *no* for them. Turn them loose and let them go, and you will be surprised at how high they will raise the bar.

Once I was asked, "As a leader, what is your goal for your church staff and people?" My answer was, "That when they come to the end of their earthly life they can look back to their days among us and say, 'Those were some of my greatest days for the Lord because I was loved, appreciated, challenged, equipped, urged, trained, motivated, and stretched to my very best for Jesus and the winning of the lost.'"

This goal will be accomplished by intentional and dedicated commitment to training and equipping which will raise the bar and stretch the people. The goal is to move believers beyond *improvement* to a level of personal *transformation*. Did you catch that?

TRANSFORMATION

Raising the bar implies that standards are getting higher and higher and to succeed at such standards is growing more and more difficult. Using the high jump record for the last century, it was confirmed that the bar had been rising a long time for the high jump. Sullivan and Harper in their book *Hope Is Not a Method* concluded from the study of the high jump two lessons that are critical to Christians today, especially those of us in North America.

The first lesson is understanding the difference between *improvement* and *transformation*. In high jumping there have been plateau periods where athletes struggled to be champions by just improving the process and technique. The extraordinary advances came only when someone transformed the process. When transformation of the current process and techniques occurred, the bar did not just go up a little; it took a huge jump. Then the sport of high jumping was transformed as everyone began to make that adjustment.

OPPORTUNITY

The second lesson is that *opportunities to create transformation and break away from the same old results do come, but not often.* The Warrior Leader realizes that raising the bar is not something that just mysteriously happens; it is a commitment you make, by the grace of God, and you set out to live and die by that commitment. The high jumpers who transformed their records did not do so by just sitting around staring at one another and the high jump bar. There was tremendous commitment that brought about extraordinary breakthrough transformation.

The evangelical churches of North America today must experience transformation and break away from their same old results in the spiritual war for lost souls and the soul of this nation. This is imperative.

The Southern Baptist Convention could serve as an example that can be applied to every church and Christian in the twenty-first century. Like the high jumper, the SBC has been caught in a prolonged plateau in reaching the lost, baptizing them, and assimilating them into local churches. While there have been, for years, some ups and downs in improvements, there still has been no God-size breakthrough—no transformation. But it appears that the four elements for "raising the bar" in a transforming way are now present.

Opportunity. The opportunity for a God-size evangelism transformation can be seen in the SBC's stated goal of baptizing one million people in 2005. Because of the kingdom focus across the Convention and the desperate need for kingdom expansion, this is a perfect opportunity at a perfect time.

People. Make no mistake about it, ordinary churchgoing Christians of a million variations will be the ones to accomplish this as the power of the gospel moves through them to lost souls who live in their sphere of influence. These Christians can do this and *will* do this if given leadership, training, and encouragement. But they must be believed in, cheered on, and told, "You can do it, with God's help."

Transformation. To witness, win, and baptize for Christ one million people in one year would truly be a transformation. It would transform eternities, lives, current processes and approaches, as well as leadership and kingdom causes. Such a breakthrough would catapult the evangelical churches of North America in the twenty-first century, enabling them to reclaim their priority and biblical distinctive of soul winning, which declares Jesus as the only Savior and Redeemer.

Leaders. Yes, this will be done by the people—but not without leadership. Leaders at all levels will be faced with one huge challenge. None will feel this challenge more than SBC leaders. The challenge is not the one million baptisms. In fact, that could become routine if leaders will meet their true challenge.

The one big challenge is how to create mass for the sake of soul winning. (Read "Mass" under "The Twelve Ways To Win" on pages 150–52). The power of mass is not only mobilization but also spiritual synergy. Those who break the code will experience unparalleled transformation. Such an opportunity for an evangelism transformation exists now for the Southern Baptist Convention. There has never been a time when the SBC needed to regain its unity of purpose more than now. However, we must remember that such opportunities to create transformation do not happen often, and they do not last long.

THE *EVERYONE CAN* KINGDOM CHALLENGE FOR EVANGELISM

The *Everyone Can* Kingdom Challenge for Evangelism represents my very best efforts as president of the Southern Baptist Convention to join with leaders, pastors, and people to promote a conventionwide initiative to maximize our potential for accomplishing exactly what is urged in these pages—Raising the Bar—and doing so almost immediately! The objective is to create a *unity of purpose for evangelism* that will result in baptizing one million in one year between June 2005 and June 2006. One million baptisms in one year will more than double the present one-year SBC baptism record.

Two things must be present to mobilize multiplied millions of believers in such a short time:

First, the plan must be extremely simple and highly effective while centering on Christ, God's Word, and evangelism.

Second, the plan must allow each and every Christian and every church to use their own individuality, uniqueness, diversity, timetable, schedule, and methods in carrying out the plan during the one year. It must touch their own family, friends, and acquaintances. The Six Points of Challenge are the ministry points that each church and Christian must accomplish sometime, in some way, within the year of June 2005 to June 2006. These points should unify every Southern Baptist who loves souls.

THE SIX POINTS OF CHALLENGE

1. Witness and Equip. Yes, with God as my Helper, I accept the challenge to train and equip myself and others by participating in the classes offered by my church that I may learn to be more effective personally in reaching out to those with ministry needs and to those who are lost and need Christ as their Savior, including my family and friends.

2. Witness and Win. Yes, with God as my Helper, I accept the challenge to witness and win others to Christ by participating in the ministry and evangelism visitation efforts offered by my church and Sunday School class in order to express Christian love, concern, and care to those around us, beginning with family and friends. I understand that if you witness, you win; if you don't, you lose.

3. Baptize. Yes, with God as my Helper, I accept the challenge to help another to follow Christ in believer's baptism. Further, I'll do my best to help at least one person to be baptized at our church on this coming Easter Sunday and another person on the last Sunday in August, which may be some of my family and friends.

4. Stewardship. Yes, with God as my Helper, I accept the challenge to learn and apply biblical teachings on stewardship for the expansion of His kingdom through my life, through His church, and in cooperation with other SBC churches.

5. Vacation Bible School. Yes, with God as my Helper, I accept the challenge to be personally involved in some way in the upcoming Vacation Bible School. In today's world I am convinced we must engage and reach our children and their parents for Christ now.

6. Start New Units. Yes, with God as my Helper, I accept the challenge to do my best to encourage and help to start new Sunday School classes and/or new churches. At least I can encourage the start of one new Sunday School class.

These six points of challenge can easily be woven into a church's life and become its priority for twelve months. It will be achieved by leaders encouraging people to seize their opportunity and thereby become God's agents of transformation!

BEFORE THE NASHVILLE CONVENTION, JUNE 2005

The Nashville Convention will be the time and place of the official launch of the *Everyone Can* Kingdom Challenge for Evangelism.

Of course most churches will not actually engage in the Six Points of Challenge until some weeks after the Nashville Convention.

In the months leading up to the Nashville Convention all leadership at every level together with all pastors and people are urged to stir themselves and all others to pray, plan, prepare. and unite in a way that will shake the gates of hell and defeat Satan himself!

I will attempt to extend myself as far as humanly possible to help and encourage this stirring and preparation across the country. Among a number of things I will do is the *Everyone Can* bus trip to all fifty states and Canada in twenty-five travel days (a plane will be needed for Alaska and Hawaii). My goal for the bus stops at churches in each state is to put together a mosaic of who Southern Baptists are across the land and at our roots. All the while the unifying call will be for each and every church, pastor, and person to come join together with us in this great and glorious venture for souls—the *Everyone Can* Kingdom Challenge for Evangelism!

Regardless of size, situation, or state, the message will be that each and all of us can come together in this twelve-month effort to "do all we can, with all we have, where we are, *now!*" I believe the press will help get out this message from the bus to others. Also, I will contact state leadership along the way for their help.

AFTER THE NASHVILLE CONVENTION

After the Convention launch, my prayer and hope will be that in the next twelve months everyone, everywhere across the SBC, will at some time, in some way, do all we can, with what they have, where we are, to accomplish the Six Points of Challenge. This will require a Warrior Leader effort, and the SBC has the leadership, pastors, and people who can do this for the sake of Christ's kingdom and souls!

This is not the easiest leadership task in the world, but it is the most urgent and most worthwhile. When leaders devote themselves totally to this effort, for the sake of the great mission, all of us should rally to them with prayer, cooperation, coordination, encouragement, and our best efforts to be a part of that spiritual synergy to rescue souls from hell and to expand the kingdom of God.

If spiritual synergy for the sake of lost souls cannot be achieved soon, then the mediocrity of cooperation and coordination for lesser causes will drain our hope and our vision. Then each of us will be forced to ask, What future is there for a high jumper with no hope and no vision? But this transformation is possible now and only waits for us to seize it. Again, the SBC's opportunity serves as a good example that can be applied to every church and every Christian.

The Warrior Leader model of leadership is one way to accomplish transformation. Those who are willing to make the commitment to the Warrior Leader life are experiencing transformation and a breakaway to new victorious spiritual-war fighting as well as accomplishing the Great Mission. The critical need of this day is as the prophet Ezekiel observed in the valley of dry bones in Ezekiel 37:1–14. We need a fresh breath of God in us and a shaking of our bones that will extend to our feet and force us to become "an exceedingly great army" (Ezek. 37:10 NKJV) for the glory of God and the redemption of souls.

The Warrior Leader lives for such a widespread transformation and believes that this is the time and place for "an exceedingly great army" to raise the bar of commitment to reach a lost and dying world with the gospel. It begins with each of us. We must raise the bar.

⚜ ⚜ ⚜

THAT COLD, GRAY, DEAD FACE

*T*he officers of the unit were on the verge of leading their warriors into combat. Silence fell over the room where these fifty or so military officers were assembled. All that could be heard was the commander's jump boots pacing back and forth. This was reminiscent, I'm sure, to some of those in the room of their days in high school or college when their coach was preparing them for the greatest game of their lives. But this was no game! These war fighters who stared at their commander were no longer boys. With his head down looking at the floor as he paced, the commanding officer knew that this was one of the most important things he would say to these war fighters. This would probably be the last thing many of them would hear him say.

Earlier, these officers and a group of noncommissioned officers, twice their number, had been listening together to the commander outside the room. There was serious talk there as well. But when the commander instructed the colonel to dismiss the non-commissioned officers and have the officers reassembled inside the building, a far deeper mood fell on the group.

"Afghanistan, Iraq." As he said those words, each officer straightened his back and leaned forward in his chair trying to get his ears closer to these words as the commander named several other areas of the world. "These are places you and your men are going to war," he continued.

Their chairs were not organized in neat "dress right dress" military rows as might be expected. They were casually disorganized in a way that distanced them from formality and drew them in closer as fellow warriors and friends linking heads, hands, and hearts for a do-or-die mission. Yes, this was a "band of brothers" going to war. But the commander's crowning lesson was that they were going to war as Warrior Leaders. They must never forget the expectations and responsibilities that fell upon them as a leader of soldiers in war. No man in that room would ever forget how he drove that point into their hearts and souls that day.

"Men, when those body bags containing your own warriors begin coming to you . . ." Then he paused, closed his eyes, and faced toward the ceiling. There he was, this veteran warrior of many combat fights, battles, and wars, his uniform giving testimony of such an authentic Warrior Leader. No soldier in that room expected any tears from this war horse, but for a split second they wondered as his jaws clenched while he was racing back through horrors upon horrors just before he revealed his thoughts.

"And believe me, men, those body bags will come to you as they have to me more than anyone would ever want to remember. And when they come, it is your responsibility and obligation—no one else's. This is the body of your own soldier. You owe it to this warrior. You open that body bag and personally identify this brave soldier yourself." The officers' eyes were like lasers locked on a target, and their lips were beginning to tighten in rapt attention. The commander moved slowly among them now with his eyes locking into every face in the room.

"Then you run your hands down into that body bag and turn that cold, gray, dead face of your own soldier to look into your face. Then ask yourself this question, 'Did I train, equip, and lead this warrior in such a way that he had his very best opportunity to live and to win?' That is your responsibility and obligation to those who follow you. You must not fail those who follow you in this war!"

Frankly, after he said that I cannot remember one other thing that occurred in that room or in the remainder of that entire day. But since then I've thought many times about the leader's responsibilities and obligations.

Whatever your leadership position in this life in spiritual warfare—father, mother, sister, brother, preacher, teacher, or whatever else—each of us owes something to those who look to us for leadership. We have a responsibility and obligation to them. Look into the faces of those who look to you and ask yourself, "Am I teaching, training, equipping, and leading this war fighter in such a way that he has his very best opportunity to live and win?"

They have the right to expect that you will do just that. The Warrior Leader will give his all to meet those expectations.

WARRIOR EXPECTATIONS

Issues may vary tactically and technically in the course of spiritual-war fighting, but when it comes to interpersonal expectations among warriors, they must not change. In fact, these shared personal expectations between the led and the leader are what the Lord uses to raise the bar as well as raise the warrior himself personally and victoriously above the inevitable combat surprises. The apostle Paul pleaded with the Roman Christians, "I beseech you therefore, brethren, by the mercies of God, that ye present your bodies a living sacrifice, holy, acceptable unto God, which is your reasonable service" (Rom. 12:1).

You have never seen or heard as much screaming, running, and jumping as in a military basic training company. The tempo is almost impossible to describe. In a brief period of weeks, usually around eight weeks, a herd of young men and women from every imaginable background and orientation must be molded into a unified team of war fighters.

I served as a company grade officer "pushing troops" through basic training at Fort Hood, Texas. I remember one of our most effective tactics. In order to imprint an important truth upon new recruits who would be in combat within months, we would have a full inspection. Since these soldiers had not had any off-post leave time, the incentive for them to do their best was an eight-hour pass into town. If you did well in the inspection, you would get a pass. The energy and morale of troops were high for this inspection.

As hundreds of these new recruits stood on the parade field awaiting their personal inspection, non-commissioned officers and other officers were inspecting their barracks and personal items with a fine-tooth comb. (Even drain covers in the showers were to be removed by the recruits for this inspection. Officers would use a white cloth and push it into the drain to detect any "unauthorized or unfit" dirt.) Afterwards the troops were surrounded on the inspection field, and they were inspected one by one. Officers lifted pant legs to assure sock tops were at the same height. Caps had to be two fingers above the eyebrows. A dozen details were inspected on each soldier. Each recruit, with a few exceptions, had prepared himself meticulously for this inspection. I often thought how proud their parents and families would have been.

Then the awaited moment came as the commander mounted the platform to give the results of the inspection. As he spoke of how well the soldiers and their barracks had been prepared, you could feel the excitement rise as smiles began to appear on their faces. He told them how proud he and the other instructors were of their efforts. Just as they were about to burst with joy and throw their caps into the air, he concluded, "However, *no one* will receive a pass for this weekend."

First, there was silence as they looked at one another in disbelief. Then they began to mumble about the unfairness of all of this. (They were not using Sunday School language either!) After a few seconds of this the company commander would call all of them back to attention in his most forceful command voice.

Then he used this entire day's work to burn into their memory a lesson that would perhaps save their lives in combat one day. I know it did mine! The company commander made what may have been his most important point in all of basic training: "Soldier, what you have done today is nothing more than what is expected of every soldier in this army on every day of his life. This is your expected service. Soldiers do not get the Medal of Honor and other awards of valor on the field of battle by doing what is expected of them. But many do lose their lives because they fail to meet daily expectations."

The Bible calls this "our reasonable service"—not extraordinary service but our daily expectations before our Commander-in-Chief. There are warrior expectations for the Warrior Leader and those whom he leads. Many lives and souls have been lost to our enemy and to hell because spiritual-war fighters did not take expectations seriously.

Consider warrior expectations in three groups: (1) the leader's expectations of himself—how he leads, (2) the expectations of those whom he leads, and (3) the leader's expectations of the led.

THE LEADER'S EXPECTATIONS OF HIMSELF

Outside of my own personal list, I cannot remember all of the sources from which I compiled the following group of helps. I do know this list has inspired me many times to try to do better as a leader.

- Leaders don't run things; they lead.
- Leaders don't major on managing.
- Leaders have a vision that is clear, bold, and specific.
- Leaders fill other people with vision and passion.
- Leaders are inspired, captivated, and possessed by an idea for the future.
- Leaders have vivid imagination and bold faith.
- Leaders are energized and driven.
- Leaders are able to energize others.
- Leaders hunger to keep things simple.
- Leaders accelerate action.
- Leaders get other people to reach levels that they do not think possible.
- Leaders look for ways to make things better, bigger, and smoother.
- Leaders get other people out of their comfort zones.
- Leaders pull people out of their box.
- Leaders long for people to be more excited and to do more worthwhile work.
- Leaders have the greatest passion and the greatest dreams feeding each other.
- Leaders spark the system.
- Leaders let people get loose.
- Leaders put the best people on the biggest opportunities.
- Leaders provide excitement and do not wait for it.
- Leaders make things exciting.

- Leaders are not interested in running *things* but in building *people*.
- Leaders focus on improvement, not always on the set goal.
- Leaders measure how far people have come.
- Leaders draw everyone around them to a vision.
- Leaders are interested in everyone understanding and running with the vision.
- Leaders don't just talk about vision; they lead it.
- Leaders develop vision and implement vision.
- Leaders spread enthusiasm like wildfire and fire up the group.
- Leaders allow people to participate and have responsibility.
- Leaders feel a need for more vision and more enthusiasm.
- Leaders draw out workers' energy and creativity.
- Leaders understand they cannot do everything by themselves.
- Leaders have the confidence to build teams of the brightest and best.
- Leaders often have team members who are brighter than themselves.
- Leaders try to live with energizing and inspiring action every day.
- Leaders display strong wills to accomplish the task.
- Leaders are not seen as ivory tower commentators but are obsessed with vision, passion, compassion, and excitement.
- Leaders learn how to swallow their ego, lose their identity, and expend themselves for others and the good of the vision.
- Leaders have simple messages, and they keep repeating them over and over.
- Leaders know they are learners, and learners can always improve their leadership.

Anyone who reads this list and thinks about it each day cannot help but become a stronger leader. Those whom we lead also have expectations of the leader as well.

EXPECTATIONS OF THE LEADER FROM THOSE HE LEADS

Everyone who follows a leader in spiritual warfare has a right to expect certain things of him. Following is a checklist of these expectations:

- He tries to live a Spirit-filled life.
- He lives by core values.
- He follows the correct motivation, mind, mission, and maturity.
- He leads by example.
- He cares for those whom he leads.
- He equips followers to become Warrior Leaders.
- He reflects confidence.
- He is trustworthy.
- He lives the attributes of a Warrior Leader.
- He admits his own mistakes.
- He continues to learn.
- He listens to those whom he leads.
- He is decisive.
- He has humility.
- He is a field soldier, not an officer.
- He expands a force-multiplying army.
- He accomplishes the Great Commission.
- He encourages those whom he leads as well as other leaders.
- He plans and prepares.
- He appreciates and recognizes improvement.
- He is challenged himself, and he challenges others.

As surely as those led have expectations of their leaders, their leaders have expectations of those whom they lead.

THE LEADER'S EXPECTATIONS OF THOSE HE LEADS

- They try to lead a Spirit-filled life.
- They follow the correct motivation, mind, mission, and maturity.
- They are willing to try.
- They encourage the led and the leader.

- They are committed to learn.
- They are teachable.
- They live core values.
- They care for others.
- They equip themselves to become Warrior Leaders.
- They are trustworthy.
- They live the attributes of Warrior Leaders.
- They are humble.
- They set a good example.
- They listen to others.
- They have confidence.
- They are decisive.
- They expand a force-multiplying army.
- They accomplish the Great Commission.

EXPECTATIONS IN UNCERTAIN TIMES

The Mission-Vision and warrior expectations are things the Warrior Leader must know and practice. All along the Warrior Leader journey, he will do well to know and be prepared to practice four time-less leadership principles, especially in times of uncertainty.

Captain Vincent R. Lindenmeyer, U.S. Army and a member of the Officers Christian Fellowship, writes out of his experiences to help us stay prepared for times of uncertainty and spiritual-war fighting.

A cadet approached me, his eyes expressing the need to talk. Since 11 September, my counseling load as a tactical officer at the United States Military Academy (USMA) had decreased, as if cadets baring their souls would somehow validate the horrifying reality. This second-class cadet was at the mid-point of his cadet career, with four semesters completed and four more to go. He was failing thermodynamics. A USMA Preparatory School graduate and a prior-service U.S. Army Ranger, he said, "My best friend, who was my team leader in the battalion . . . they've been alerted; I know it, 'cause I can't get in touch with him and his wife keeps calling me telling me to get word to him." He stopped, searching for my reaction.

I nodded. He continued, "But the worst thing, sir, I feel like I've trained my whole life for this . . . this war. My brothers are deploying, every training mission was for naught if I can't be there with them. I feel like I should be there serving alongside them. Academics . . . thermodynamics, doesn't seem important right now."

I nodded again, but this time there was a longer pause. In the distance, I could hear an ambulance siren. He was silent and seemed ready for me to do more that just nod, to say something intelligent and help him make peace with his conflicting thoughts. I felt qualified to empathize with him; however, helping him see through his haze of uncertainty seemed daunting. It occurred to me that between studying and watching CNN, cadets had forfeited the time to process the enormous consequences of 11 September and the uncertain future. Ready or not, it was my turn to talk.

"Cadet, your mission is to *prepare*. As a cadet at the United States Military Academy, you are called to prepare yourself for whatever our country's future missions may be." The words had hardly left my mouth when it occurred to me that we are all preparing every day for an uncertain future— as officers and as witnesses. The mission to prepare may lack the glory of serving in the front lines of battle, but it is just as critical. As a mentor to cadets, I struggle not only with trying to understand the events of the day, but also with my own faith.

In this struggle, the Word of God offers a timeless account of Divine leadership principles in order to help someone like me grasp what "preparation" entails. Current events demand that Christian leaders know themselves, not through the world's lens, but through Christ's call to be His disciples.

In seeking scriptural guidance, I traveled to the time when the apostle Paul was calling others to prepare for an uncertain future at the church at Colossae. Heresy threatened Christianity as the believers of Colossae lost direction and entertained beliefs from other religions. The false teachings, Gnostic in nature, threatened their understanding of who Christ was. The Colossians began thinking that if Christ was only a "connecting element" between God and the world, then there must be other deities worthy of worship. Paul advised the Colossians to get back to the basics—the fundamentals, such as fellowship, accountability, truth, and prayer, focused on Christ Jesus—or forever be lost as a religion in a new emerging world. Paul states that the Colossians have been given "fullness" in Christ (Col. 2:9 NKJV).

Paul's charge to believers of AD 61 remains applicable to believers today. We must use his timeless leadership principles to prepare ourselves for an uncertain future.

Principle 1

Authentic leaders quiet themselves and pray, which yields gifts of endurance, patience, joy, and a spirit of thankfulness.

"For this reason, since the day we heard about you, we have not stopped praying for you and asking God to fill you with the knowledge of his will through all spiritual wisdom and understanding. And we pray this in order that you may live a life worthy of the Lord and may please him in every way: bearing fruit in every good work, growing in the knowledge of God, being strengthened with all power according to his glorious might so that you may have great endurance and patience, and joyfully giving thanks to the Father who has qualified you to share in the inheritance of the saints in the kingdom of light" (Col. 1:9–12 NIV).

Paul charges Christian leaders to be role models who demonstrate specific qualities or traits that will aid us to prepare for the future. Paul emphasizes that God will fill the

Colossians with the knowledge of His will through all spiritual wisdom and understanding. With knowledge that God's will "will be done," the Christian officer must prayerfully step out in faith and serve God with confidence and joy, resulting in a spirit of thankfulness.

Fortunately, God paired me with a wife who is a "prayer warrior." Too often, I am easily angered, short of patience, and (sometimes) miserable to be around. Thankfully, my wife reminds me to pray. Prayer gives us confidence in Christ to be vulnerable for the sake of God's kingdom. Through prayer, leaders will look at their careers with endurance and patience. This is the only way to ensure that family and faith are not sacrificed to career. Prayer allows patient leaders to risk themselves for the sake of leading subordinates.

As a tactical officer at West Point, I have been charged to inspire my company. Humbly, I have learned that authentic leadership is straight from the heart. No other method better inspires cadets. For instance, in lieu of giving the routine "safety briefing," I told them the personal story of losing a soldier to a POV accident because he simply did not wear his seat belt. I did not try to "shock" them with gory details, but I did share the anguish and disappointment of losing a soldier.

Paul states that those who are living a Christ-centered life will "bear fruit." Any success for the kingdom of God, no matter how small, gives us an attitude of joy and thankfulness. Therefore, the first general order of preparing yourself is to pray, and a spirit of patience, confidence, thankfulness and joy will emerge.

Principle 2

Christian leaders focus on the unchanging, timeless principles of the Bible, not the most recent fad.

"See to it that no one takes you captive through hollow and deceptive philosophy, which depends on human tradition

and the basic principles of this world rather than on Christ"
(Col. 2:8 NIV).

Paul's second timeless principle talks about remaining true
to the fundamentals—in this case, Jesus Christ our Lord.
General Douglas MacArthur, in his farewell address to the
Corps of Cadets in 1962, stated, "And through all this welter
of change and development, your mission remains fixed,
determined, inviolable—it is to win our wars." Senior officers
will give you their top three to five priorities in an operations
order. These are fundamental military disciplines. Likewise,
fundamental disciplines exist for Christians: fellowship,
accountability, truth, and prayer.

I can admit to not sustaining myself properly. I was a task
force commander in charge of all of the trucks and maintenance for a National Training Center rotation. I wasn't praying, studying the Bible, or finding time to fellowship with my
unit chaplain. When finally pushed to the edge when we
didn't meet our vehicle turn-in goal, I lost my temper and
stormed across the deserted motor pool, blaming circumstance for the unit's predicament. I embarrassed myself.
Successful leaders remain true to the fundamentals; they
maintain their wellness, spiritual fitness, and accountability,
in order to remain encouraged.

Principle 3

Genuine leaders know themselves (their own personality and temperament) and are able to work with others: "Let the peace of Christ rule in your hearts, since as members of one body you were called to peace" (Col. 3:15 NIV).

One of the main themes of Colossians teaches that a right relationship to the exalted Christ manifests itself not in spurious otherworldliness but through the real human relationships and structures of life in this world. The Colossians' true identity in Christ became unclear because of the many confusing religions competing for their attention. They readily accepted other religions' teachings and traditions of faith because they did not know their true identity in Christ. Instead of preparation, the Colossians sought the fast-food approach to ultimate knowledge in turning to Gnostic teachings. It takes meditation and prayer to know oneself. Leaders who know themselves are genuine, confident leaders who easily work well with others.

Before learning about counseling, I did not understand how critical knowing yourself—how you generally react to situations and other people—would determine what you did in current and future situations. Sun Tzu, a Chinese general around 500 BC and author of *The Art of War,* explained, "If you know the enemy and know yourself, you need not fear the result of a hundred battles. If you know yourself but not the enemy, for every victory gained you will also suffer a defeat. If you know neither the enemy nor yourself, you will succumb in every battle."

The Colossians were slowly succumbing to heretical teachings, and Paul saw that the battle for Christian truth was waning. As Christians, we can represent Christ as ambassadors charged to "go and make disciples" with confidence, joy, and endurance. Knowing ourselves allows a spirit of peace to transcend our daily existence and actions. With the power of the Holy Spirit, a Christian officer's peace should be a greater component that allows us to work with anyone.

Principle 4

Servant leaders work for their true employer.

"Whatever you do, work at it with all your heart, as working for the Lord, not for men, since you know that you will receive an inheritance from the Lord as a reward. It is the Lord Christ you are serving" (Col. 3:23–24 NIV).

Thankfully, a Christian officer can have accountability. There are bound to be other Christian officers, such as a mentor at the same installation or a peer in your organization, who desires exactly what you do—accountability in pursuit of Christ's call. If confident and competent junior officers pursue the Christian disciplines and bear fruit, then their true boss is glorified. Unfortunately, life becomes busier than we care for and missions take priority over Christian fundamentals. Our desire to "be" the Christian as parents, officers, or spouses can be clouded easily by the operational tempo of the unit that we serve. Through accountability, you have a way, a Colossian way, to be reminded that family and faith can be a priority in a successful professional's lifestyle. Be encouraged, and know that you will "receive an inheritance from the Lord as a reward" when you work "for the Lord" and "not for men."

The young second-class cadet remains a cadet at the Academy. Currently, he is proficient in thermodynamics and continues to prepare for the uncertain future. As a tactical officer, I am encouraged because I can clearly see the practical application of Christian principles enriching the character development of the future leaders of our Armed Forces and our Nation.[38]

The Warrior Leader has those same expectations of himself and those whom he leads. They also have expectations of the Warrior Leader in both certain and uncertain times.

Ask yourself this question: Do I train, equip, and lead spiritual warriors in such a way that they have their very best opportunity to live and to win? If your answer is no, please start, because everyone—including the Lord Jesus—expects it of us.

❖ ❖ ❖

LEADERSHIP WITH A WILL

*T*here is a need to highlight some of what I would classify as "attributes" that represent the Warrior Leader. These will also become some of the expectations for the leader as well as those whom they lead. Used here is a memory device the U.S. Army adapted with their list of values. Together, the first letter of each spells L-D-R-S-H-I-P for *leadership*. I've added an additional letter at the end, W for *will*. Following is "Leadership with a Will."

One Army leadership manual says, "Leadership is not a natural trait, something inherited like the color of eyes or hair . . . . Leadership is a skill that can be studied, learned, and perfected by practice."[39] The Warrior Leader will study, learn, and attempt to perfect the following attributes, and then pass them on.

Below is a digest for a quick reference of these leadership traits, followed by expanded insights into each trait.

Loyalty	unswerving faithfulness
Duty	Fulfill your obligations
Respect	Do unto others as you would have them do unto you
Selfless service	others before me
Honor	reputation for living the Christ life
Integrity	Do right

Personal Courage   positive actions facing fear, danger, or adversity
Will   compelling inner drive

LOYALTY: UNSWERVING FAITHFULNESS

Loyalty shows true faithfulness and allegiance to Christ, the cause of His kingdom, the church, and fellow soldiers of the cross. Loyalty is a matter of believing and devoting yourself to those things. Loyalty is a two-way street. You should not expect loyalty from others without being willing to give it as well. Loyalty cannot be demanded or won by simply talking about it. The Warrior Leader is given loyalty as a gift when he deserves it—when he trains and equips his people well and cares for and treats them as colaborers and examples of the Warrior Leader Christ life he talks about. No loyalty is more true and long-lasting than that of fellow soldiers who trust their leader to take them through the risks and dangers of spiritual combat.

Brigadier General Samuel L. A. Marshall said, "Loyalty is the big thing, the greatest battle asset of all. But no man ever wins loyalty of troops by preaching loyalty. It is given to him as he proves his possession of other virtues."[40]

DUTY: FULFILL YOUR OBLIGATIONS

Fulfill your obligations as a follower of Christ even if no human being is watching or if you don't get any credit for it. This is an important responsibility that is not reserved just for special occasions. In a pre-war letter to his son, Robert E. Lee said, "Duty . . . is the most sublime word in our language. Do your duty in all things. . . . You cannot do more—you should never wish to do less."[41]

There is an expectation that for the cause of Christ we all should be ready and willing to exceed our normal duty. The nation's highest award, the Medal of Honor, is given to those who act "above and beyond the call of duty." General John A. Wickham, former Army Chief of Staff, said, "The essence of duty is action in absence of orders or direction from others, based on an inner sense of what is morally and professionally right."[42]

RESPECT: *Do Unto Others as You Would Have Them Do unto You*

Treat others with dignity and value, expecting them to do the same. This means giving others the same consideration we would like to be given by others. The church mirrors the diversity of the people of our country and world. Respect shows value and appreciation for the best in other people. It is not possible to develop a cohesive and effective spiritual-war fighting team and army without respect.

Self-respect is a vital ingredient in teamwork and is reflected by digging down deep to put forth your best effort to accomplish the mission. Such a selfless effort of service and duty is the spirit that builds trust and regard among fellow believers. This is also what earns you their respect. Respect reminds you and them that your people are your greatest blessing.

In an address to the U. S. Corps of Cadets, Major General John M. Schofield said:

The discipline which makes the soldiers of a free country reliable in battle is not to be gained by harsh or tyrannical treatment. On the contrary, such treatment is far more likely to destroy than to make an army. It is possible to impart instruction and to give commands in such a manner and such a tone of voice to inspire in soldiers no feeling; but an intense desire to obey, while the opposite manner and a tone of voice cannot fail to excite strong resentment and desire to disobey. The one mode or the other of dealing with subordinates springs from corresponding spirit in the breast of the commander. He who feels the respect, which is due to others, cannot fail to inspire in them regard for himself, while he who feels, and hence manifests disrespect toward others, especially his inferiors, cannot fail to inspire hatred against himself.[43]

SELFLESS SERVICE: OTHERS BEFORE ME

Put the welfare of others before your own. It is service before self. This does not mean that you should neglect your family or yourself. In fact, such neglect weakens the leader and can cause more harm than good. Selfless service means you do not make decisions or take action based upon how these decisions may personally benefit you or your future. This type of living and serving means that we understand our mission is much larger than we are.

The best way to demonstrate selfless service is to dedicate yourself to teamwork where you set the example for everyone to go a little further, endure a little longer, and look a little closer to see how the team can be more effective in accomplishing its mission. Selfless service is larger than one person. It is a kingdom cause inspired by our Savior's selfless service for the world and us in order that souls may be saved.

General Omar N. Bradley, former general of the Army, said, "The nation today needs men who think in terms of service to their country and not in terms of their country's debt to them."[44]

The kingdom of God today must have Warrior Leaders who think in terms of selfless service for Christ and His cause and not in terms of their own personal agendas.

HONOR: A REPUTATION FOR LIVING UP TO THE CHRIST LIFE

This does not mean you are perfect. It does mean you have a reputation for being dedicated to the pursuit of living the Spirit-filled life. The Warrior Leader makes honor a matter of daily living, developing the habit of making choices, decisions, and actions that demonstrate a keen sense of right and wrong.

Living honorably develops a moral climate that strengthens not only you but others as well. Again, it is very instructive to observe the Medal of Honor. Those who receive this highest award did not get it by doing only what was expected; they went beyond the ordinary. It is fitting that the word used to describe this distinguished achievement is "honor." The honor above all honors is to have the Lord Jesus declare to us, "Well done, good and faithful servant."

Lieutenant General Thomas J. ("Stonewall") Jackson said, "What is life without honor? Degradation is worse than death."[45]

INTEGRITY: DO RIGHT

W. W. J. D. are familiar initials to most Christians—"What Would Jesus Do?" He would of course *do what is right.* W. W. J. D. is a good question to ask in every situation. People of integrity are people who have established a habit of consistently acting according to godly and biblical principles that cause them to do what is right. They are convinced and convicted that God blesses what is right.

Integrity demands that we do or say nothing that deceives or misleads anyone. The Warrior Leader says what he means and means what he says. He does so because people of integrity do the right thing not because it is always easy or because it brings them pleasure or profit. They act with integrity because their Christian character permits no less.

PERSONAL COURAGE: POSITIVE ACTION IN THE FACE OF FEAR, DANGER, AND ADVERSITY

Personal courage can be both physical and moral. Nowhere is it said that fear must disappear so courage can be displayed. General George Patton observed, "If we take the generally accepted definition of bravery as a quality which knows no fear, then I have never seen a brave man."[46]

The Warrior Leader knows courage can be developed in people. He knows that personal courage, physical courage, and moral courage can be developed and built up by making it his habit to stand up for others and to act upon the things that he knows are right. He seeks to exemplify this, and he trains others to do the same.

Physical courage has to do with overcoming the fear of bodily harm in order to do your duty. In contrast, moral courage is overcoming fears and standing firm on beliefs, values, principles, and convictions—even

102

when threatened. Moral courage is practiced when leaders, as well as those whom they lead, take responsibility for their decisions and actions, even when things go wrong. It is often expressed by candor. Candor means calling things as you see them, even when it is unpopular or when it is in your best interest to remain silent.

Circumstances requiring physical courage are rare, but situations requiring moral courage occur frequently. Don't forget, consistent moral courage is as important as fleeting moments of physical courage.

Robert E. Lee said, "You must study to be frank with the world. Frankness is the child of honesty and courage."[47] In spiritual-war fighting, physical and moral courage are often brought together. Sometimes the right thing to do can be both dangerous and unpopular.

The Warrior Leader understands there are three aspects of courage: personal, moral, and physical, and each can be built up in people. He is committed to develop examples and teach these aspects of courage.

WILL: COMPELLING INNER DESIRE

Colonel Dandridge M. Malone said, "The will of soldiers is three times more important than their weapons."[48] Our will is the inner desire that compels us to keep going when it would be easier to quit.

The test of your will is when everything seems to go wrong and you are exhausted, confused, afraid, and desperate and events seem to be out of control and it appears you are about to lose to the enemy. At times like this the Warrior Leader knows he must draw upon his inner reserve of determined drive and keep pressing on. During these times the spiritual-war fighter may be certain that the Holy Spirit will enable him because we as believers are promised, "When we are weak, He is strong," and that nothing will happen to us that we cannot handle, with the Lord's help.

Athletes know that when great physical demands are made on them, it is possible for them to reach another plateau of strength which they call their "second wind." The Warrior Leader has both a physical and a moral "second wind" that is provided by the Holy Spirit living inside. No human's will or demon's force can be victorious over the

Warrior Leader who lives and fights in the fullness of the Holy Spirit's power and will.

A city was occupied by enemy forces. The U.S. leadership had determined that if the city could be taken from the enemy, there was a real possibility the war could be shortened and thousands of lives would be saved. But the only way such a victory could be accomplished was by paratroopers jumping into the area, surrounding the city, and then overrunning it. There was no other way.

The problem was that no paratroopers were available within that region of the war. There were plenty of soldiers in the area, but none were parachute-qualified. In fact, most of the soldiers had never even been on an airplane.

While the American leadership agreed that this was a great opportunity to shorten the war, defeat the enemy, and save many lives, most of them were ready to abandon such a vision of victory because of the lack of paratroopers. But a few leaders were determined to find a way to prevail.

These leaders assembled their troops and laid before them one of the most heroic challenges imaginable. "We realize you men are not parachute-qualified to jump from planes. But there is no other way to win. Will you soldiers put on parachutes for the first time in your lives, get on the waiting airplanes, and then jump into the combat zone around the city, fight your way into the city, and take it?"

Can you picture these soldiers' astonishment? When I heard this story, it seems that only one question was asked of the leaders who made such a request of their soldiers, "Sir, will you go with us?" The leaders answered in the affirmative. The soldiers donned their chutes, boarded the plane, and roared off toward the city. When the doors of the aircraft opened, those leaders and their brave warriors jumped and captured the city, won the victory, and accomplished their mission. It was later determined that, comparatively speaking, these men had no more injuries and fatalities than such a jump with trained paratroopers would have produced.

The force that won the victory that day was *will*. The leaders had the will to find the way. They had the will to lead the way. The warriors had a will to follow their leaders. All of them together had a will to win.

Much is said about vision, but little is said about will. Far too often visions of victory have been replaced by a few excuses because leaders did not find the will to go on. Such is totally unacceptable when it comes to the eternal souls of people. The Warrior Leader is called by God to take on the attributes of leadership for the sake of those souls. We must remember that the enemy will use every trick and deceitful device to deny the Lord's army the victory. But the will can overcome.

BOOBY TRAPS, LAND MINES, AND AMBUSHES

"In the way in which I walk they have secretly set a snare for me."
PSALM 142:3 NKJV

"Stand against the wiles of the devil."
EPHESIANS 6:11

CAUTION: It is still difficult for me to remember this account without tears. If you will be upset by graphic descriptions of a war wound, you should skip ahead a few pages, then resume reading.

"To Hell and Back," an essay that appears later in this book (see p. 198), is where I tell of my time in the hospital as the result of combat wounds in Vietnam. By the time I was able to try to walk, there were several tubes running out of my left side and more tubes coming out of other parts of my body. These tubes went into glass jugs sitting on the floor. Finally, we got all the jugs in a cardboard box, then put the box with the jugs into the seat of a wheelchair. I stood behind the wheelchair with the goal of pushing that contraption down the aisle. This aisle was formed by all the Army hospital beds facing foot first toward one another. These were my first steps since I had been shot, and it took all I had to make them.

Every few steps I was forced to stop and rest, usually leaning up against the foot of a bed. Halfway down the aisle I had to stop. When I did, I looked up at the soldier in the bed in front of me and almost passed out. My mouth fell open, I became sick to my stomach, and sweat broke out as my knees weakened. Bending forward over the back of the wheelchair, I tried to tighten my grip on it. *Don't look at him again!* I kept saying to myself. *You'll pass out if you do! Don't look at him again!*

Something else inside me seemed to shout back, *You must look at him! This is your brother in arms, a fellow soldier. He deserves your attention. Look at him!* Before any more arguing inside, I looked again at him and immediately had all those sickening feelings again. I grabbed the railing at the foot of the soldier's bed, locked my eyes on him, and held on for dear life. This poor, pitiful soul had somehow picked up a booby-trapped object with both hands. He had lifted it toward his face to get a closer look. When he did, the explosive inside went off right in his face.

The blast had blown off both hands and lower forearms. What was left of them were now pulled up from his bed and kept out in front of him by cables running to each stub from an overhead bar. Both stubs jerked violently and pulled the cables as if his nerves were screaming for those flailing nubs to break loose from the wires.

His head had been shredded by the blast and had swollen to twice its normal size. He faced me like a melting mound of raw hamburger meat. I could not identify his eyes or mouth. There were no ears or any other distinguishing characteristics. From all areas of this mass there oozed fluids which drained to several white towels that were being used to sponge up the fluid and what might have been some of his tears. His head had some of the same jerking motions as his arms, although not as much or as violent.

Not only was I frozen at the foot of that dear man's bed, glaring at his wounds and torment, but that picture at the same time was being frozen into my mind and heart. The only thought I had was, *Surely, God will be merciful and not let him live.* With help from a nurse I made it back to my own bed. Over and over for hours, two thoughts burned in my brain: *What a high price some of these brave soldiers pay for our country and our freedom! And what staggering damage one enemy booby trap can do.*

Why do I tell such a graphic and horrible story? Because we Christians are in a real war against a real enemy who seeks to use everything he can to rob, steal, kill, and devour us, our families, children, grandchildren, and everyone around us. Furthermore, the horror and torture of that poor soldier's wounds do not compare to the eternal torment of those who go to hell. We must not get tricked, trapped, sidetracked, wounded, or taken out of action until we have accomplished the Great Mission.

There are hundreds of ways to get killed in a war. But sometimes the enemy does not want to kill you; he just wants to slow you down. If a soldier is wounded, three or four or five other soldiers are usually taken out of action—the wounded and those who must carry and care for him and his equipment. In World War II some of the enemy soldiers had bullets with wooden projectiles. When a soldier was hit he probably would not be killed immediately but would become infected and sick until he died from a slow death.

In Vietnam there were the infamous "pungi pits" and "pungi stakes." These were bamboo sticks sharpened on the ends. Their points were plastered with human excrement, then placed in a hole and covered over. If you stepped in or fell into one of those pits and your skin was penetrated by the stakes, you were not dead—but you had severe problems.

These things—along with booby traps, land mines, and ambushes—were devised by the enemy in order to lure you into a vulnerable position. Then by surprise and deadly force, he would either kill you or severely wound you.

Booby traps are things that look harmless and also have an appeal that makes a person want to handle them. These traps might be a jewelry box, an unusual weapon, food, or equipment. Sometimes a booby trap is a gate or a door that offers what appears to be an easier way to travel. When skillfully placed, a booby trap then waits for some unsuspecting, untrained, or careless soldier to make a deadly misjudgment.

Land mines are explosive devices that are placed just beneath the ground's surface. They are most effective when placed along routes of least resistance—perhaps a mountain trail with a cliff on one side and a steep slope up the other side, or in an open area but on a road crossing the open area. A soldier who is tired, in a hurry, untrained, unwilling, or unable to take the difficult route will lose feet, legs, and even his life when he touches the land mine.

Ambushes are by far the most deadly trap imaginable. Ambushes are the combat soldier's greatest fear and worst nightmare. They have an element of surprise, synchronized with murderous small arms and machine gun fire, along with explosives. These traps are almost inescapable once they are sprung and you have been caught in the ambush zone. I have set up ambushes and lain for hours and days with my men with no food, no speaking, no noise—just waiting for the enemy to be lured into our trap. Trains, boats, vehicles, men, women, boys, and girls have been lost to ambushes. Churches and Christians can be, too.

Following are several things the Warrior Leader will encounter along the path of victorious spiritual-war fighting in order to accomplish the Great Mission. These things are much like booby traps, land mines, and ambushes. The things, in and of themselves, are not always dangerous or deadly. In fact, they may be good and useful. But what gets attached to the thing is what ends up blowing up in your face and causing irreparable damage and denying us the ultimate victory for our Lord.

The potential troubles discussed have been broken down into *Trap, Triumph, Truth,* and *Test. Trap* indicates how the enemy uses a good thing as a cunning device against us and God's mission. *Triumph* is the way to diffuse the device and get on with our primary mission. *Truth* indicates the nugget of truth that grows out of the *Trap-Triumph* interaction. *Test* is a simple question that can help us detect the device that might be used by the enemy to hinder our offensive for souls.

BE CAREFUL ABOUT WITNESSING

Trap: Every witness knows that all the love in the world is to be displayed when sharing the gospel. There have always been a few people, however, who are hyper-extended with criticism about personal witnessing or even giving an evangelistic invitation at church. Sometimes the insinuation or accusation is that to do so is self-centered, faulty, high pressured, non-biblical, deceitful, shallow, and will cause all forms of dissension, division, false conversion of believers, and will kill off their form of outreach (which is usually slim or none).

Triumph: The Warrior Leader is convinced that both personal soul winning and public invitations are thoroughly biblical and clearly exemplified by Jesus, the apostles, the disciples, and the early church. The Warrior Leader is totally committed to do the same and to equip and train a force-multiplying army to do likewise.

Jesus said, "Not everyone that saith unto me, Lord, Lord, shall enter into the kingdom of heaven" (Matt. 7:21). Jesus had Judas. Christ reminded His followers that not all seed falls on good ground. Many people have argued that Jesus, in the parable of the sower, was indicating that He was expecting only a 25 percent return on His witnessing efforts. If that is true for the Lord, what of us?

Remember that God had only one Son, and He made Him a personal soul winner who went everywhere giving a public invitation to everyone. The Warrior Leader had rather stand before God having witnessed to too many than to too few. You can bear it if you ask too many people to go to heaven, but you will not be able to bear it if you allow too many to go to hell.

Truth: It is impossible to share the gospel with the wrong person.

Test: Do both your private and public witness and invitation reflect confidence in the example of Jesus and the power of the gospel?

PRAISE AND WORSHIP

Trap: In recent years the terms "praise and worship" have come to be used to describe church worship services or at least the music portion. Every believer should be committed to praise and worship of our Lord. We will never have too much of that. However, the elements of outreach and evangelism should be equally present in all aspects of our worship, including music, message, and invitation. To omit the outreach and evangelism elements is as shortsighted as omitting the praise and worship elements.

Triumph: The Warrior Leader will insist that the church services reflect the role of the forward operation base that worships, equips, consoles, cares, and encourages evangelism in order to rescue the lost and the unchurched. To minimize evangelism in our worship services is a certain path to implosion as opposed to an outward explosion.

Truth: Explosion, not implosion.

Test: Do our services minimize outreach and evangelism in music, message, and invitation? Does our invitation include evangelism?

CHURCH GROWTH EMPHASIS

Trap: It is shocking how many church leaders do not understand the difference between *church growth* and *growing the church.* Church growth is about filling a building with people. Growing the church is about equipping and mobilizing the people in the building so they can leave the building to go out into the world and fill the kingdom with souls whom they rescue off the road to hell.

Triumph: The Warrior Leader is committed to church growth. But he is convinced that if the emphasis is always placed on equipping the people to fill the kingdom, the King will take care of His church's growth.

Truth: Growing the church is the biblical way to church growth.

Test: Does our church have a continual year-round training and equipping emphasis that equips the members to win and disciple their own world in their lifetime?

FAVOR DISCIPLESHIP

Trap: Every believer and every church leader wants his or her ministry to have a balance between discipleship ministry and evangelism. Every believer is also aware that if we are allowed to go in the direction of least resistance, we will always end up doing more discipleship ministry to those we already know rather than going to the lost whom we do not yet know or love. We are like an automobile with a front end that needs alignment; we drift toward one direction unless there is some force applied to the steering wheel that holds it in the road.

Triumph: The Warrior Leader will always favor evangelism because he understands that it is the only way for a ministry to maintain balance. Otherwise the church will drift off the course set by the Lord and render itself unable to accomplish the Great Mission.

Truth: Favor evangelism for a balanced ministry.

Test: Do we have a balanced ministry in our emphasis, services, classes, budget, and staff that favors evangelism?

DEPEND ON LARGE CHURCHES

Trap: Large churches cannot win North America. It has already been declared that the Warrior Leader is for church growth and that every church should grow as large as God will allow it. Still, it is not possible to grow enough churches large enough to reach, assimilate, and disciple all the lost and unchurched people. Time and square footage constraints will not permit this. It is a mistake to depend only on large churches to win the world.

Triumph: The Warrior Leader, while committed to church growth, does not depend on that to win North America. His obsession is to equip and motivate all the members to become the church-at-large. That is to enable the church not to be restricted to what I call "facility-

-based evangelism" at one location but to get loose in their world with the gospel.

The large church cannot win North America. But the church-at-large can win not only North America; it can win the entire world!

Truth: Depend on the church-at-large to win this large world.

Test: Are you relying primarily on people to come to your church's "facility-based evangelism" in order for them to be reached?

SMALL-CHURCH PASTOR

Trap: For a pastor in a small membership church to believe *I'm just a small-church pastor* is Satan's kiss of death. The same is true for the member who says, "I'm just in a small church." Such statements generally indicate little hope to do much that is very big. This is a lie straight out of hell! If God called you to that church as a pastor or a member, you are the greatest pastor and the greatest member in the greatest church in the world.

Triumph: When crisis hits—a tragic automobile accident, a marriage disaster, incurable cancer, or a thousand other things that are common to members of both large and small churches alike—who shows up at the emergency room or at a dozen other places at 2:30 in the morning? It's the greatest pastor and the greatest members from the greatest church in the world! The TV evangelist and world-famous preacher will not be there when it matters most—it will be you! And those people will see you as the greatest pastor and people in the world, warts and all. Use that influence to equip them to win their family and friends to Christ.

Truth: Christ in you, the hope of glory.

Test: Am I and our church living in the fullness and greatness that comes when Christ fills and controls us?

REWARDING SOUL WINNERS

Trap: If those who are effective and successful at winning the lost are the only persons who are celebrated, recognized, applauded, and appreciated, then your effectiveness will be limited. Rewarding only successful soul winning is an example of settling for good but giving up the best.

Triumph: Teach your people to love fishing, not just catching. Every person who makes an attempt to witness and minister should be celebrated, recognized, applauded, and appreciated. That way people learn the value of faithfully trying. They will stay after it, and sooner or later the Lord will bring about much fruit for their efforts.

The fisherman doesn't go through all he does just for the catch. Naturally, the catching is wonderful, but they stay out there no matter what because they love fishing and not just catching. If people love catching only and not the fishing, they will soon stop fishing. But if they learn to love fishing, they will stay after it—and catching will come sooner or later.

Truth: Teach the people to love fishing, not just catching.

Test: Is your ministry area an environment of celebration, recognition, and encouragement to those who are faithful to "keep on keeping on" regardless of the outcomes?

THE GIFT OF EVANGELISM

Trap: A multitude of scholars believe that there is the gift of the "evangelist" (see Eph. 4:11) but not the gift of "evangelism." I agree. Whether you believe there is the gift of "evangelism" or not, it does not change the fact that each of us is under a clear mandate from God to do evangelism.

Triumph: The Warrior Leader knows he must not only exemplify personal evangelism; he must never stop trying to get every Christian man, woman, boy, and girl to perform evangelism. It is not only the driving imperative of those whom we lead; it is the leader's immovable duty. Leaders must not allow those whom they lead to become disoriented and thereby fail to rescue family and friends from the devil and hell.

Truth: Every believer must do evangelism.

Test: Has our Lord's Great Commission of evangelism become a job for only a select few, or are you and many others committed to doing evangelism?

NEED MORE PASSION

Trap: "We need more passion for the lost!" That statement is only half correct at best. To be sure, everyone everywhere would do better for themselves, lost souls, and the kingdom of God if they had more passion. Passion is that spirit and emotion in people that causes them to be excited. You'll witness passion at a football game, a gospel singing, and a thousand other places. Passion is great, and we need more for lost souls. But compassion is at least equally the need of our hour. To me, compassion is merely having enough *commitment* connected to *passion* (com-passion) to cause people to actually do something with their excitement. Passion without compassion will cause you to be spiritually alive at church and spiritually dead in the world.

Triumph: You can have all the passion in the world and never get outside your church house or comfort zone. Not so with compassion. Every time you find compassion in the life of Jesus and the Bible, it is accompanied by action. Compassion says, "Yes, something must be done and I am not going to stay here any longer. I am going out there to do something about it."

Truth: Be moved with compassion.

Test: Are you just mostly passionate or are you moved with compassion?

I'M ONLY A LAYPERSON

Trap: Usually "I'm only a layperson" is intended to be translated, "Don't expect too much out of me." There are probably lots of reasons many church members come to reconcile themselves to that station of Christian living, but it is a trap of the enemy.

Triumph: If you are a Christian layperson, you are exactly what the Lord needs and is looking for. Frankly, His entire plan and purpose depend on you, the average, ordinary Christian man or woman. There is not one thing God wants to do that He cannot do through you or any other layperson. We must yield to His lordship and will. D. L. Moody said, "The world is waiting to see what God will do with the life of one person who is completely surrendered to His will."

Mr. and Mrs. Layperson, you're it! The Great Mission will never be accomplished unless you become a Warrior Leader.

Truth: Loose the laypeople and watch them go.

Test: Do the laypersons in your ministry area believe everything rises and falls on their commitment to the Great Mission?

FACILITY-BASED EVANGELISM

Trap: Last year I was in a meeting with a group of Southern Baptist denominational leaders with responsibility for church evangelism across the nation. It was surprising to me that their collective opinion was that only about 5 percent of Southern Baptist churches have a program by which they regularly involve themselves in going out and visiting people who never have attended their church, with the intention of sharing the gospel with them.

This indicates that only a few congregations are doing what most consider New Testament evangelism. At best the remainder of the churches are requiring people to first visit their church and then the church will return the visit. Their approach is, "If you will visit us first, we may visit you later." That's one of the reasons I call this "facility-based evangelism"—because a person must make contact with your facility before you will attempt evangelism.

Triumph: Jesus' model and instruction are for the church to go into the highways, byways, and waterways to reach the people. This approach was certainly not "facility-based evangelism."

Truth: Go into all the world.

Test: Does your ministry strategy equip and urge people to share the saving gospel with people whenever and wherever they meet them?

Leading a small team of soldiers on a long-range reconnaissance patrol through what was considered "no man's land" (an area where neither side has control), we were certain of the enemy's presence nearby. "I can smell them, Sir!" my point man whispered. The terrain offered ideal conditions for us to be ambushed by a larger unit of the enemy forces that could wipe us out. Finally we were back into safer surroundings and compared notes. We agreed that the enemy was lying in wait for us. But we were puzzled about why they had not hit us.

Before that day was over, an American unit much larger than our little patrol was ambushed in that exact location, and they suffered a number of casualties. It was later determined that the enemy allowed us to pass through because of how we were equipped, the way we moved, and the belief that we had detected them and were ready to fight. Their element of surprise was lost, and we were saved.

The Warrior Leader will be vigilant in preparing those whom he leads in such a way that they will not be surprised, outnumbered, overrun, or taken out by the enemy. Remember that principle: "If the way is easy, it is probably mined or booby-trapped or has an ambush site!" Always be on guard for those things along the way that will keep you from accomplishing the Great Mission. There is one thing for certain: If you attempt to win the lost to Christ, you will get opposition. But you will be doing what pleases the Lord, and you can expect that He will help you win His victory. The Warrior Leader knows to watch his step and avoid booby traps, land mines, and ambushes.

⚜ ⚜ ⚜

NO MAN LEFT BEHIND

The slogan "No man left behind" is an expression of one warrior's love, concern, commitment, and care for another warrior. These words mean, "No matter what it takes, someone cares enough to make certain you will not be left alone and abandoned." When the Warrior Leader brings those spiritual-war fighters he leads to *know* that this expression is a fact, all of them rise to a new level of victorious war fighting.

"Moving stealthily through the night, Special Forces executed a bold raid to save a private." This is how the account of the famous rescue of U.S. Army private Jessica Lynch begins. Follow the story of that mission and her survival, and know how committed the U.S. military is to leaving no person behind. As you read, try to identify similarities in this story that should apply to Christians and their fallen fellow war fighters.

She was hiding in her bed, just after midnight, when the Special Ops team found her in a room on the first floor of Saddam (naturally) Hospital in An Nasiriya. A soldier called her name, and without answering she peeked out from under the sheets.

"Jessica Lynch," he called, "we're United States soldiers and we're here to protect you and take you home." The American approached the bed and took his helmet off and she looked up at him and replied: "I'm an American soldier, too."

The operation had launched less than an hour before. As helicopters carrying the Special Ops forces landed outside the hospital, predator drones circled overhead, sending pictures back to intelligence officers, who briefed commanders in the super secure Joint Operations Center. One detachment of Marines made a diversionary attack on another part of the city, while the main force landed at the hospital and began searching for Lynch. When they found her, she "seemed to be in a fair amount of pain," officials later recounted, and she was strapped to a stretcher to be carried down a flight of steps and outside to a helicopter. As her chopper took off, she grabbed the hand of the Army doctor and pleaded, "Don't let anybody leave me."

In the Joint Operations Center, Air Force Capt. Joe Della Vadova followed the raid as it happened, and as soon as Lynch was in the air phoned Jim Wilkinson, the top civilian

communications aide to CENTCOM, General Tommy
Franks. "She is safe and in our hands," he reported. The
whole operation, expected to take 45 minutes, was over in 25.
Next Della Vedova called General Vince Brooks, the No. 2
operational officer at CENTCOM. "Mission Success 1," he
said tersely, indicating a successful rescue of Lynch. "Mission
Success 1 and 2" would have meant they'd achieved the
raid's other objective: to capture Saddam's cousin Ali Hassan
al-Majeed, the sinister "Chemical Ali" who had an office in
the hospital. They missed him that time, but a few days later
U.S. officials announced that he was believed to have been
killed in a bombing raid on his home.

Pfc. Jessica Lynch had entered Iraq as an unheralded private, a 19-year-old clerk in a rear-echelon supply unit that
had the misfortune to take a wrong turn in the desert. But she
left it last week as the one enlisted soldier almost every
American could recognize by sight—the first U.S. prisoner to
be rescued from behind enemy lines since World War II. Her
return to safety after 10 days in Iraqi hands was a welcome
reminder to Americans that their forces could strike almost at
will in Iraq, coming just as the coalition resumed the advance
that took them to the streets of Baghdad last week. It was
heralded from the White House—where President George W.
Bush was described by a senior official as "full of joy
because of her rescue and full of pride because of the rescuers"—to the tiny hamlet of Palestine, West Virginia, where
church bells rang and the roadside signs left no doubt about
who deserved the credit: "Thank You, God, for Saving Jessie!
Prayer Brings Miracles Home."[49]

An Iraqi doctor led the Americans to the makeshift graves of as
many as eleven coalition soldiers. Without shovels, the Special Ops
team dug up the bodies with their bare hands. Later nine names were
moved from "missing" to "killed in action."

This is one of the most touching and exemplary aspects of the entire operation—brave rescuers digging up dead bodies of fellow soldiers with their bare hands so there would be "no man left behind." Their statement was heard not only throughout the military but around the world: "Come what may, we care enough for each other that no one will be left alone or abandoned!"

These kind of actions communicate that warriors do not neglect their responsibility to care for other soldiers. Bringing those you lead to *know* this fact is one of the most powerful things a Warrior Leader can do. The Warrior Leader must instill in those whom he leads the confidence that he loves and cares for them. They, in turn, should be trained to do the same for those around them. This is precisely one of the things that is telegraphed by the leader when he is insistent on being around the front lines of battle and also why the leader is always last to eat, after those he leads have been fed.

These and other similar actions cause people to say, "He does not ask us to do things he will not do himself." Translated, this means, "Our leader is as concerned about us as he is about himself." Leaders should always find opportunities to demonstrate love and care for the people whom they lead. The word *CARE* is a good way to remember the efforts leaders should make to achieve this objective.

C is for *Concern.* Look at a person's life, work, children, marriage, health problems, and time for opportunities to express concern.

A is for *Action.* It is not enough to just discover and speak about concerns. We must show concern through helpful actions.

R is for *Respect.* Regardless of age, station in life, income, background, race, creed, education, or position, respect always shows the same Christlike attitude for everyone. This should be done personally and publicly. Respect should also be shown when speaking of someone who is not present. Those who are listening will judge how you respect all people by the way you show respect to some when speaking in private.

E is for *Enrichment.* One primary goal of leaders is to invest in and enrich the spiritual lives and futures of those with whom we serve.

They and their families should be able to point to certain aspects of their spiritual journey that are better because they have been with you.

First Sergeant James Karolchyka said, "Never get so caught up in cutting wood that you forget to sharpen your ax." The Warrior Leader must never get so caught up in what he is doing that he fails to care for those whom he leads. Like professional military war fighters, the Warrior Leader realizes that he will not accomplish anything without those whom he leads. And those whom you lead must know you care and that you won't forget them.

Frederick the Great said, "The commander should appear friendly to his soldiers, speak to them on the march, visit them while they are cooking, ask them if they are well-cared-for, and alleviate their needs if they have any."

"All this talk about super weapons and push button warfare is a pile of junk," said General George Patton. "Man is the only war machine. . . . Always remember that man is the only machine that can win the war. . . . It's nice to have good equipment, but man is the key. Remember the French Revolution? That battle was won with brooms, sticks, and stones—by a bunch of angry women. Get a determined bunch of men and women and they will win the battles no matter what the odds or what kind of equipment they use."[50]

The Warrior Leader realizes the need for buildings, resources, and equipment, but nothing is more important than training, equipping, and caring for the people. Jesus came and died for people, so people must always be the main thing. General Patton declared, "The soldier is the army. No army is better than its soldiers."[51]

The Warrior Leader must never forget that he is in the battle for the people—both those who are saved and those who are lost.

III.

ATTACK, ATTACK, ATTACK!

The Warrior Leader's Mission ("Do")

THE COMBAT INFANTRYMAN BADGE

This medal is awarded for skill and heroism to the field soldier engaged in active combat in the trenches of front-line war fighting.

YOUR COMBAT INFANTRYMAN BADGE

As the Warrior Leader you will receive your combat Infantryman Badge as an award for do-or-die efforts made on the front lines of spiritual-war fighting for souls and God's kingdom. This not only reflects distinguished commitment but also the reason for which the Warrior Leader was saved and the Great Mission he is to *do*.

THE WARRIOR LEADER'S MISSION ("DO")

This is what the Warrior Leader is to *do*, and it is what forms and defines his commitment.

"CONTINUE THE ASSAULT"

A ll ammunition expended, bayonet fixed and bloody, one hundred dead enemy all around me, my arms and weapon stretched forward into battle, and my last breath shouting, "Attack, attack, attack!" This was the answer of one combat soldier when I asked him, "As a warrior of many wars, what do you want your last words to be?"

That soldier's words were almost the same comments that came out of a circumstance in Afghanistan. The true story was recounted recently of a few Special Forces team members trapped in a fierce battle. After a number of days attempting to fight off a much larger enemy force, they were about to be overrun and killed by the enemy.

Finally, the team leader was contacted by radio from headquarters. Those seeking to locate and help this team that was about to be killed asked, "What is your present condition?" As the radio signal weakened and then stopped, the team leader's last words were: "Here is our condition: We have not slept in four days, we have not eaten in two days, we are out of water, almost all of our ammunition is gone, I have redistributed ammo, ten rounds per man—and tonight we are prepared to attack, attack, attack!"

This brave team of Special Forces combat soldiers was declaring, "It doesn't matter how the conditions of our situation may appear. We are disciplined, trained, and equipped warriors who know our mission. We are determined to die giving all our effort to accomplishing our objective!" Thankfully, the team lived through this near-death episode, and it was probably due mainly to their determination to stay on the attack even unto death.

The Christian life and the Great Mission of our Christian life are not static but dynamic. The Warrior Leader understands that to go forward in an all-out offensive and to refuse to rest upon past accomplishments does not mean we are ungrateful or forgetful about the past. It means that we refuse to die in the past and that we had rather have victory for our own future and for that of coming generations.

Often the Warrior Leader will not have all he needs to mount a victorious attack, but he will continue the assault nevertheless. General George Patton recalled a major offensive attack in which he was involved.

On December 19, 1944, General Eisenhower had a meeting at Verdun with General Bradley, General Devers, and myself and the members of his staff present. The decision was made for the Third Army to attack the southern flank of the Bulge. I was asked when I could make the attack. I stated that I could do so with three divisions on the morning of the twenty-third of December. I had made this estimate before going to Verdun and had taken exactly eighteen minutes to make it. General Eisenhower stated that I should wait until I got at least six divisions. I told him that, in my opinion, a prompt attack with three was better than waiting for six—particularly when I did not know when I could get the other three.

Actually the attack of the III Corps with the 80th, 26th, and 4th Armored Divisions jumped off on the morning of December 22, one day ahead of the time predicted. In making this attack, we were wholly ignorant of what was ahead of us but were determined to strike through to Bastogne, which we did on the twenty-sixth. I am sure that this early attack was of material assistance in producing our victory.

The Battle of the Bulge was the last major German offensive of World War II, and it caught the allied forces off-guard, completely surrounding the 101st Airborne and elements of other units. The Allies had generally assumed that the Germans had been defeated and that the war was drawing to a close. Patton and others understood, however, that if the German all-or-nothing offensive succeeded, the war would be prolonged at a great cost. Pushing back the offensive and rescuing the surrounded 101st required immediate action. Patton believed that he could not wait for ideal conditions. Leadership is often a matter of balancing timing against available resources. Opportunities are easily lost while waiting for "perfect conditions."[51]

The Warrior Leader is committed to *do* the Great Mission. It is his assignment given by none other than Jesus Himself: "As You sent Me into the world, I also have sent them into the world" (John 17:18 NKJV).

The Warrior Leader has been assured that he and the church have the power to overrun the enemy: "I will build My church, and the gates of Hades shall not prevail against it" (Matt. 16:18 NKJV).

The Warrior Leader knows full well that his Commander is expecting him to focus on His mission assignment: "For whoever is ashamed of Me and My words, of him the Son of Man will be ashamed when He comes in His own glory, and in His Father's, and of the holy angels" (Luke 9:26 NKJV).

The Warrior Leader is committed to *attack, attack, attack!* because time is critical and he already has been given the *go* for the Great Mission: "Go therefore and make disciples of all the nations, baptizing them in the name of the Father and of the Son and of the Holy Spirit" (Matt. 28:19 NKJV). "I must work the works of Him who sent Me while it is day; the night is coming when no one can work" (John 9:4 NKJV).

So why are we waiting? Let's get moving to the front lines.

⚜ ⚜ ⚜

GOING TO THE FRONT LINES

Amy Carmichael wrote the following disturbing essay about Christians who are unmoved and unconcerned about the plight of the unsaved.

The tom-toms thumped on all night, and the darkness shuddered round me like a living, feeling thing. I could not go to sleep, so I lay awake and looked; and I saw, and it seemed like this:

That I stood on a grassy sward, and at my feet a precipice broke sheer down into infinite space. I looked, but saw no bottom; only coiled shapes, black and furiously coiled, and great shadow-shrouded hollows, and unfathomable depths. Back I drew, dizzy at the depth.

Then I saw forms of people moving single file along the grass. They were making for the edge. There was a little woman with a baby in her arms and another little child holding on to her dress. She was on the very verge. Then I saw that she was blind. She lifted her foot for the next step . . . it trod air. She was over, and the children over with her. Oh, the cry as they went over!

Then I saw more streams of people flowing from all quarters. All were blind, stone blind; all made straight for the precipice edge. There were shrieks as they suddenly knew themselves falling, and a tossing up of helpless arms, catching, clutching empty air. But some went over quietly and fell without a sound.

Then I wondered, with a wonder that was simply agony, why no one stopped them at the edge. I could not. I was glued to the ground, and I could not call. Though I strained and tried, only a whisper would come.

Then I saw that along the edge were sentries set at intervals. But the intervals were far too great; there were wide, unguarded gaps between. And over these gaps the people fell in their blindness, quite unwarned; and the green grass seemed blood-red to me, and the gulf yawned like the mouth of hell waiting for them.

Then I saw, like the picture of peace, a group of people under some trees, with their backs turned toward the gulf. They were making daisy chains. Sometimes, when a piercing shriek cut the quiet air and reached them, it disturbed them and they thought it rather a vulgar noise. And if one of their number started up and wanted to go and do something to help, then all the others would pull that one down. "Why should you get so excited about it? You must wait for a definite 'call' to go. You haven't finished your daisy chains. It would be really selfish," they said, "to leave us to finish this work alone."

There was another group. It was made up of people whose great desire was to get some sentries out; but they found that very few wanted to go, and sometimes there were no sentries for miles and miles at the edge.

Once a girl stood alone in her place, waving the people back; but her mother and other relations called, and reminded her that her furlough was due; she must not break the "rules." And, being tired and needing a change, she had to go and rest awhile; but no one was sent to guard her gap, and over and over the people fell, like a waterfall of souls.

Once a child caught at the tuft of grass that grew at the very brink of the gulf; the child clung convulsively, and the child called but nobody seemed to hear. Then the roots of the grass gave way, and with a cry the child went over, its two little hands still holding tight to the torn-off bunch of grass.

And the girl who longed to be back in her gap thought she heard the little one cry, and she sprang up and wanted to go; at which her relatives reproved her, reminding her that no one is necessary anywhere— the gap would be well taken care of, they knew. And they sang a hymn.

Then through the hymn came another sound like the pain of a million broken hearts wrung out in one full drop, one sob. And a horror of great darkness was upon *me,* for I knew what it was—the cry of the blood.

Then thundered a Voice, "The voice of the Lord, saying, Whom shall I send, and who will go for us? Then said I, Here am I; send me. And He said, Go, and tell this people," "Jesus said, 'Go ye into all the world, and preach the gospel to every creature,' and, lo, I am with you always" (Isa. 6:8–9; Mark 16:15; Matt. 28:20). But most just stayed there making daisy chains![53]

SENT TO WAR

I graduated from the Special Forces school at Fort Bragg, North Carolina, and I got to return as the graduation speaker for a class. This was an unforgettable experience for me. A large class of graduates from the U.S. Army John F. Kennedy Special Warfare Center and School and a record crowd of attendees filled the civic auditorium. However, nothing was more unforgettable than what I heard as I handed out diplomas to these unique warriors.

The men themselves were worn and torn, having been out of the woods only a few hours before after successfully completing what is one of the toughest military training courses in the world. In this graduating group, one soldier had been killed in training. He received his diploma and Green Beret posthumously. Another had been wounded, and he got out of his wheelchair to limp up to receive his diploma. All of them showed bruises and cuts, but none could have looked prouder. These were not kids, regardless of their age. Some had already been in combat, and they wore the medals to prove it, but now they were receiving that coveted Green Beret.

They received their diploma from me. I embraced their firm hand shake, and from the bottom of my heart I said to each man, "God bless you!" These men and everyone present knew where they were headed, so each responded sincerely to my benediction over them. But what came next was the unforgettable thing.

Passing by me, after receiving their diploma, they immediately came face-to-face with the school's commanding general. Major General (now Lieutenant General) "Jerry" Boykin is an imposing and fit figure who is probably one of the most decorated officers on active duty. General Boykin is almost legendary in the Special Forces and Special Operations world.

"Soldier," Boykin said to each man, as if that were his first name.

Then he would declare, "You are a warrior and I am sending you to war!" Then continuing, as if to prophesy, he declared, "You won't let us down—you will make us proud!"

I could almost hear the back bone of each soldier cracking as he stood a little straighter and taller just before giving his earnest and strong reply, "Yes, sir!"

Then the general's voice would become more fatherly as he gripped "Soldier" by the hand and shoulder, bidding him farewell. "God bless you, son—God bless you. Now go to war." Again, "Soldier" responded as if pledging himself to die before he would disgrace duty, honor, and country: "Yes, sir!"

Unforgettable! Hearing that exchange well over one hundred times that day as the warriors went off to the front lines of war was a moving experience.

There is no time for distractions and daisy chains. The Warrior Leader is commanded to go to the front lines to *do* the Great Mission. He is a warrior sent to a war. The Warrior Leader is following the command and example of his Lord, and he knows that on the front line is where the war is won.

⚜ ⚜ ⚜

THE VICTORIOUS BATTLE PLAN

*T*he person with a vision is always at the mercy of the person with a plan." I agree with whomever made that statement, but it is essential to have a vision *plus* a plan if you are to execute a victorious strategy.

Strategy is the plan used by the Warrior Leader to fulfill the Mission-Vision and accomplish the Great Commission. Strategy is far more than just imagining a plan and hoping for future possibilities.

Without effective strategy you, your family, friends, and church will perish. They will wander aimlessly into an enemy-infested wasteland of religious activity while souls—those for whom Jesus died and whom we are commissioned to win—miss heaven and plunge headlong into hell.

Strategy is the connector between dreams and reality. It is the link between now and later. It is the difference between life and death, dreams and nightmares, victory and defeat, heaven and hell. The Warrior Leader is always conscious of this truth. His mind is always focusing on the strategy he will *do*.

The Warrior Leader knows how he will move and maneuver the strategic plan from ideas, concepts, and means to practical execution that results in accomplishing the Great Mission. A clear illustration of "strategy as a bridge" is given by General Gordon R. Sullivan, former Army Chief of Staff. Our graphic places on the "nearside" the means, ideas, concepts, and resources we have to work with. On the "farside" the vision is placed. The "nearside" is where we are, and the "farside" is where God wants us to be.[54] (See figure #1.)

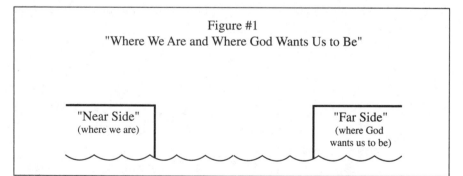

Figure #1
"Where We Are and Where God Wants Us to Be"

"Near Side"
(where we are)

"Far Side"
(where God
wants us to be)

What connects where you are to where God wants you to be is the bridge, the strategy, the victorous battle plan. (See figure #2.)

Whatever strategic approach (bridge) is chosen, the Warrior Leader will evaluate its effectiveness by one simple biblical standard. "Is my strategy effective in discipling and developing victorious spiritual-war fighters who are able to multiply themselves through others, who form an army committed to win souls and then continue this cycle until the Great Mission is accomplished?"

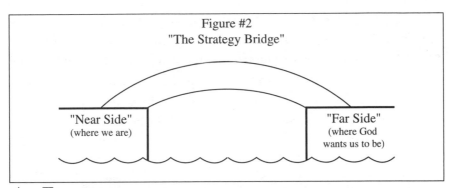

Figure #2
"The Strategy Bridge"

"Near Side"
(where we are)

"Far Side"
(where God
wants us to be)

AN EXAMPLE

Warrior Leaders all across America and in other countries have discovered that the FAITH Sunday School Evangelism Strategy is an effective plan and bridge to move them from where they are to where God wants them to be. Let us apply the FAITH concept to Sullivan's illustration of strategy.

Nearside illustrates that our resources and means are represented by the Bible, the Holy Spirit, and the church.

Farside is the Warrior Leader's stated Mission-Vision, which is his ultimate goal.

Sunday School small group ministry is the backbone of the FAITH strategy bridge. Everything revolves around, in, and out of the small group. Sunday School small groups become the foundational span for the bridge of FAITH strategy. Now see how effectively FAITH moves the Warrior Leader from where he is to where God wants him to be. (See figure #3.)

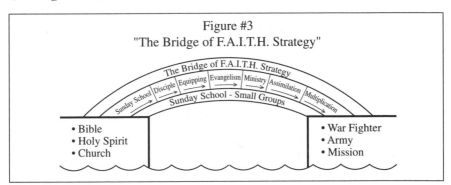

Figure #3
"The Bridge of F.A.I.T.H. Strategy"

The Bridge of F.A.I.T.H. Strategy

Sunday School | Disciple | Equipping | Evangelism | Ministry | Assimilation | Multiplication

Sunday School - Small Groups

• Bible
• Holy Spirit
• Church

• War Fighter
• Army
• Mission

It is interesting that years ago when missionary Robin Hadaway and other leadership in Brazil began to strategize on how to spread FAITH across that great country, their Portuguese translation of the name came out precisely, "Bridge of FAITH." Their logo became a bridge connecting to two sides. Also, the Warrior Leader will have deep appreciation for the fact that Sullivan correctly allows his illustration to use *values* as the bedrock that provides the foundation for the supporting pylons for the bridge. (See figure # 4.)

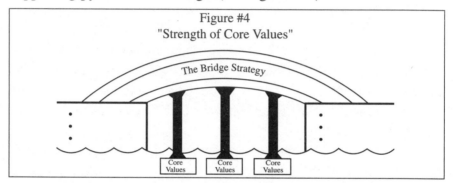

Figure #4
"Strength of Core Values"

The Bridge Strategy

Core Values   Core Values   Core Values

Sullivan explains, "Your *values* capture who you are and how you will operate. Your *vision* illuminates your purpose. It is the spark that ignites everything else. Your *strategy* outlines how you will achieve your vision within the context of your values. Strategy without vision is meaningless, just as vision without values has no legitimate basis. Taken together, however, they create a gestalt that is the basis for successful action."

It is amazing how many churches have well-phrased vision statements, yet they are not equipping their people to accomplish the Great Mission. Vision without a strategy to accomplish the Great Commission is a pathway to kingdom failure.

One key to developing an effective strategy is for the Warrior Leader to mentally position himself on the *farside* at the Mission-Vision and look back toward the other side, the *nearside*. Looking back allows him to better view the ideas, concepts, resources, and means in order to develop and construct a plan, a bridge, a strategy.

As the Warrior Leader looks back to devise a strategy for church members to win and disciple their world in their lifetime, he knows it will require more than the pastor and staff continually repeating the Mission-Vision. It will take more than inviting a few lost and unchurched people into "the fort" on special occasions. It will take more than a few soul-winning specialists making occasional small raids into enemy territory.

Remember the Warrior Leader's Mission-Vision?

- To develop victorious spiritual-war fighters
- who form a force multiplying army
- that accomplishes the Great Commission

If the vision is just to fill a building with a crowd of people, we must admit that such is not God's ultimate vision. The Lord's vision is a kingdom strategy by which every believer is to be intentionally active in winning all the lost to faith in Christ and then discipling them to go and do the same.

It is almost impossible to find another biblical strategy, other than FAITH, that is able to accomplish so much so effectively in one single approach and effort. Each week with only one organization and one effort, FAITH enables the pastor and church to impact all the key functions of the church—evangelism, discipleship, assimilation, ministry, fellowship, small groups, and worship—along with the care and nurture of members.

Nothing has more clearly illustrated the comprehensiveness of FAITH than a pastor whom I saw in a box. That's right, a pastor in a box! I know you're chuckling right now saying, "I've seen pastors in a corner, in a jam, in a mess—but never in a box!" Well, I did!

To illustrate all that FAITH had done for him and his church, he used a box. On each of the four sides of the box he had written the words *Evangelism, Ministry, Discipleship, Sunday School, Assimilation,* or the like. He had removed both the top and the bottom of the box so he could stand inside the box, hold it up, and run from one side of the platform to the other. He said, "Here was my life before FAITH. Someone would cry out, 'Evangelism!'" (He turned that word toward the audience and ran to the other side of the stage.) Then someone would cry out another of the words and he would again run to the opposite side.

He continued this until all words had been called out and began to be repeated. Standing with the look of frustration and exhaustion, he exclaimed, "That's the way my life was before FAITH!" Then he got out of the "rat race" box and declared that FAITH had simplified it all by doing all those things in one effort at one time. He concluded, "FAITH has become the all-in-one ministry strategy for our church!"

The twenty-first-century church must look and think toward its future strategically if it expects to survive and to be victorious.

General Douglas MacArthur said, "A good soldier, whether he leads a platoon or an army, is expected to look backward as well as forward; but he must think only forward."

It is entirely possible as you look back and then think forward toward your future that the bridge of FAITH is exactly the strategy that will connect where you and your people are now to where you know the Lord wants you to be for His kingdom and for souls in the future. It certainly has become such for thousands of churches and hundreds of thousands of Christians.

The Warrior Leader's strategic battle plan will go forward along certain guidelines that have become history's advice on "the ways to win." Following are several principles of victorious spiritual-war fighting that are in fact "The Twelve Ways to Win."

✤ ✤ ✤

THE TWELVE WAYS TO WIN
(PRINCIPLES OF VICTORIOUS SPIRITUAL-WAR FIGHTING)

*"The art of war owns certain elements and fixed principles.
We must acquire that theory, and lodge it in our heads—
otherwise, we will never get very far."*
FREDERICK THE GREAT[54]

*T*he Twelve Ways to Win" are the principles of war. These principles of war summarize the characteristics of victorious war
fighting. This set of time-tested guidelines comes from vast
military experience. The greatest value of these principles to the
Warrior Leader is educating him to understand and analyze what must
happen to win against the enemy. Some of these winning ways do not
apply exactly the same in all situations and therefore should not be
viewed as just a checklist.

Through the years, experts in military warfare have listed the principles of war, generally numbering them from four to fifteen. The
shorter listing is usually a combination of those on the long list. Today
the United States Army's list contains nine guidelines. The Warrior
Leader's list has twelve.

In order for the Warrior Leader to execute spiritual-war fighting
victoriously, he must know and have focused in his mind at least the
following twelve principles. All these principles are biblical, they are
found in the life of Christ and others, and they are effective in gaining
victory in spiritual combat.

There will always be some overlapping of core values with these
twelve principles of war. However, core values are non-negotiable and
are connected in a progressive way, whereas the twelve principles of
war are guidelines that may vary with the situation.

Following is a quick overview of the twelve principles, followed
by expanded explanations.

1. *Objective.* A clearly defined, decisive, attainable goal that contributes directly to accomplishing the Great Mission. Expected result:
Focus.

2. *Offense.* Initiating intentional aggressive action to advance
against the enemy and accomplish the Great Mission. Expected result:
Advance.

135

3. *Intentionality.* This is the essential active ingredient in all offensive actions. Expected result: *Initiate.*

4. *Intelligence.* Information that produces confidence by giving us advantage and denying the enemy unexpected advantage. Expected result: *Confidence.*

5. *Force Multiply.* Training and equipping that increases the force and enhances success. Expected result: *Expansion.*

6. *Mass.* Concentration of forces to overwhelm the enemy, gain control, and accomplish the Great Mission. Expected result: *Synergy.*

7. *Mobility.* Movement that allows us to take advantage of situations and keeps the enemy at a disadvantage. Expected result: *Flexibility.*

8. *Simplicity.* Concise instructions that ensure complete understanding. Expected result: *Understanding.*

9. *Surprise.* Striking at a time and place or in a manner that catches the enemy off guard. Expected result: *Unprepared.*

10. *Reinforcement.* Additional persons who strengthen the force and effectiveness of our efforts to achieve the Great Mission. Expected result: *Strengthen.*

11. *Unity of Command.* Leader authority to generate coordination and cooperation. Expected result: *Synergy.*

12. *Communication.* Exchange of information that produces help and support to fulfill the Great Mission. Expected result: *Help.*

PRINCIPLE #1: OBJECTIVE

Every effort of the Warrior Leader should be expended toward a clearly defined, decisive, and attainable *objective* that contributes directly to accomplishing the Great Mission. This principle objective drives all other war fighting activities. The Warrior Leader must have a clear vision of the end result and must also convey a clear understanding of how all actions will contribute directly to the final goal.

General von Clausewitz said, "No one starts a war—or rather, no one in his senses ought to do so—without first being clear in his mind what he intends to achieve by the war."[56]

Long before General von Clausewitz came on the scene, the Bible made this observation clear: "For which of you, intending to build a tower, sitteth not down first, and counteth the cost, whether he have sufficient to finish it?" (Luke 14:28). "What king, going to make war against another king, sitteth not down first, and consulteth whether he be able with ten thousand to meet him that cometh against him with twenty thousand?" (Luke 14:31).

The Warrior Leader must build willing acceptance and support from all those in his area of influence. Otherwise, the efforts and actions will deteriorate and the objectives will become unobtainable.

If the individual Christian warrior is deceived by the enemy into believing he is fighting all by himself or that his fighting does not directly contribute to the Lord's Great Mission, he will develop an attitude of "what's the use to keep fighting?"

Jesus Christ, our Commander-in-Chief, has given us an overall objective and individual assignments. He has put in the grasp of every warrior the power for the victory. The Warrior Leader must make the objective so clearly defined, decisive, and attainable that every Christian warrior will be influenced to stay on the front line and keep fighting until the Great Mission is achieved. The objective is primary. Can you state your objective?

PRINCIPLE #2: OFFENSE

Yes, for Christians it is true that the war has already been won and the victory has been declared. However, there are more battles to be fought as we approach the final battle in this "mopping-up" campaign. Meanwhile, the Warrior Leader obeys the Lord's orders to maximize all efforts and resources to rescue from the enemy's possession those he holds captive as he waits to plunge them into eternal torment. Such requires an all-out offensive.

The offense determines victory or defeat for souls; therefore, more information is shared on this critical principle than others. Many Christians and Christian leaders are failing because they don't understand offense. Please read carefully and continuously apply the

137

following observations to your individual life, your family, class, church, and world.

Offense is to initiate intentional aggressive advance against our enemy, Satan, to accomplish the Great Mission. Offense is the essence of victorious war fighting. This cannot be emphasized too strongly.

General George Patton risked his reputation and career on the belief that he should initiate an intentional aggressive advance against the enemy or be relieved of his command. His philosophy was attack or quit. Patton recalled, "General Omar Bradley called up to ask me how soon I could go on the defensive. I told him I was the oldest leader in age and in combat experience in the United States Army in Europe, and that if I had to go on the defense I would ask to be relieved. He stated I owed too much to the troops and would have to stay on. I replied that a great deal was owed to me, and unless I could continue attacking I would have to be relieved."[57] Patton's conviction was to attack or quit. He was not relieved.

Without offense it is impossible to win—whether in your personal spiritual life, your family, or accomplishing the Great Commission.

Consider the expressive words used to define offense: "initiate, intentional, aggressive, advance." None of these terms and actions is confrontational to people to whom we minister. The Warrior Leader understands that to be hostile, defiant, and rude to people is unacceptable and counter productive to our intent. However, the Warrior Leader's offensive actions are intended to be perceived by Satan as hostile, defiant, and rude.

To *initiate* is to take the initiative in dictating the terms of action. It is the ability to self-start, to take it to the enemy before we receive a devastating blow ourselves.

Intentionality is action that is focused on a certain purpose. The Warrior Leader is not just doing "church stuff." He is doing ministry with a dedicated purpose.

Aggressive is to be tenacious, bold, and courageous against obstacles that the devil sends against our efforts.

Advance is to make progress in the direction that accomplishes the *mission.*

These expressions are hot-hearted fighting words. The Warrior Leader knows it is impossible to go forward without such an offense. James Wilson, in his "application of military theory to contemporary spiritual conflict," is correct: "Whether the offense is made along the whole front or at a decisive point, it has several basic characteristics. In attitude it is bold; in direction it is forward toward the enemy at the objective; in means it uses effective weapons."[58]

Jomini emphasizes the powerful expression of offense: "They want war too methodical, too measured; I would make it brisk, bold, impetuous, perhaps sometimes even audacious."[59]

All successful war fighters, both military and spiritual, subscribe to what General Patton called "The Golden Rule of war: speed, simplicity, boldness." He emphasized this offensive rule by saying, "We're advancing constantly and we have no interest in holding on to anything except the enemy." His summary on the subject of offense was, "When in doubt, Attack, Attack, Attack!"[60]

This offensive attitude will seem contrary to some Christians. To many Christians it appears that a retiring, passive, defensive attitude in their spiritual life is considered a virtue, more Christlike. To them an intentional offensive approach toward the enemy would be out of character for a Christian, perhaps even sinful.

These often portray themselves as being defenders, hoping that such a position will overcome the enemy and accomplish the Great Mission. The Warrior Leader is convinced that a prolonged defensive posture will inevitably lead to defeat. Defensive postures are deceptive because they convey a false sense of safety when actually you have made yourself a stationary target. This is the most deadly position to have in a fight.

This combat truth is precisely why experienced commanders urge their soldiers, "You keep moving and the enemy cannot hit you. When you dig a fox hole, you dig your grave!"

Paul the apostle understood the dangers that sitting still brought to spiritual war fighters such as himself: "Brethren, I do not count myself to have apprehended; but one thing I do, forgetting those things that are behind and reaching forward to those things which are ahead, I press toward the goal for the prize of the upward call of God in Christ Jesus" (Phil. 3:13–14 NKJV).

Yes, some Christians may draw back from such intentionality. But the Warrior Leader will not. The Warrior Leader is like me and countless thousands of other believers who have stood knee deep in carcasses and blood of mothers, fathers, sons and daughters, marriages, families, futures, homes, and churches, to say nothing of our dear nation. All because good people stood by sucking their spiritual thumbs, hoping something good was about to happen, while the enemy devoured their loved ones, friends, and the world around them.

The Warrior Leader will not stand by because he is a Christian who is convinced beyond a doubt that we are in a blood-and-guts battle for souls. The Warrior Leader refuses to occupy himself with spiritual pacifiers, playing silly parlor games, making daisy chains, and the like. *No!* the Warrior Leader is compelled on every front to rise up in the warrior spirit of Christ and mount an all-out offensive assault, declaring as Jesus did, "The gates of hell shall not prevail against [us]" (Matt. 16:18).

That expression is the clear embodiment of the Warrior Leader as he leads the offensive charge for the sake of souls and our Lord's kingdom. Offensive actions are taken to dictate the nature, scope, and tempo of war fighting. The Warrior Leader is determined to expend all energy and resources to impose upon the enemy and the situation God's will to win souls and to disciple them.

The war fighter on the offensive will always have a morale advantage as well as a physical advantage over the enemy at the point of contact in combat. The intentional aggressor has made decisions and plans; the defending enemy's reaction is forced upon him by the attacker. The Warrior Leader knows it takes less force to mount an offense against one point than to defend all points.

140

The Warrior Leader has two general approaches to conduct an offensive attack—the conventional approach and the unconventional approach. I choose the term *conventional* because it describes what most people understand war fighting to be—large numbers of soldiers lined up on two opposing sides facing and fighting each other. Such an approach requires one side to have an overwhelming number of troops, weapons, resources, and superiority to be victorious and overpowering. But the Warrior Leader understands it takes more to win than numbers and resources massed in one location. This is exactly why he is aware that large churches cannot win North America. Of course, all churches should grow larger for the sake of souls, but they cannot be effective in accomplishing the Great Mission through size alone.

If the offensive strategy of the church is what I call "facility-based evangelism"—bringing people to the church facilities in order to expose them to a life-changing experience with Christ—it will be impossible to get all the needy souls into the churches, even if they would come. There are just too many!

Further, it is impossible for Christians to get all their family and friends into a church. The idea that we can build enough churches that will be large enough to attract enough people in order to carry out the Great Commission is absurd. While facility-based evangelism can be useful in a limited way, it is at best a half-hearted effort and is doomed to failure in accomplishing the Great Commission.

Please understand that I am all for growing churches larger and larger and planting more and more new churches. But individually, locally, nationally—and especially internationally—our mission is doomed if this is our primary offensive strategy.

The New Testament approach that Jesus gave is not dependent on large churches. Rather, it depends on the "church-at-large." The church-at-large can win not only North America but the entire world. When observing a church's effectiveness, the question should not only be, "How large is it?" but "How at-large is it?" How effective are the members at reproducing themselves and carrying out the Great

Mission when they are away from the facility base of the church building?

This truth brings us to the second approach to conducting an offensive attack against the enemy—the unconventional approach. This term denotes an approach unlike that of the conventional. It is unconventional because rather than depending on the largest congregations, it depends on the smaller units. All size churches, small groups, and small teams can mount the offensive and decisively defeat the enemy locally, nationally, and internationally. This focuses on training and equipping people to function as victorious war fighters as a small team or as individuals. The focus is now upon "persons-at-large" and not upon the large church or facility-based evangelism.

The wholesale advantage of this more unconventional approach is apparent. Regardless of the size of a church congregation, each and every Christian can and should be equipped, trained, and mobilized to conduct victorious war fighting and to set captives free, whether or not those captives ever make it into our church facilities.

Doesn't it seem likely that God's primary plan is not to invite non-Christians, a few at a time, into an over concentration of Christians where these believers preach the gospel over and over to one another? His plan is to empower, equip, and loosen the believers from a church to go into an over concentration of lost souls (their world) to reach them for Christ.

Once such a kingdom view and approach is linked to the force-multiplier approach, there is forged an unparalleled spiritual-war fighting offensive that will achieve the Great Mission.

The decisive battlefield "tilt point" will come when there is a sufficient number of force-multiplying small groups from all size churches to create a mass able to fulfill the Great Mission on the largest scale possible. That date and point in time is undeniably within the grasp of this generation. But we need believers who dare to rise up to be Warrior Leaders of a force-multiplying army, regardless of the size of their churches.

Large-scale strategic planners make their best contributions to such a massive victory by:

- Being personally engaged in front-line spiritual-war fighting with a small group force-multiplier team. (The ruin of an army comes when leaders lose their taste and smell for the victory of front-line trench warfare and when they fail to move among the troops and share their risk and sacrifice.) Strategic leaders must be front-liners.

- Devising, resourcing, and mobilizing the small group force-multiplier approach on a worldwide scope. This supports tactically and technically those who are locked in combat on the front lines of the offensive locally and globally. This is biblical kingdom strategy that God will bless.

The Warrior Leader has concluded, as have military experts, that there are three aspects to conducting a victorious offensive. Whether the offensive is on a small or large scale or from an individual, a Sunday School class, or a national denominational convention, these three aspects are (1) seize, (2) retain, and (3) exploit. These are to be sought in the initiative.

To *seize* is to take intentional action to renew progress and advancement toward the Great Mission. Not only do most churches need to do this, but every evangelical denomination is also in desperate need of this strategy.

To *retain* is to focus unrelentingly on making progress and advancement.

To *exploit* is to use the momentum of the progress and advance to the greatest gain possible without relenting too soon. Look at your efforts to equip and train your people, your efforts to reach the lost, your efforts to baptize, and your efforts to assimilate and to minister. Can you identify places where the offense needs to be seized, retained, and exploited? How could you begin such an offensive effort?

PRINCIPLE #3: *INTENTIONALITY*

Intentionality is not synonymous with *confrontational*. When I kiss my wife I am intentional but I'm not confrontational! Sometimes, in an attempt to cast a dim light on witnessing, people will call it confrontational. Usually in so doing they try to give the idea that all types of intentional witnessing are rude and insensitive toward others. No one should be confrontationally rude and insensitive in attempting to speak for Christ, but everyone should be intentional if they intend to witness for Christ.

Intentionality is action that is focused on sharing the saving grace of God with lost souls. The Warrior Leader will demonstrate intentionality in many ways, but none more than in three situations: (1) When attempting to share the gospel with a lost person, (2) when giving a private invitation for a person to profess Christ as his Lord and Savior, and (3) when giving a public invitation for a person to make known publicly his commitment to Christ. Intentionality is the essential, active ingredient in all offensive actions. It is to initiate action as a self-starter, for the sake of souls.

PRINCIPLE #4: *INTELLIGENCE*

"Lest Satan should take advantage of us; for we are not ignorant of his devices" (2 Cor. 2:11 NKJV).

Intelligence is essential elements of information (EEI) that never permit the enemy to acquire an unexpected advantage over us while at the same time providing us the advantage over our enemy.

According to James Clavell's translation of the Chinese language, Sun Tzu believed that to remain in ignorance of the enemy's ways and conditions was the height of inhumanity, that one who neglected this intelligence was no leader, no help to his sovereign, and no master of victory. What enabled this general to strike, conquer, and achieve things beyond the reach of ordinary men was foreknowledge—intelligence.[61]

The lack of intelligence is inhuman because without it, battles and wars are extended, victory is denied, and the Warrior Leader loses an advantage in carrying out his primary mission. Consequently, thousands upon thousands of souls continue to go into hell, which, in fact, is the apex of inhumanity.

There are two effective ways to gather reliable intelligence on the devil that will result in the Warrior Leader's ability to wage victorious combat against the enemy. The *number one resource* is God's documentation of EEI (essential elements of information) found in His inerrant orders given to us in His Word. The *number two resource* is "converted spies" who have come over to the Lord's side from the enemy's side.

Sun Tzu's most appreciated advice comes from the use of spies to gather intelligence.[62] He proposed that there are five classes or kinds of spies: local, internal, doomed, surviving, and converted spies. It seems obvious that we who are saved away from Satan are the "converted spies" in this spiritual war for souls. Captives who have been freed from the devil's bondage bring a storehouse of EEI about the hellish devices the devil uses to ruin lives and souls. These reports from converted spies are real-life illustrations of God's EEI from us and those in the Bible.

The Warrior Leader will develop accumulative EEI along three avenues: (1) Who is our enemy? (2) What is our enemy's objective? (3) How does our enemy attack and make war upon us? By answering the third question, the answers to all three questions become obvious. The EEI assures us of three things: (A) Satan has definite predictable devices to use against us. (B) Satan has definite limitations and vulnerability. (C) Satan has a defeating weakness that must continually be assaulted.

The predictable *devices* that our enemy uses against us can be summarized from Ephesians 6:11–12: "Put on the whole armor of God, that you may be able to stand against the wiles of the devil. For we do not wrestle against flesh and blood, but against principalities, against powers, against the rulers of the darkness of this age, against spiritual hosts of wickedness in the heavenly places" (NKJV).

Note the following *devices* used by Satan:

- *Identification.* Satan seeks to confuse us into thinking individuals are the enemy.
- *Army.* He has vast numbers of organized helpers.
- *Unseen.* His army is not of flesh and blood.
- *Power.* He has powers, rulers of darkness of this world, and spiritual wickedness in high places.
- *Leaders.* Satan personally masterminds and leads his forces.
- *Offensive.* He is always on the offensive attack, unlike too many Christians and churches.
- *Tactics.* He uses search-and-destroy tactics as he constantly patrols for men, women, boys, and girls to devour (1 Pet. 5:8).
- *Attacks.* He will usually attack with force at your weakest point.
- *Timing.* Knowing his final defeat is to be consummated soon, he hurries to murder, destroy, ravage, and take captive to hell all souls possible before his time is up.

Now note the following *definite limitations* of our enemy.

- *Identification.* Our enemy has already been definitely identified. While he and his forces may be unseen, we know our enemy is the devil and no one else.
- *Army.* Our enemy's army may be large and evasive, but it is not everywhere at once.
- *Power.* The enemy's force has power but not superior, omnipotent power.
- *Leader.* The enemy's leadership is no match for our Commander-in-Chief.
- *Offense.* The limitation of the enemy's offensive attack is that (1) we have the EEI on him and (2) our God is omniscient and omnipotent.
- *Tactics.* Souls will not long and hunger for an adversary who searches and destroys, but they do long and hunger for an advocate who seeks and delivers.
- *Attacks.* The Warrior Leader is fortified by the armor of God and the omnipresence of God.

- *Timing.* The Warrior Leader is defined by his obsession to win souls and his unceasing efforts to do it now while the harvest is plentiful and before night comes when no one can work.

Now note the following two *defeating weaknesses* of our enemy.

1. *Satan is vulnerable to the truth.* The Warrior Leader will mass all his people, reserves, and weapons to break the enemy's hold on souls at the enemy's most vulnerable point. The Warrior Leader's most valuable EEI is that the enemy is crushed and defeated every time he is confronted with the truth. The truth that "God so loved the world that he gave his only begotten Son, that whosoever believes in him should not perish but have everlasting life" (John 3:16) is confirmed by the death, burial, resurrection, and ascension of the Savior of souls— Jesus. This will always be the truth that drives Satan and his demons toward hell and sets captive souls free. In the Bible, whenever this truth confronts the devil, he trembles and flees.

2. *We can confront Satan.* Mark this fact plainly. The Warrior Leader is convinced that Satan must be confronted with this liberating truth. We must intentionally and aggressively get to the places where the captives are held in bondage by the enemy. These locations are not in the church but in the world. If you were assigned the responsibility to perform a rescue mission of as many captives as you could possibly free, what would you do? Would you have a big meeting inside your fort and hope that some of your soldiers might be able to locate and bring home a few captives, with the hope that others might hear the truth and be rescued?

Would you not instead equip, train, and mobilize warrior teams to go into the areas where most captives are found and attempt the rescue? The question here is not which approach is easier, more convenient, or less risky, but which method is likely to rescue the most captives. Which tactics would you want used if one of those captives were your son, daughter, mother, dad, sister, or brother?

Most importantly, which action did Jesus practice and teach in the New Testament and the early church? Everyone knows the correct answer. It is to go into the world, the enemy territory, and to attempt such a rescue. However, few churches and Christians have an equipping strategy that takes the truth into the enemy's territory in an intentional and aggressive manner. The Warrior Leader is determined to change that.

Having developed intelligence about the who, what, and methods of our enemy, the Warrior Leader is emboldened with confidence. He is able to lead an offense of truth that liberates lost souls from satanic strongholds.

PRINCIPLE #5: FORCE MULTIPLIER

Spiritual leaders in the church understand that they are engaged in a real war. The objective of war is victory, not fighting. Fighting always results in casualties and not necessarily victory. War fighting that minimizes casualties and maximizes the likelihood of a speedy victory always goes forward on one element. This element is correct strategy. Leaders must have a clear understanding and command of the correct strategy. The concept of *force multiplier* is the New Testament strategy for the Christian, the church, and the kingdom.

In response to the terrorist attack on America on September 11, 2001, the Special Forces Green Berets entered into enemy territory in Afghanistan. Their mission was described as "force multipliers."

Afghanistan was 90 percent dominated by the Taliban enemy forces while only 10 percent of the country was a refuge for a relatively small force of anti-Taliban freedom fighters. This small number was ineffective against their overpowering enemy. The U.S. Army Special Forces placed small teams of well-trained and clearly focused soldiers among the freedom fighters and equipped those fighters to achieve a speedy victory. These small teams multiplied themselves in others and created a much larger, effective, and victorious force.

In a way, the force multiplier is like a small amount of yeast that is placed into dough, which then causes that larger mass to expand far beyond what would otherwise be expected or predicted.

Second Timothy 2:2 describes the biblical mandate for the Christian to be a "force multiplier," which is often seen as discipleship or mentoring: "And the things that thou hast heard of me among many witnesses, the same commit thou to faithful men, who shall be able to teach others also."

The evangelical churches of North America in general and Southern Baptists in particular must enlist, train, and activate an army of spiritual force multipliers across America that will equip "the saints for the work of ministry" (Eph. 4:11 NKJV). Without such an army, rooted in and led by the local church, our spiritual future in this country is bleak. Thousands of people are committed to the belief that the force multiplier is the way and that now is the time for each church to focus on winning and discipling its world in its lifetime by "equipping the saints for the work of ministry."

Imagine pastor, staff, and each member of the church not only finding a way to grow and be more deeply and continually discipled themselves, but also finding a way to extend and expand their life in others for the sake of God's kingdom. Each of us, our friends, our church, our country, and our world need to be empowered to become force multipliers.

As I say again and again, many people do not understand the difference between *church growth* and *growing the church*. One concentrates on filling the building while the other focuses on equipping the people who fill the building. Without a doubt we do need force *motivators* from the pulpit to the larger crowd, but we will fail if we do not have an effective way for each believer to be empowered as a force multiplier.

- Are you involved in such a biblical strategy?
- Is that strategy being transferred and multiplied into others?
- How can we significantly change our world without each of us becoming a force multiplier?

Spiritual Warrior Leaders across the land are committing to enlist, train, and empower an exceedingly great army of force multipliers for the sake of the kingdom of God, the world, and eternity. The FAITH Sunday School Evangelism Strategy is designed to be an effective force-multiplier approach.

PRINCIPLE #6: MASS

Mass is bringing together and focusing the united combat powers of a number of forces on one mission. It is the concentration of war fighting forces to overwhelm the enemy, gain control, and accomplish the mission.

Mass is demonstrated when everyone prays for the same outcome (see Matt. 18:19). Mass occurs when the church directs its resources, energy, organization, and leadership toward accomplishing the Great Mission. Mass is effected when all the small groups and Sunday School classes are focused on equipping, discipling, and on-the-job training as force multipliers to reach their objective. Mass can occur throughout an entire denominational body. This is rare, due to territorialism at many levels and the lack of leadership focus and resolve to include unity of command. However, mass was demonstrated in the Southern Baptist Convention's battle for the inerrancy of Scripture and the conservative resurgence.

The tragedy of present-day denominations, including the SBC, is that they have not been able to create sufficient mass to mount an effective offense nationwide to advance the Great Mission beyond the declining condition that now threatens us. It is possible for mass to occur across a denomination. This will happen with the emergence of thousands of single-minded Christians who are driven by the Warrior Leader's obsession to carry out the Great Mission (see "Raising the Bar," p. 74).

Some good points on the subject of mass can be made by examining Nathan Bedford Forrest, a Confederate general in the Civil War. "I git thar firstest with the mostest," he declared.[63] General Forrest likely did not use the double superlative in the quote, but he certainly knew how to use the principles of war even though he was not a West Point graduate. In fact, in this one short quote there are four principles implied. *Git*—that's offense; *thar*—that's objective; *firstest*—that's mobility; *mostest*—that's mass. *Mostest* is mass by bringing the largest amount of combat power to bear on one objective. Our goal in spiritual warfare is not to fight prolonged battles but to win as soon as possible with the fewest casualties and maximum rescue of the enemy's captives.

You may have some limited effectiveness as a "Lone Ranger" witness and may feel most comfortable that way. However, you have no hope of realizing your maximum combat capacity in advancing the Great Mission unless you are equipped and able to multiply and create mass. This is true for the church, denominations, and individuals.

Luke 10:1–2 applies the principle of mass to spiritual warfare: "After these things the Lord appointed seventy others also, and sent them two by two before His face into every city and place where He Himself was about to go. Then He said to them, 'The harvest truly is great, but the laborers are few; therefore pray the Lord of the harvest to send out laborers into His harvest'" (NKJV).

In this passage Jesus is calling for a creation of mass in His offensive effort. He applies mass to prayer and to people. These efforts are for more manpower to seize, retain, and exploit the offenses for the great harvest. In Matthew 28:18–20, Jesus appealed to all Christians through all ages to focus their efforts on one thing—His Great Commission. Now that is massive mass! It's exactly what is needed today.

Paul came to the point where he would hardly mount a spiritual offensive without the hope of concentration of forces: "Furthermore, when I came to Troas to preach Christ's gospel, and a door was opened to me by the Lord, I had no rest in my spirit, because I did not find Titus my brother; but taking my leave of them, I departed for Macedonia" (2 Cor. 2:12–13 NKJV).

Troas was an open door to the gospel that was passed by because of a lack of help. The opposite was true in Macedonia. There Silas and Timotheus joined Paul and became the beginning of a concentration and a force-multiplying team that produced "much people" for the Lord.

> When Silas and Timothy had come from Macedonia, Paul
> was constrained by the Spirit, and testified to the Jews
> that Jesus is the Christ. But when they opposed him and

blasphemed, he shook his garments and said to them, "Your blood be upon your own heads; I am clean. From now on I will go to the Gentiles." And he departed from there and entered the house of a certain man named Justus, one who worshiped God, whose house was next door to the synagogue. Then Crispus, the ruler of the synagogue, believed on the Lord with all his household. And many of the Corinthians, hearing, believed and were baptized. Now the Lord spoke to Paul in the night by a vision, "Do not be afraid, but speak, and do not keep silent; for I am with you, and no one will attack you to hurt you; for I have many people in this city" (Acts 18:5–10 NKJV).

Even though Paul probably never used the words *mass* or *concentration,* no doubt this principle is why the Holy Spirit caused Paul to write the admonition for the New Testament believers to use the force-multiplier approach: "And the things that you have heard from me among many witnesses, commit these to faithful men who will be able to teach others also" (2 Tim. 2:2 NKJV).

Just as stated in the Mission-Vision, the Warrior Leader is committed to building an army of force multipliers. They in turn will do the same thing, generating an even larger mass of force multipliers. What are some things you could eliminate and/or begin, to create mass for the sake of souls and the Great Mission?

PRINCIPLE #7: MOBILITY

Mobility is the flexible movement of war fighting power in a way that keeps the enemy at a disadvantage. Effective use of mobility keeps the enemy off balance by making him deal with new situations and problems faster than he can handle them. The Warrior Leader knows that maneuvering with mobility reduces his own vulnerability and extends the success of the effort. In truth, mobility is actually a force multiplier because of the ability to do more with less.

In Vietnam I served as a combat leader of a battalion reconnaissance platoon of the First Air Cavalry Division. Both the division and the men of my leadership were fitted for flexible, fast movement and maneuvering. The First Cavalry Division had been made "air mobile" by extensive use of helicopters. All of us in this division were trained and equipped to take the offensive attack to the enemy. Additionally, my platoon sergeant and I had trained our twenty-eight men to be "ground mobile" after we left the mobility of the choppers. We did this through reducing equipment to a minimum, hard training, long stays in enemy territory under harsh conditions, cold food, and no fires.

What was the payoff for our mobility? Mobility saved our lives and others more than once and defeated the enemy again and again. The Warrior Leader knows that mobility empowers war fighters to "go."

Read in Luke 9:57–10:16 the dynamic course the Lord Jesus laid out for His personally trained force multipliers as they prepared to launch their offensive for souls. He emphasized the flexibility and speed of being mobile to these Warrior Leaders as they got prepared for conflict, combat, and war fighting (Luke 10:3–4).

Their pay-off? They returned alive. They were victorious. They rejoiced because demons were put on the run and brought to submission by them through the name of Jesus (Luke 10:17). It is noteworthy that our Lord reminded them that the Great Mission was for more names to be written in heaven (Luke 10:20).

Both in the illustration of Jesus and the disciples, as well as my division and men in Vietnam, an important point is obvious. Mobility must affect both the larger group and the lone individual to produce the "go" demanded to realize the Great Mission.

With the church and the Christian, mobility is a matter of obedience to our Commander's orders to *go*. The Warrior Leader will mobilize the largest number of people possible. This is done by mobilizing the largest manpower organization available. This is one of the primary reasons the FAITH Sunday School Evangelism Strategy mobilizes the small group classes within the Sunday School organization. As the large group organization is being mobilized to go as a unit, the small groups are further mobilized into three-person teams.

When I was an A-team leader in the 20th Special Forces (Green Berets), these teams were referred to as "go teams" because of their mobility and their reputation for moving quickly. The individual Christian must function with regularity on a "go team" if he is to become a force multiplier who is victorious in his missions.

When the September 11 attacks happened in the United States, our church experienced extraordinary mobility. This was because of more than twenty-one years of continual, regimented equipping and on-the-job training in the approach mentioned above. Almost immediately, all of our teams were transferred to a special effort to seize, retain, and exploit the offensive opportunity presented by 9/11 to reach people and share the gospel.

In the days after 9/11, many people prayed to receive Christ and hundreds of others were helped with ministry. It is not surprising that over a year later we were still reaping souls—the rewards of understanding and applying the principles of offense and mobility.

Any spiritual-war fighting group that does not have mobility loses the capability of attacking, evading, or even retreating. All that's left for them is to defend until surrender and the end. The Warrior Leader refuses to think in such terms and develops mobility to assure victorious spiritual-war fighting.

PRINCIPLE #8: SIMPLICITY

Simplicity means to see it big and keep it simple. Simplicity is communicating clear, uncomplicated plans and concise instructions in a way that ensures complete understanding. This is a principle of war because simplicity reduces misunderstanding and confusion. These are the things that lead to defeat. Simple plans and instructions carried out on time are better than detailed plans executed too late.

One combat-seasoned general was reported as saying, "Every defeat and every failure can be traced back to two words . . . *'too late!'*" For the Warrior Leader, simplicity will eliminate such defeats and failures in spiritual combat.

God committed His love in clear terms that no one could misunderstand. Jesus committed the same love in uncomplicated expressions that were summarized on the cross and the empty tomb. No clearer demonstration of love has ever been shown. God's plan for redemption of lost souls is often referred to as the Lord's simple plan of salvation. Jesus gave us the Great Mission to accomplish. It is concise, clear, and easy to understand.

The Warrior Leader is attuned to the fact that conducting spiritual warfare requires communication, enlistment, mobilization, teaching, equipping, on-the-job training, organization, exemplifying, ministry, discipling, and assimilation. All of these must be done simply. But no element of carrying out the Great Mission demands simplicity more than the evangelism approach and presentation. This is true for several reasons.

First, you must make your point simply and quickly because people will not pause for long conversations. Second, most people do not have a home church or much theological understanding. Third, the Warrior Leader's commitment is to equip everyone possible and not just a few "elite soul winners." Fourth, these truths must be transferable facts that are easy to grasp.

Have you ever read a church mission statement that said, "We exist to keep people out of hell and to get them into heaven." If you ever do, you can believe that church has the right idea about the principle of war known as simplicity. A congregation like this is able to "see it big and keep it simple."

PRINCIPLE #9: SURPRISE

Surprise means to strike at a time and place or in a manner that catches the enemy off guard. Joshua illustrated surprise by the way he caught the enemy unprepared at the battle of Jericho (Josh. 6:1–21). Gideon's attack of the Midianites was a surprise in all three areas. The *time* was at night, the *place* was on three sides of the camp, and the *manner* or method consisted of lamps, torches, voices, and trumpets (Judg. 7:1–23).

There is no example of a victorious offensive surprise that can top Calvary and the empty tomb of Christ. Even though these events had been forecast in prophecy, they were still overwhelming and they caught the devil unprepared.

The Warrior Leader is certain our enemy, Satan, will be surprised:

- When Christians are equipped to be consistently effective at evangelism, discipleship, ministry, and assimilation.
- When Christians are empowered as force multipliers to pass on to others this training.
- When Christians will do this for the long haul, month after month and year after year.
- When these equipped believers will go to homes of "prospects" night or day.
- When these equipped believers will talk to persons whom they do not know and who have never been to their church.
- When these Christians become Warrior Leaders in their home, church, and small group training teams.
- When those won to Christ are then discipled and become force multipliers themselves.
- When pastors, staff, and church leaders become Warrior Leaders who develop such an army of laypersons.
- When we stop saying *no* for our laypeople and lead them.

When these things happen, Satan will be surprised and we will win.

The Warrior Leader enjoys an advantage of surprise in being indwelled and commanded by the Lord Jesus. God is omniscient but Satan is not. God cannot be surprised. This is not the same with the devil. He can be surprised not only by the things mentioned earlier but by the never-ceasing, victorious power of the love of God through the gospel message itself: "For when we were still without strength, in due time Christ died for the ungodly. For scarcely for a righteous man will one die; yet perhaps for a good man someone would even dare to die. But God demonstrates His own love toward us, in that while we were still sinners, Christ died for us" (Rom. 5:6–8 NKJV).

It is obvious from this text that the love of God and Christ demonstrated through Jesus' death and resurrection was not expected by the enemy. In time, place, and manner, it is still surprising to Satan. The devil is not surprised by the gospel in a church preaching service on Sunday. But Satan is most surprised when an army of laypersons from that church is trained and mobilized to go anywhere at anytime and share the gospel. In truth, Satan is shocked. Talk about "shock and awe" warfare!

The Warrior Leader will seize these tactics of surprise as opportunities to take the initiative and win the day for Christ's sake. Opportunities are lost while waiting for better conditions when surprise will create better opportunities for victory. Hebrews 4:12 sounds out a devastating surprise: "For the word of God is living and powerful, and sharper than any two-edged sword, piercing even to the division of soul and spirit, and of joints and marrow, and is a discerner of the thoughts and intents of the heart" (NKJV).

The Warrior Leader has settled in his mind what his greatest surprise tactic is. It is the gospel of God and Christ taken by ordinary laypersons to people all around them in times and places and in a manner that catches the enemy off guard and rescues souls from Satan's bondage.

An older Christian man shopping in a grocery store with his wife asked a store employee about an item on the shelf. Their conversation continued, and the man shared the love of Christ with the female employee. She prayed to receive Christ right there in the aisle of the store. The woman was soon baptized and joined a church. It was discovered that she was in the final stages of terminal cancer, and she died six months after becoming a Christian.

She had been quiet and shy and had lived a very modest and humble life. The funeral was to be simple and inexpensive. Everyone wondered if anyone would be there since she probably had few acquaintances or friends.

The pastor was surprised when he entered the room for her funeral. While not many people were present, eighteen large funeral wreaths were placed around the casket. Each of these wreaths had been placed there by a person whom this shy, unassuming young woman had led to Christ in the past six months! An army of "ordinary laypersons" like her will not only surprise the enemy; it will change the entire world and eternity.

PRINCIPLE #10: REINFORCEMENTS

Reinforcements can refer to a variety of items, but here it applies to individuals. Reinforcements are additional people who strengthen the force and the effectiveness of our efforts.

While *reinforcements* is not formally labeled as a principle of war, it is certainly implied. Many battles have been won and lost, based on the timely or untimely arrival of reinforcements. The role of reinforcements is vital to performing the Great Mission.

I am often asked how many people we have trained and equipped in FAITH since 1986, with two sixteen-week semesters each of those years. I always laugh and reply, "I don't know and if you know, please don't tell me because I'd be depressed." The reason for this reply is that I'm certain we still don't have enough people on the front line of weekly war fighting, even with the large number we have trained. I am grateful for all those and their efforts to advance toward our mission. However, what I am really urgent about is how many will show up this week and the next week to help us go out into the highways and byways to battle the enemy for souls.

Reinforcements have made us successful in our combat area of operation. If we have 450 to 500 people out for FAITH in a week, likely only 8 to 10 of those people have been in the battle for the entire 21 years. The other 440 or so are reinforcements. Without reinforcements our church would be out of existence and out of the fight.

What a mistake leaders make when they train and equip a number of people and then depend on that same group to stay on the front line forever. The Warrior Leader expects casualties, drop-outs, and stay-behinds. He will lay out plans several times a year to recruit a fresh group of reinforcements. Jesus, Paul, and others called for reinforcements again and again: "Laborers are few . . . pray . . . to send out laborers into His harvest" (Luke 10:2 NKJV); "Do thy diligence to come shortly unto me" (2 Tim. 4:9).

Reinforcements bring energy, excitement, and freshness to those who are showing battle fatigue. Reinforcements will be eager and successful. They will make their leader more committed, confident, and thankful. Reinforcements are willing to move on from learner to leader. Again, force multipliers will supply your front-line offense with a continual flow of needed reinforcements.

PRINCIPLE #11: UNITY OF COMMAND

Unity of command is where a leader with the authority to unify the action of the forces is in charge. Cooperation and coordination are required to have unity of command. However, at this point is where this principle of war is often lost, and this leads to loss of the war.

It is possible to have a high degree of cooperation and not be victorious. While the components may interact in cooperation with one another and coordinate to some extent, without unity of command it is practically impossible to produce the most victorious results.

Failure to understand and deal with this is what robs most bureaucracies of their best war fighting ability. This happens even in denominations. Such a problem does not indicate a lack of leadership. But there needs to be *one leader*—whether a person or a group of persons—with the authority to unify all the forces, resources, and actions. Without this, there is no way to create offensive mass on the largest and most victorious scale.

Smaller groups are not immune from a problem with the unity of command. However, smaller groups that require more direct action leadership usually do produce an effective unity of command.

Cooperation that yields coordination is essential in succeeding at unity of command. *However, it is possible to be so preoccupied with cooperation that unity of command is lost and victory gives way to defeat.* Please read that statement again. Again, entire denominations have lost focus and victory at this point.

The United States barely avoided a horrible defeat in the Pacific during World War II because this principle of unity of command was not applied properly. When Admiral Chester Nimitz and General Douglas MacArthur brought their forces together in the Philippines, there was no single commander on site who was in charge. If the Japanese admiral mounting the assault had not decided to withdraw, for no apparent reason, the American forces might have been dealt a decisive defeat. This would have brought a staggering effect upon the outcome of the war. The American forces had overwhelming strength, cooperation, and coordination. The forces also had the greatest leaders. They were committed to victory. However, all this was almost for nothing because no single leader was in charge. There was no unity of command.

The Warrior Leader realizes that Christians have unity of command first and foremost in Jesus Christ, who is with us always (Matt. 28:20). Where the breakdown of this principle occurs is not, of course, in Christ, but in the individual Christian combatants. When this happens, there is a deterioration of cooperation, coordination, and concentration of forces. This leads to defeat.

The great deterrent to unity of command, cooperation, and concentration is pride. The Warrior Leader must never forget that he is like the Roman centurion who confessed to Christ, "I am a man under authority, having soldiers under me" (Matt. 8:9). The Warrior Leader is under the Commander-in-Chief, and he is also responsible for leading others. Neither area of personal responsibility can afford to become contaminated by personal pride. Pride will keep you from being led to victory. Pride will keep you from leading others to victory. Pride is an arch detriment to accomplishing the Great Mission.

No wonder God's attitude toward pride is so explicit (see Prov. 6:17; 16:18; 1 John 2:16). Daniel 5:20 points out that pride was the downfall of one leader, Nebuchadnezzar: "But when he was strong his heart was lifted up, to his destruction, for he transgressed against the LORD his God by entering the temple of the LORD to burn incense on the altar of incense" (2 Chron. 26:16 NKJV).

If pride can do this to a secular leader, how much more so to a Christian? Pastors are in the church to assure unity of command in order that all forces may be massed and mobilized in order to advance toward carrying out the Great Commission.

PRINCIPLE #12: COMMUNICATION

Most combat leaders are convinced that communication is the most critical aspect of victorious war fighting. This is true not only in secular warfare but in spiritual warfare as well. Communication among individuals, groups, and organizations is essential for efficient and effective accomplishment of the Great Mission. Accurate information must pass back and forth from leaders and subordinates.

The enemy will always have as a primary objective to jam, cut, and disrupt communications. spiritual-war fighting is no different. Satan wants to cut us off from higher headquarters and our Commander. If he succeeds at doing this, he can bring about our defeat and destruction.

In military combat, the enemy will always try to knock out or kill the communications as soon as possible—preferably even before the battle is joined. As an intelligent gathering reconnaissance team, we would often have several radio operators with our unit. These radio specialists with their equipment were easy to spot. They would be the first soldiers fired upon when we made contact with the enemy. Loss of communications would halt our ability to call in help or air power. I would never allow these radio operators to walk next to me because not only did the enemy want to knock out communications from out-side; they wanted to do the same inside the unit. The person closest to the radio operator was usually the commanding officer, so he was always the second person who drew enemy fire.

If the enemy can cut off communication to outside help and knock out the leader on the ground, it is likely he will win the battle.

Prayer is our line of communication with the Lord. Nothing must keep the Warrior Leader from constant prayer. This is the great means to the Great Mission.

⚜ ⚜ ⚜

MISSION CHECKLIST

*H*ave you ever observed the pilot of a plane holding a card in his hand while going through his pre-flight checklist? He does not trust anything to memory or chance because too much and too many people are at risk. There is never a flight that he does not consult and follow that same checklist, often doing so many times in one day. And aren't we glad he uses a checklist!

The military's combat leader's field guidebook emphasizes at least twenty checklists that are critical to the leader's success at his mission. Checklists are quick review points that leave nothing to chance and risk while keeping everyone on mission. The following is a mission checklist that will be used by the Warrior Leader over and over to great advantage: M-I-S-S-I-O-N.

M = Mission Objective
Am I clearly defining a decisive, attainable goal that contributes to accomplishing the Great Mission? Yes___ No___

I = Individual Life
Am I and others living, exemplifying, and teaching the Warrior Leader's core values? Yes___ No___

S = Strategy
Am I committed to a bridge plan that produces victorious war fighters and a force-multiplying army that accomplishes the Great Mission? Yes___ No___

S = Stress Training
Am I stressing and providing on-the-job training that equips the saints to win and disciple their world in their lifetime? Yes___ No___

I = Intentionality

Am I practicing, exemplifying, and training the people to initiate intentional actions to accomplish the Great Mission? Yes___ No___

O = Offense

Am I continually initiating aggressive action against the enemy and accomplishing the Great Mission? Yes___ No___

N = New Reinforcements

Am I consistently bringing into our strategy fresh new persons who strengthen and expand our offense to accomplish the Great Mission? Yes___ No___

Every time I review this checklist, the Lord brings me to recommit myself to the Great Mission. As one who strives to be a Warrior Leader, I intend to keep this checklist always before me because—even more so than with the pilot—"too much and too many people are at risk!"

⚜ ⚜ ⚜

AGAINST ALL ODDS

Often when the Warrior Leader looks at the mission before him, it seems overwhelming. Many times the best spiritual-war fighter thinks, "What's the use; I can't do this all by myself." The enemy loves it when he can get us to believe that the odds are stacked against us. He delights for us to fail to trust the Lord because we feel that our victory would be "against all odds."

There is an exquisite bronze art piece by Ken Payne in Sedona, Arizona. The art piece is of a U.S. Army cavalry soldier of 1865 atop his horse running all-out cross country. "Against All Odds" is the title of this work. The soldier depicted on his horse is Sergeant Charles L. Thomas of the 11th Ohio Cavalry.

There were 416 soldiers decorated with the Medal of Honor during the Indian Wars of the 1860s to the 1890s. These decorations were for valor, and one of the most outstanding accounts was that of Sergeant Thomas.

These wars consisted of running gun battles and scattered skirmishes across vast terrain. Because of such dispersement of troops, the noncommissioned officers became the backbone of these small fighting detachments. Their courage, knowledge, daring, and ability made the difference in these battles.

Late in the summer of 1865 the right column of the Powder River Expedition Dakota Territory containing 1,400 men became lost. Wandering hopelessly, they were unable to reconnect with their larger force. Lost for ten weeks without food, the column was in total despair.

Sergeant Thomas was the only soldier to step forward and attempt to execute a mission to find and bring back the troops, who were headed for certain death. He was one man against overwhelming odds.

Early in the morning Thomas, with two Pawnee Indian scouts, struck out from a larger group across a country that was infested with hostile Indians. After a day or so, Thomas and the two scouts were attacked by Sioux warriors, and a running battle developed. The mighty Sioux were hungry for scalps of the "Long Knives." For hours they fought off their Sioux pursuers. On September 17, 1865, after thirty-six hours in the saddle, Thomas found the lost soldiers surrounded by the enemy. He fought his way through the lines to discover the scurvy-ridden soldiers, who were out of food and totally demoralized. Not one of the officers knew the direction toward safety.

Thomas rallied the troops and formed them into a fighting formation. They were successful in forcing back the Sioux. Thomas further organized the soldiers and pushed them to fight their way over 150 miles to a supply depot camp. This heroic action by one man who was willing to step forward and lead the attack warded off the death and destruction of the entire lost column. Thomas was victorious, against all odds.

Long before Sergeant Charles L. Thomas prevailed against all odds, the Lord demonstrated His saving power over and over again on behalf of His spiritual-war fighters. Consider Joshua at Jericho, Moses at the Red Sea, Gideon facing the Midianites, Daniel in the lions' den, the three Hebrew young men in the fiery furnace, the New Testament apostles and disciples facing opposition, Jesus against Satan and hell, and all the others who have been victorious—even when it appeared they were "against all odds."

KEEP ON KEEPING ON

When I grow discouraged in the battle, some of the most encouraging words come to me not only from the Bible but also from a story recounted by Leslie B. Flynn. "Keep On Keeping On" tells about a young man from Massachusetts who was stubbornly persistent.

A lad saw a want ad in a small Massachusetts paper, asking for a young man to assist the office manager of a brokerage house in Boston. Applications were to be mailed to Box 1720, Boston. The young man wrote the best letter of application he knew how. When no reply came he wrote a second letter. Still no reply. Though discouraged he did not quit. He rewrote his letter, changing the wording, improving the construction. Still he received no reply from his third letter.

The lad knew that success required persistence. So he took a train to Boston, went directly to the post office and asked, "Who rents Box 1720?" The clerk replied that to give out such information was against the law.

The boy hunted for Box 1720, then waited for hours until someone came to the box. He followed the person to one of Boston's large brokerage houses. When the manager heard his story he said, "My young friend, you are just the type we are looking for. The job is yours." Thus began the career of Roger Babson, one of America's illustrious statisticians.

Do you ever feel like giving up your Sunday School class, secretarial job, or superintending position? The qualities demanded of

Christians include perseverance, fidelity, and steadfastness. Paul ordered, "Let us not be weary in well doing: for in due season we shall reap, if we faint not" (Gal. 6:9). Flynn points out that Galatians 6:9 actually deals with three ideas: well-doing, weariness, and waiting.

WELL-DOING

This concept is first in the text. If we follow the original Greek, it reads, "In well-doing let us not be weary." Although some people become tired before doing anything, the usual order is well-doing before weariness.

The immediate context would amplify well-doing as restoring fallen Christians, bearing burdens, sharing income with the Lord's servants, and doing good to all people, especially those of the household of faith. Stretching the context back into the fifth chapter, well-doing embraces the fruit of a spirit-filled life: love, joy, peace, longsuffering, gentleness, goodness, faith, meekness, and self-control. In a general sense, well-doing involves all elements of Christian character and service.

But in well-doing always lurks the danger of weariness.

WEARINESS

Weariness here does not mean physical weakness, but it carries the idea of losing courage, flagging, fainting, relaxing one's strength, becoming despondent in the task. Weariness may be caused by the lack of results as one teaches week after week without apparent impact. Monotony and lack of cooperation can also take their toll.

How easily Paul could have grown discouraged in his long, arduous travels and the persecution he suffered—beaten, shipwrecked, weak, ill, rejected by churches he had founded, facing martyrdom constantly. Yet he knew the secret of an unwearied life. Someone has pointed out how frequently he used the word *always*.

- "always abounding in the work of the Lord" (1 Cor. 15:58)
- "I exercise myself, to have always a conscience void of offence" (Acts 24:16)

- "always confident" (2 Cor. 5:6)
- "alway rejoicing" (2 Cor. 6:10)
- "praying always" (Eph. 6:18)
- "giving thanks always" (Eph 5:20)
- "always having all sufficiency in all things" (2 Cor. 9:8)

A man handed out tracts for years on a certain street corner. Because there were no results, he gave it up. Returning to the same corner two years later, he saw a man giving out tracts on the same spot. Striking up a conversation, he learned that the man had become a Christian through a tract given out there just over two years before. He added, "Many a time I've come back here to find the man to thank him, but he never came back. So I decided he must have died and gone to his reward. That's why I've taken his place."

We need not only initiative but *finish-iative.*

WAITING FOR THE CERTAIN HARVEST

A dying soldier asked the hospital chaplain to send a message to his Sunday School teacher. "Tell her I die a Christian and that I have never forgotten her teaching." A few weeks after he sent this message the chaplain received this reply from the Sunday School teacher: "May God have mercy on me! Only last month I resigned my Sunday School class because I felt my teaching had done no good through the years. I am going back to my pastor at once to tell him that I will try again in Christ's name and that I will be steadfast to the end."

We should learn a lesson from the farmer. He plants, waits, and waits some more, but though discouragement abounds, the reaping finally comes. Just as the farmer is supported by the hope of a sure harvest, so every Christian teacher should sow, weep, pray, and work in the hope of reaping fruit in God's appointed time.

A missionary goes to a field for a term, but few respond to the message. Discouraged, he almost resigns from the mission board. But he returns to find a ready harvest, due mainly to his faithful sowing during his first term. Another missionary works in Muslim territory. After forty years he can count the converts on the fingers of one hand. He dies. Another missionary is sent. Hundreds of people are converted under his ministry, the result of the first missionary's faithful, plodding service.

The least promising person in a woman's class was a shabbily dressed boy named Bob. The superintendent secured new clothes for him. After three Sundays Bob was missing. The teacher visited him, only to discover that his new clothes were torn and dirty. The superintendent gave him more new clothes. Bob returned to Sunday School. After attending twice his place was empty again. Once more the teacher learned that the second new clothes had gone the way of the first. Utterly discouraged, she told the superintendent she was going to give up on Bob.

"Please don't do that," urged the superintendent. "I'll give him more new clothes if he'll promise to attend regularly." Bob did promise. He did attend regularly. He became an earnest Christian, joined the church, became a teacher, and eventually studied for the ministry. He became Dr. Robert Morrison, honored missionary to China. He translated the Bible into the Chinese language and opened the gate to teeming millions in that country.[63]

The Warrior Leader is so confident in his Commander-in-Chief that he is committed to "keep on keeping on" and to *attack, attack, attack!* until the Great Mission is accomplished. The Warrior Leader realizes he has the battle plan and the methods to get the job done.

We can win this war regardless of how stacked against us the odds may seem. Don't forget that you and the Lord Jesus add up to the majority. It's glorious to think about how many spiritual-war fighters have gone into battle as a minority and come out as the majority. That's your destiny as a Warrior Leader. We can only imagine what follows for the Warrior Leader when his days of service on earth are completed.

Meanwhile, even when it appears that we are struggling against overwhelming odds, *attack, attack, attack!* Stay on the offensive and accomplish the Great Mission.

✤ ✤ ✤

FOXHOLE BUDDIES

*I*n the hours of the early morning, snoring coming from a soldier in a foxhole will attract an enemy probing team like a rare roast beef draws a junkyard dog. I was only a few yards away, and I could hear the snoring loud and clear. In fact, I could hear two men snoring in the same foxhole that I was crawling toward. After moving another foot or two, I could make out the situation clearly—two soldiers in one foxhole, and both sound asleep.

One was crumpled up, face down, with his weapon behind him. The other was undoubtedly the one who was supposed to be on watch. He was to the side, with his head tilted back, his mouth wide open, and he was making noises like a broken-down sawmill. His weapon had slipped from his hands and fallen outside the foxhole, with the barrel down in the dirt and the stock still near him.

I slipped one leg over the top of his weapon and sat on it so he could not use it on me if he awoke suddenly. Already I had eased out my meat cleaver from its holster. I was getting ready to strike this sleeping sentinel right in the head in a way that he and his foxhole buddy would never forget.

L.Z. (landing zone) "Box" was on a ridge where our unit had set up position for the night. Sergeant Watts and I were foxhole buddies. Both of us were happy to have an old cardboard ration box flattened out and placed between our bodies and the wet cold ground. Our ponchos covered us from the damp of the mountains in the north central highlands of Vietnam. We had pushed hard all day in some scary places and were extremely glad to rest. However, Watts and I took turns each hour all night long, crawling around "checking the guard."

Our troops were teamed up in foxholes. One man in each foxhole had to stay awake to keep the enemy from crawling up on us during the night. The foxhole buddies would take turns staying awake and standing guard, but Watts and I had to check to be certain they were awake. One sleeping sentinel could get us all killed.

It was my turn to check the sentries, and I was crawling from fox-hole to foxhole. If a soldier was sleeping or was only half-awake while on guard, he was doubly dangerous. If I surprised him he might shoot me before he realized what was going on. When I heard the two sol-diers snoring, I was both angry and scared. My intentions were to ven-tilate both feelings in a way to teach these two a lesson.

Straddling the soldier's weapon, I turned the meat cleaver over so the cutting edge faced away from the man and the butt side was com-ing down on his head. I screamed right in his face as that meat cleaver came down on his steel helmet just above his eyes. When he grabbed for his weapon I grabbed him. The other sleeping soldier woke up and realized what was happening.

In the most graphically threatening words I could muster, I com-manded him to get back on his duty before he got us all killed. My reassurances to him were that I would be crawling back here before daybreak. If I found him asleep again I would throw him down the ridge, and he knew what the results of that would be. As I crawled back up the ridge away from the foxhole, I could hear his foxhole buddy taking up where I had left off. He was fussing and cussing at the guy about the likelihood of his sleeping getting them both killed.

Foxhole buddies end up together in order to strengthen and help each other. However, within the course of a war you can end up fight-ing beside some interesting people. The Warrior Leader will find him-self again and again linked with and leading an assortment of foxhole buddies with whom he must fight and win. The Bible describes some of those characters with whom we must work, fight, and lead in order to accomplish the Great Mission.

Paul the apostle, as the Warrior Leader, was about to make his final and eternal change of duty stations. In prison and facing certain death by having his head chopped off, he was at the end of his road. He could look back over thirty years on this road that began in Damascus and now was about to end in Rome.

All along the way of his advance in spiritual-war fighting for the sake of lost souls and the kingdom, he found himself fighting beside a variety of fellow soldiers in the Lord's army. In 2 Timothy chapter 4, he reviewed some of his most unforgettable foxhole buddies: "Be diligent to come to me quickly; for Demas has forsaken me, having loved this present world, and has departed for Thessalonica—Crescens for Galatia, Titus for Dalmatia. Only Luke is with me. Get Mark and bring him with you, for he is useful to me for ministry. And Tychicus I have sent to Ephesus" (2 Tim. 4:9–12 NKJV).

Soldiers are great at nicknaming one another. These soldiers described by Paul could easily have been called:

- Wonderboy
- Quitter
- G.I.
- Top
- Doc
- Re-Up
- Runner
- The Old Man

WONDERBOY: THE DEDICATED SOLDIER

Paul instructed Timothy, "Do thy diligence to come shortly unto me" (v. 9). Timothy was the young lieutenant leader type. He was Paul's young leader lieutenant as well as his friend and chief associate. He came from a very strong Christian background. He grew up in a Christian home that was fully engaged in spiritual-war fighting.

Timothy probably would also have been looked upon as a "ninety-day wonder." That's a nickname given to young officers who have had little training before they are placed in responsible leadership positions. Hence, he was a "Wonderboy."

Timothy was young, but he was made of the right stuff. Likely he was converted under Paul's ministry, and the apostle saw his potential.

He became the "commander's aide" to Paul, who poured Jesus, the gospel, and himself into this young firebrand soldier of the cross like a father would do to a son. The apostle referred to Timothy as his "beloved and faithful son in the Lord" (1 Cor. 4:17 NKJV) and his "true son in the faith" (1 Tim. 1:2 NKJV).

This young, dedicated leader did not disappoint Christ or Paul. He became an evangelist and an encourager. He was strong, sensitive, affectionate, and loyal. He had sterling character, and he set a good example. According to some accounts, Timothy became the first bishop of Ephesus.

Warrior Leaders are always willing to pour themselves into younger Christians with the hope that some will emerge to bless the Lord and the cause of His kingdom. Timothy reminds us all that young leaders have important roles. When the Lord saves and calls a young soldier, he can equip and enable him to serve Him and lead for Him. Blessed is the Warrior Leader who provides places, experiences, and opportunities for worthwhile ministry among young adults and youth. Young men and women will quickly catch a vision and step out with enthusiasm and faith. They are teachable and trainable.

There has never been a time when the church needed more "Timothies" than it does right now. Do you have some around you? If not, find them. Paul and the early church can testify that they can become good foxhole buddies.

QUITTER: THE DESERTER SOLDIER

"Demas has forsaken me, having loved this present world, and has departed for Thessalonica" (v. 10a NKJV). Demas was a disgraceful deserter. He was no doubt a believer and at one time served the Lord and was named among the faithful who ministered to Paul during his first imprisonment. But now he was a disgrace. No true Christian can fall from grace. But there is no state of grace from which it is impossible for a person to fall into disgrace! Beware of a Christian profession that does not separate a person from the world. This foxhole buddy did the most disgraceful and dishonorable thing imaginable.

172

He crawled out of his position and went over to the side of the enemy. Paul said, "He loved this present world and departed."

"Love not the world, neither the things that are in the world. If any man love the world . . . the lust of the flesh, and the lust of the eyes, and the pride of life, [he] is not of the Father, but is of the world" (1 John 2:15–16).

What ruined Lot's wife? The world. What ruined Achan? The world. What ruined Judas? The world. What ruined Simon Magus? The world. What ruined Demas? The world. What is most likely to ruin us if we're not separated from it? The world.

When this foxhole buddy turned his back on Paul and crawled off to the enemy, he also turned his back on the Lord Jesus. The chink in the armor of a soldier who allows his consecration to run out will be the same spot where his courage will also run out.

Be on guard for "deserting Demases." Keep them close to you. Make clear to them the certain and present dangers that lure every soldier of the cross. Place other good warriors around them. Call for their accountability. Make them look at the deserter's cause. Help them know how deserters rob heaven and fill up hell with souls. Then cheer them, love them, pray for them, and hang on to them—just as Christ has done for us. For they, like you, are choice, chosen soldiers whom Christ has called to victorious war fighting.

"But it is too late," you may be saying. "I've already been deserted." Have you ever been dependent on someone and they let you down, ran out on you, and deserted? Just about everyone has had some experience like that, even Christians, pastors, teachers, deacons, husbands, wives, parents, children, and Christian friends. Desertion by people you trust is very hard to take, and sometimes you can never get over it.

What do you do in those times? Paul never took his eyes off the Lord. He did not abandon the Lord because someone had left him. The mission and the blessings of God were too precious and important for him to desert and do to the Lord what someone had done to him.

It is said of David after he was betrayed by King Saul, "David went on his way" (1 Sam. 26:25). You and I, like Paul, must get on with our lives in Christ. Don't let a deserter steal that from you. Your Commander-in-Chief has supernatural reinforcements to send you right now. Call on Him. Forgive and fight on as Warrior Leaders who, like Jesus and Paul, have gone on victoriously before you.

GI: THE DISGUISED SOLDIER

"Crescens to Galatia" (v. 10b). Crescens's name is mentioned only here in the New Testament. He is never heard of again after this brief mention by Paul. We have seen in the foxhole the young dedicated lieutenant, and we have watched a disgraceful deserter leave his war fighting position and go over to the enemy. But Crescens portrays the most glorious of all fighting persons ever to serve as a soldier and crawl into a foxhole. He represents the millions upon millions of ordinary, unnamed soldiers. He was the ordinary, everyday, general utility GI (Government Issued) who looks like all the other soldiers in the trenches. Sometimes they are called the "grunts" or the "ground pounders." But regardless of what they are called, these ordinary soldiers are the most glorious of all.

General Douglas MacArthur had the following to say about the plain, ordinary American soldier:

The men in the ranks are largely citizen soldiers, sailors or airmen—men from the farm, the city, from school, from the college campus—men not dedicated to the profession of arms; men not primarily skilled in the art of war; men most amazingly like the men you know and see and meet each day of your life.

If hostilities come these men will know the endless tramp of marching feet, the incessant whine of sniper bullets, the ceaseless rustle of sputtering machine guns, the sinister wail of air combat, the deafening blast of crashing bombs, the stealthy stroke of hidden torpedoes, the amphibious lurch over perilous ways, the dark majesty of fighting ships, the mad din of battle and all the stench and ghastly horror and savage destruction of a stricken area of war.

These men will suffer hunger and thirst, broiling suns and frozen reaches, but they must go on and on and on when everything within them seems to stop and die. They will grow old in youth burned out in searing minutes, even though life owes them many tranquil years. In these troublesome times of confused and bewildered international sophistication, let no man misunderstand why they do that which they must do. These men will fight, and perchance die, for one reason only—for their country—for America. No complex philosophies of world intrigue and conspiracy dominate their thoughts. No exploitation and extravagance of propaganda dims their sensitivities. Just the simple fact, their country called.

MacArthur not only was describing the American GI; he was also describing Crescens and all those multiplied millions like him. Many of us seek to wage spiritual war as Warrior Leaders from our tiny spot in the world or on the front lines of our lives. But those lone, solitary, unnamed, and unknown soldiers are heroes to their mothers, fathers, sons, daughters, sisters, brothers, neighbors, and friends. The identity of many of these soldier heroes is kept from us. In fact, some of the most decorated soldiers in the armed forces often go unnoticed and unappreciated because they are undercover war fighters.

The Lord lists the names and some details of great heroism in the "Hall of Faith" in Hebrews 11. But the Lord also gives the same commendation, honor, and appreciation to many heroes whom He allows to remain anonymous. They are simply called "others" (v. 35).

One of my most cherished possessions is the flag that flew over the Tomb of the Unknown Soldier which was presented to me. It was given on behalf of the United States Army to memorialize the day I was wounded in combat. That tomb, and all the ceremony attached to it, honors faithful soldiers who have fallen but their names are not known. That tomb says, "We may not know your name, but we are aware of your faithful service. We love and honor you for it and will never forget you."

There are so many unnamed warriors of the Lord in the Bible who were greatly used for His glory. Think of the little boy with the loaves and fish, the unnamed man who delivered the city in Ecclesiastes, the three wise men, the centurion, and dozens of others whom God chose to use for His glory. We may be used of the Lord as unnamed and unnoticed instruments in His hand. Furthermore, we may be touched and moved by God through just such a blessing in disguise.

It doesn't matter if a person is a big name, a small name, or even a no-name. If the Lord has put him in our lives—or foxholes—we should make the most of it for Jesus.

In all your battles and war fighting with some wounds and defeats, if you ever feel downhearted, remember that "God has arranged the parts in the body, every one of them, just as He wanted them to be" (1 Cor. 12:18). And don't forget that the Lord knows your name, rank, serial number, and foxhole. The Bible says that "many that are first shall be last; and the last shall be first" (Matt. 19:30).

TOP: THE DILIGENT SOLDIER

"Titus unto Dalmatia" (v. 10c). Titus was not an ordinary GI like Crescens; he was more like Timothy. He was like Timothy for good reason: He had the same Lord in heaven and the same leader here on earth as Timothy.

According to Paul, Timothy was reliable and dependable. He had the strength and tact to bring calm to desperate situations. But above all those admirable qualities, he was a diligent soldier. Consequently, Paul entrusted him with some of his most difficult assignments.

Titus was a Greek convert whom Paul entrusted with missions in Corinth and Crete. Through his forceful and diligent leadership, he was able to calm uproars and difficulties in some hard and struggling church circumstances (1 Cor. 16:10–11). His life was a beautiful example of how a Christian should live out his faith in hard times. In the military the soldier who is the backbone of the outfit and who can always get the job done is the first sergeant. He is called "Top," meaning top sergeant. He is the most diligent and reliable soldier who can be depended on when the going gets tough. Titus certainly lived up to that name.

It has been noted that the secret to Titus's success in spiritual-war fighting was in how he himself was led: "Titus was led to Christ, for Christ and by Christ."[64] Just as the Lord used Paul to lead Timothy to Christ, He also used Paul to lead Titus to Christ. Paul never seemed to get that out of order. He always got the soul to Christ first. Then other things would follow. Too many people today try to "sneak up" on a person. They try to get a lost person involved in many things before he actually gets involved in Christ as the main thing, and they end up with nothing. Do not be timid or afraid to share the gospel. It is not you who will convert people. It is the power of the gospel that does it—the power of the gospel unto salvation!

Next, Titus was led *for* Christ. It is obvious that much nurturing and discipling were given to Titus. Because Titus had been led *to* Christ and *for* Christ, he was easily led *by* Christ into many wonderful and fruitful opportunities for spiritual victories and the winning of souls. Since Titus followed Christ closely, he followed Him well and as a result he led well, too. This made Titus the "man of the hour" a number of times. He was assigned the responsibility of completing the collection for the poor believers of Jerusalem as well as strengthening the churches by teaching sound doctrine and good works (Titus 1:5).

It is a wonderful thing for your foxhole buddy to be not only a dedicated, reliable soldier but a person who is also diligent for Christ. When the fire starts falling and the bullets start whizzing by, Titus is the foxhole buddy you want. He stands his guard, and he covers your back. You will never have to worry where he is or what he's doing.

DOC: THE DISTINGUISHED SOLDIER

"Only Luke is with me" (v. 11a). Luke was the medic, the medical officer, the "doc" of this detachment. Front-line medics are some of the bravest and most revered people in uniform. Most of the time they have excellent training, which is surpassed only by their extraordinary courage to stay in the forefront of the hottest battles, treating wounds, extending lives, encouraging the hopeless, and comforting and praying with dying soldiers. The last person on earth whom a dying combat soldier usually sees is a fellow soldier or a medic.

These warriors abandon their weapons, defenses, and usually their good sense—all for the sake of rescuing or caring for the wounded and dying. (At least six to eight of these dear souls were necessary for me to make it out of Vietnam alive. Every one of them worked over me as if I were their own brother or son.) I hope there is a monument somewhere in our country to honor such outstanding warriors. None are more deserving than these medical men and women.

Luke was Paul's "fellow laborer" (Philem. 24 NKJV), and he is the person who wrote the Gospel of Luke and Acts. There are only three personal references to Luke in the Bible. He was a Gentile physician, or "the beloved physician" as Paul called him (Col. 4:14), and the only non-Jewish writer of a New Testament book.

Some interpreters believe Luke might have been the brother of Titus—but this is only a guess. It is certain that Luke was a brother in Christ, and he accompanied Paul on some portions of all three of his missionary journeys. When Paul wrote these words in 2 Timothy, Luke was with him.

As expected of a Christian and a physician, Luke was a person of humility who had a gift of mercy. This was revealed in his deep concern for the poor, sick, outcasts, and especially lost souls. This comes through in the Gospel of Luke. He was a constant encouragement to everyone, especially Paul. He probably treated people's physical ailments, perhaps even Paul's eye trouble.

Everybody needs a "doc" sooner or later. Even without a medical degree, we can be merciful and encouraging to others. It is amazing how many people have thanked me for being a powerful helper to them personally. My "doctoring" consisted of nothing more than listening to their heartaches, encouraging them, and praying with and for them. That little dose of attention has been a miracle-working prescription through the years. I have been "doctored" on myself in the same way with wonderful healing results.

Most of us know more medicine and "doctoring" than we are practicing. The Warrior Leader understands that the sickest soul on this planet who needs the most urgent care is the lost soul. Sin sickness not only ruins life now; it ruins it eternally. Don't say, "I can't help!" Of course you can, with God's help working through you. Go, comfort, encourage, and pray. Show you care to some person, and watch the Lord Jesus bless him and you. There's a hospital full of "docs" in our churches. They just need leadership to get them out and into practice.

No wonder God allowed "doc" Luke to write His eternal prescription: "Then the angel said to them, 'Do not be afraid, for behold, I bring you good tidings of great joy which will be to all people. For there is born to you this day in the city of David a Savior, who is Christ the Lord'" (Luke 2:10–11 NKJV).

RE-UP: THE DETERMINED SOLDIER

"Take Mark, and bring him with thee: for he is profitable to me for the ministry" (v. 11c). If you as a soldier rejoin the military, you "re-up." That is, you reenlist in the army.

Mark had been one of the most promising young recruits ever, but he dropped out after Paul and Barnabas had begun the first missionary journey. This must have been something similar to what happened with Demas. Because of this, Paul refused to let Mark go along on the second missionary journey. Can you think of anyone like that? Have you ever just dropped out? Perhaps you quit and were rejected later because you had developed a reputation as a person who would not stay the course. If you have ever done that, here's some great news.

There are many stories about people who have become successful after an experience of failure and defeat. One day while reading a devotion from *Our Daily Bread,* I came across just such an account.

Nathanial Hawthorne, for example, lost his position in the custom house at Salem, Massachusetts. Feeling very low, he told his wife the bad news, expecting her to share his dismay.

179

But to his surprise, she responded with delight, "Now you can continue work on your book." With her encouragement, he got busy and finished *The Scarlet Letter,* which literary critics say is one of the finest novels ever written in the United States.

Phillips Brooks failed miserably as a teacher, but later went on to achieve great prominence. When he couldn't make it in the classroom, he decided to prepare himself for the ministry. He became very successful, and his name appears in lists of the best known American clergymen.

So if you are despondent because of a failure, don't give up hope. Ask God to help you learn from your experience, and then begin anew. You may be down, but you are not out unless you give in to an attitude of defeat.[65]

John Mark—the dropout, the quitter, the failure, the runaway who came back to "re-up" for a second chance—became the constant companion of Simon Peter, much like Timothy was for Paul. He eventually became a preacher, an evangelist, and he wrote the Gospel of Mark. This resulted in Mark preaching and winning souls even unto this very day—all because a dropout came back to a God of the second chance. I have hoped many times that Demas did the same as Mark. I don't know about Demas, but I do know about you and me.

One time, before I entered the ministry, I did just like Demas and Mark. But by the grace of God, I had the same joy as Mark when I returned to the God of the second chance. Do you need a second chance? Then come back and return as the wayward son did in Luke 15:11–24. Please read that thrilling story. You can have the same results as all these who did not let failure become a permanent state in their lives.

Never forget the millions of people who desperately need an encounter with our Lord of the second chance. Be the Warrior Leader who will comb the highways and byways with the glorious truth of God's love and a second chance to "re-up."

RUNNER: THE DEPENDABLE SOLDIER

"And Tychicus have I sent to Ephesus" (v. 12). Tychicus was an Asian Christian who traveled with Paul. He was more fully described by Paul in other places as "a beloved brother," "a fellow servant," "a faithful minister" (Col. 4:7–14). When you link those expressions—brother, servant, minister—it is plain to see why Tychicus was such a trusted and dependable colaborer.

He had exactly the character needed to be the messenger for Paul in the early church. He was responsible for communications from Paul to others. In more recent decades he would have been called by the military a radio operator. But in New Testament days, they might have called him a runner because of all the going he did.

The person responsible for relaying messages is critical. Are you aware that in military communications the word *repeat* is never used? Once when it was used, it was misunderstood as *retreat.* And that miscommunication cost many soldiers their lives. Instead of *repeat,* the military expression is *say again.* This expression is drilled into the average soldier. Even after their military days are over, they almost never stop saying "say again."

How important the messenger is because of the message he carries. The codes that were used by my Army reconnaissance unit for radio messages were always changing for security reasons. Therefore, they were impossible to memorize. I required the radio operator to have that code tied around his neck with two separate cords. Two other soldiers were then appointed to get that code off his body and bring it directly to me or the platoon sergeant if the radio operator was killed or disabled. This was to be done at the risk of their lives.

No doubt about it, the message and the messenger are critical. The Warrior Leader will risk his own life and that of others to be certain that the gospel message of Christ is communicated. The Warrior Leader, like Tychicus, must be a trusted and dependable soldier of the cross with the message of Christ.

THE OLD MAN: THE DEVOTED SOLDIER

"Do thy diligence to come shortly unto me" (v. 9). Don't forget that Paul was also a soldier who was numbered among these foxhole buddies. The Warrior Leader believes there is no higher honor than to be a field soldier in the army of Christ. Paul was many different things in the kingdom of God, but he always remained a field soldier on the front lines of spiritual-war fighting, rescuing lost souls.

In military terms, Paul as leader of this detachment was the CO—commanding officer. Of course, Christ is the Commander-in-Chief, but the Lord commissions soldiers to lead here on earth. No matter how old the CO is, soldiers generally call him "the old man." Although it is an expression of respect and recognition, it would never knowingly be uttered in the presence of the commander himself. Paul qualified as "the old man" in both age and responsibility. If Paul had ever heard this term used in reference to him, he probably would have replied with something like President Ronald Reagan's declaration: "I'm not going to hold these younger men's youth and inexperience against them."

Paul was a weather-beaten, scarred-up old war horse full of experience who was loved and revered by those of the church who served on the front lines. He was much like Jesus as the Warrior Leader. He had spent time with many believers and Christian leaders and was now leaving behind a force-multiplying army of effective warriors who have been his "foxhole buddies." He developed them into Warrior Leaders so they could go on to accomplish the Great Mission.

Our great concern as Warrior Leaders should be, "Are we developing a force-multiplying army not only to work for the kingdom now but who will be left to continue to accomplish the Great Mission when we are gone?" Take a careful look at who you are leaving behind to accomplish the Great Mission.

Paul had some interesting characters to show up beside him as foxhole buddies. In the providence of God, it had taken all kinds of people to fashion Paul as one who would "finish the fight" as he waged victorious war fighting. God knows who you have encountered on

182

your journey, and he knows why they have crossed your path. Know for certain that the Lord can use each of them to make you a stronger and more faithful servant soldier of the cross.

But no soldier ever won a battle by lying in a foxhole trying to figure out his buddy. Get up from there and *charge!*

"In all these things we are more than conquerors through Him that loved us" (Rom. 8:37 NKJV).

⚜ ⚜ ⚜

WHO DARES TO BE THE WARRIOR LEADER?

*T*here are many ways that people attempt to live their lives as professing Christians that are far less demanding, challenging, and adventurous than that of the Warrior Leader. So why would you dare to be a Warrior Leader? I believe that Lieutenant Colonel Jonathan J. Smidt, a framer of the U.S. Army leadership materials, recorded a response to that question when he remembered a part of one of General Douglas MacArthur's speeches.

Twenty campaigns on a hundred battlefields around a thousand campfires had led the General to conclude about war fighters: "Your mission . . . is to win our wars . . . you are the ones who are trained to fight. Yours is the profession of arms, the will to win and the sure knowledge that in war there is no substitute for victory; that if you lose, the nation will be destroyed."[67]

Make no mistake about it: What this heroic war fighter concluded about secular warfare has a definite application to spiritual-war fighting. Such words speak to each of us who claim the name of Christ as our Lord and leader. We are not only locked into spiritual combat for souls; our mission is to win these spiritual wars. We are responsible for equipping the saints to have the will to win, and there is no substitute for victory. To lose is to fail God, eternity, and souls—as well as the soul of our beloved nation.

Every person in the sphere of your leadership is someone's son, daughter, brother, mother, sister, or father. As spiritual Warrior Leaders, they too, just like you, are capable of extraordinary feats of courage, self-denial, sacrifice, and victory. The spiritual warriors who came before them have proven over and over their faithful determination. Those new Warrior Leaders will show up again and again to mount the attack regardless of how frightening, exhausting, risky, or bloody the battle. And what they ask of you in return is compassionate, competent, committed, conquering leadership as the Warrior Leader. Your people deserve nothing less.

General J. Lawton Collins said, "The most precious commodity with which the Army deals is the individual soldier who is the heart and soul of our combat forces." [68]

Following are four reasons why we should strive to be Warrior Leaders now, strive to continue to be Warrior Leaders, and continue to be committed to die as Warrior Leaders.

BLESSINGS ARE BEYOND BELIEF

"A faithful man shall abound with blessings" (Prov. 28:20).

One man, out with two others on a visitation team, found himself at a stranger's home sharing the gospel. The elderly man with whom they had shared prayed to receive Christ and wanted to become part of a church. On the way out of the house the man who had shared the gospel discovered that the older man who had just received Christ was his biological father, whom he had never known. Blessings beyond belief! That would never have happened if the young man had not been willing to try to win other people to the Lord.

A certain pastor had enjoyed a good ministry in his church over a number of years. But he had come to a place of despair because of the

184

sameness of everything and the church's lack of reaching others. Once he recommitted himself personally to reaching others and to equipping and motivating the church to do the same, everything changed. The blessings are now beyond belief. He observed that "these years are now the happiest years of my life."

A young husband and wife, both medical doctors, thought there was no way they could find time to train and visit for the Lord through their church. The wife's conclusion was, "I found I did have time to do what Christ has called me to do. And I never dreamed of all the personal blessings that would come to my own life and to my family's life."

"I have a new husband!" was the exclamation of one pastor's wife. She told of how her husband had become frustrated, discouraged, and depressed because nothing seemed to go right or make any progress in the ministry and their church. He began to bring all the frustration and depression home to his family. After he committed himself to lead and train other people to get back to the Great Mission of reaching people, everything changed. The pastor's wife had gotten "a whole new husband."

"It's like Wal-Mart!" The professional-looking young man was giving a FAITH testimony, but the point of his story was about getting in on what God is up to.

"FAITH is like going to Wal-Mart. That's right; it's like Wal-Mart," he declared. "You know how you go into Wal-Mart for only one small item? Then two hours later you come out with two shopping carts full? That's the way I have found FAITH. You come out with far more than you ever expected." He went on to say he had made his commitment because he felt the need to know a simple outline that would enable him to share the gospel. He got that, but then he listed all the other blessings that came with it.

Here are a few of the extra blessings he mentioned: encouragement, new friends, confidence in the Lord, improved prayer life, closer to the Word of God, a new appreciation for the Holy Spirit, the joy of ministering to others' needs, training and teaching others, sharing the gospel, seeing and hearing miracles. Then he said, "All that on top of seeing souls saved!"

These illustrations magnify the fact that God has promised rejoicing and blessings for those who stay committed to reaching others with the gospel. And often these blessings are beyond belief.

Last year in one month, three men in our church in Daytona, Florida, lost their fathers. The blessing beyond belief was that just before these deaths, each of these men had led his own father to Christ. Hearing Mike, Rick, and Grant tell their heartwarming stories and express thanks to the staff and church for equipping them reminded me of the blessing of training and leading a church in reaching souls for Christ. Blessings beyond belief!

Of course, there is always a price to be paid in anything that is worthwhile. You cannot use a lifeboat without facing the storm and waves. You cannot save a drowning man without getting wet. You cannot work the fire escape to rescue the perishing without feeling the heat. But once you have gotten that soul in the boat, once you've helped pull that soul from the flames—especially if it is one of your dear friends or family members—at that moment you'll shout, "The blessings are beyond belief!"

We must not continue to stand idly by while those around us are perishing. We must become Warrior Leaders, stay Warrior Leaders, and die as Warrior Leaders.

THE WORTH OF A SOUL

"For what shall it profit a man, if he shall gain the whole world, and lose his own soul?" (Mark 8:36).

"A soul—is a soul—is a soul—is a soul." Thousands of times I have said that over and over. In fact, my cell phone flashes that at me between calls. None of us must lose sight of the fact that souls are the focus. It doesn't matter if the soul drives an expensive two-seater sports car down Times Square, or rides a broken-down bicycle over a jungle trail to a thatched-roof bamboo hut. Both souls are of equal value to God. He loves them so much that He sent His Son to die for them.

When God looks down from heaven, I do not believe He sees state lines, county lines, or national lines. I do not believe He sees red, yellow, black, or white. His focus is not on those things but upon the soul. He looks for souls, and He sees souls. He sees only two kinds of souls—lost souls and saved souls. His desire is for all saved souls to allow Him to live through them. He wants them to go to all the lost souls and share the love of God so they might also be saved. Then those newly saved souls are to go to other lost souls so they can also find salvation.

Do we at the grocery store see souls? At the drive-through window do we see souls? On television and in traffic do we see souls? Are we concerned that these souls are lost souls or saved souls? That is a kingdom view about the most important thing in the universe. And to think, God felt the soul is worth so much that He sent His only Son to die on a cross for your soul, my soul, and their souls. The worth of a soul compels us to become Warrior Leaders, to continue as Warrior Leaders, and to die as Warrior Leaders.

THE CONDITION OF THIS COUNTRY

The condition of this country should cause every child of God to become more intentional and aggressive in reaching our world in our lifetime.

It is shocking to realize that this statement is true: "Christianity has now become the fastest declining religion in America!" How did this happen! Where have we been? What have we done or failed to do? But most importantly, Will we wake up and come to our spiritual senses and do something now for the sake of the souls of our children, grandchildren, family, friends, and this country? (I urge you to read again and consider the section entitled "Raising the Bar," p. 74.) The condition of this country calls us to become Warrior Leaders, to continue as Warrior Leaders, and to die as Warrior Leaders

THE HORROR OF HELL

"And he cried and said, Father Abraham, have mercy on me, and send Lazarus, that he may dip the tip of his finger in water, and cool my tongue; for I am tormented in this flame" (Luke 16:24).

My Buddhist acquaintance who lives in California was a young teenage boy when an atomic bomb was dropped on his hometown in Japan. Fortunately, he and a friend were miles from the city, fishing in a valley lake hidden by mountains. After the explosion, they headed back toward the city and soon began to see people they knew—some running, some walking, some in a daze, some crawling, some moaning, some screaming, but all charred—smoking and burning. Most of them had been burned so badly that their skin seemed to be melting off their bodies.

As my friend relived that day he said, "It was like waking up in hell. It was a city on fire, torment, and screaming, with all the people burning and hopelessly and helplessly roaming about desperately searching but never finding any help or comfort."

There have been more than a few times when that true story and its comparison with hell have caused me to do something to keep people I know out of hell and to get them into heaven.

It was a rainy, foggy night when a small plane crashed into the treetops, short of the airport runway. One man was thrown from the burning plane. He was completely engulfed in flames. He ran down the hillside toward lights from traffic on the highway below. Another friend of mine returned to the scene at daylight and retraced the burning man's desperate fight to get help. He found pieces of burned skin where they had been caught in the thick bushes. One spot was marked by a shoe and sock with some flesh still attached where the man had attempted to rid himself of the fiery pain. Miraculously, the man made it to the highway and tried to stop vehicles for help.

The young man who stopped to help him said he was overwhelmed with disbelief and horror. He said the burned man was completely charred. His body was actually smoking from the flames he had endured.

188

The horror and torment of such a way of dying is overwhelming to me. The saddest of all thoughts is about a family member or loved one going to hell. Here they will not die but will continue to exist in torment and flames forever.

Hell has been described as a world without hope. I agree. Why anyone would follow Satan to a place without hope but a place of eternal torment and separation from God is beyond me. That is their self-chosen sentence if Christ is not their Savior. Some skeptics say, "You don't even know where hell is located." Anyone who makes that accusation is mistaken. The location of hell has been exactly pinpointed. Anyone will find hell located at the end of a Christless life. We do not want anyone to go there in order to find it, do we? No, and that is precisely the reason why we must be moved to become Warrior Leaders now. We must continue to be Warrior Leaders and die as Warrior Leaders.

The message had been about "why each of us should commit now to reach lost souls." Many listeners had come forward at the invitation and then returned to their seats. They had left at the altar a commitment card indicating their willingness to train and go for the sake of lost souls. The invitation was about to conclude when I saw an elderly man slowly making his way toward the front. He was barely shuffling along. A metal walker assisted him, and he was accompanied by his wife.

At first I thought he was just getting a head start on the crowd that would soon be dismissed. Then I saw it. He had his soul-winning commitment card in his hand. It was rolled and crumpled around his walker. I moved to him and asked him in the sweetest and kindest tone I could muster, "Sir, with the shape you are in physically and on this walker, what do you think you'll be able to do to reach lost people?"

He slowly turned his head and rolled his eyes toward me. He spoke to me in the same kind tones I had used in speaking to him. "Sir, I do not know what I can do to help, but one thing I cannot do any longer. I can no longer sit there in that seat when I know lost people are dying without Christ and going to hell!"

Dear Lord Jesus, help us never to forget those words: "I do not know what I *can* do, but I know what I *cannot* do any longer—I can no longer sit there in that seat when I know lost people are dying without Christ and going to hell!"

Who dares to become a Warrior Leader? I must! You must! We must! Because the blessings are beyond belief. Because of the worth of a soul. Because of the condition of our country. Because of the horrors of hell. And because there are millions of Christians sitting in our pews every week who if challenged, trained, motivated, and led will rise up and follow us as Warrior Leaders. They too will cry out, "I do not know what I can do. But the one thing I cannot do any longer is sit there in that seat when I know lost people are dying without Christ and going to hell."

The call of God to us in this hour is the same as His call to His people in the past: "Whom shall I send, and who will go for us?" (Isa. 6:8). We must respond for the sake of God and lost souls. Who dares to be the Warrior Leader? Will *you* dare?

IV.

SOLDIERS NEVER DIE

The Warrior Leader's Maturity ("Die")

THE PURPLE HEART

This medal is awarded to those of the armed forces who have been wounded or killed while engaged in armed combat against the enemy.

YOUR PURPLE HEART

The Warrior Leader will not be a victorious war fighter without incurring some combat injuries. Like Paul and all the others through the ages, your Purple Heart is for the marks (Gal. 6:17), seen and unseen, received for the sake of souls and God's kingdom. No matter how fatal the wounds may appear, the Savior's soldiers never die.

THE WARRIOR LEADER'S MATURITY ("DIE")

This is the *die* aspect of the Warrior Leader's eternal life. At this moment in time he is awarded a battlefield promotion to full maturity. As a result of this honor, he is awarded a continuation of service to his Lord and Leader. The Warrior Leader has been a servant soldier of character, competency, and commitment, and now he is allowed to continue for all eternity.

"HE IS NOT HERE, FIRST SERGEANT"

"If soldiers will face death, there is nothing they may not achieve."
SUN TZU[69]

*T*he Warrior Leader has already come to full assurance through the Bible that he can fearlessly and victoriously face death as he gives his all for the Great Mission. The apostle Paul declared, "O death, where is thy sting? O grave, where is thy victory? . . . But thanks be to God, which giveth us the victory through our Lord Jesus Christ" (1 Cor. 15:55,57). Paul also believed that "to be absent from the body" is "to be present with the Lord" (2 Cor. 5:8).

The scene was a Veteran's Day memorial service for fallen warriors. Finally, it was time for Private Gregory P. Huxley's name to be called by the first sergeant. When his name was called, there was no answer.

Again, Huxley's name was called out.

Silence.

The third time his name was shouted out.

A voice barked back, "He is not here, First Sergeant!"

Neither Huxley, nor First Sergeant Joe Garza, nor Staff Sergeant Terry Hemingway, nor Private Kelly Prewitt were there. All were members of the 3rd Brigade, 3rd Infantry Division. All had their earthly life ended in Iraq during what T. S. Eliot called "the cruelest month"—April.[70]

Death is usually the constant fear of every front-line war fighter—but not for the Warrior Leader. Thank the Lord Jesus, when the Warrior Leader's name is sounded at his last earthly roll call and the cry comes back "he is not here," he knows where he will be, because "to be absent from the body" is "to be present with the Lord" (2 Cor. 5:8). It is a fact for the Warrior Leader: "Soldiers never die!"

The following remarks were made by General Douglas MacArthur in his retirement speech before Congress:

> I am closing my 52 years of military service. When I joined the army even before the turn of the century, it was the fulfillment of all my boyish hopes and dreams. The world has turned over many times since I took the oath on the Plain at West Point, and the hopes and dreams have long since vanished. But I still remember the refrain of one of the most popular barrack ballads of that day which proclaimed most proudly that "old soldiers never die, they just fade away." And like the old soldier of that ballad, I now close my military career and just fade away—an old soldier who tried to do his duty as God gave him the light to see that duty. Goodbye.[71]

There were shouts of "No! No!" from the floor. It is said that there was not a dry eye among Democrats or Republicans as the general delivered his farewell speech. It was interrupted by wild applause and standing ovations. That legendary farewell is best remembered from the expression, "Old soldiers never die; they just fade away."

Whether the soldier leaves this earthly life as a private on the battlefield or as a five-star general in old age, it is a fact that everyone comes to the end of his days on earth. But isn't it a glorious truth that soldiers of our Savior never die? Whether young or old, *the Savior's soldiers never die.*

Upon leaving this earthly existence Warrior Leaders do not die; they experience their final and blessed transfer to their eternal permanent duty station. There they will be a celebrated part of the grand review and receive their everlasting promotion to full spiritual maturity along with awards and honors. This transfer and promotion are the last stage in their spiritual growth to maturity. They have arrived. They are now matured. They will coreign and corule in an everlasting continuation of service to their King in His kingdom. Oh glorious day!

⚜ ⚜ ⚜

HOME
FROM THE WAR

Weeks and months went by after the night of shouting, fire-works, sirens, horns, and the Big Mill whistle. But there was still an overwhelming excitement everywhere—in the air, in the streets, in the voices, on the radio, at the Mill and in the homes. And that same thrill was still on our front porch each night as Mother, Grandma, and Aunt Sibbie rocked in their high-backed chairs and I swung in the swing. We were all facing the street that ran alongside the railroad tracks, because that was where the excitement always erupted. Neighbors would walk up to the porch to "only stay for a minute." Some would sit on the steps. But regardless of how long they stayed or how long they sat, everyone talked about "the boys"—the soldiers who were coming home from the Big War.

It was taking longer than anyone thought it would for the soldiers to get home after the victory had been won and declared. But they continued to come on an unpredictable timetable—some in groups, maybe two or three at once, some only one at a time. Those returning had all sorts of battle scars on them, seen and unseen—from missing limbs to twitching heads and arms and hands. Some just went into their houses and seemed never to come out. Worse, others never came home, and it seemed their families never smiled again.

My two uncles made it back, one from the Navy and the other from the Army. But the people who met on our front porch every night were not yet satisfied. We kept looking down Williams Avenue, hoping and praying for just one more soldier to come home from this war—my Daddy.

Because I was small I could sleep with my mother on the couch that popped up into a "V" before it flattened out like a bed. It was in the front living room against a low window. Every night Mother and I would fall asleep looking out the window past our yard down the

street and across town for the biggest lighted sign in Fort Payne—
"DeKalb Theater"—because that was in the direction of the bus and
train station.

"Bang! Boom! Boom! Bang! Bang!" The noise coming out of that
pitch-black night was heart-stopping! Mother screamed and jumped
out of bed. I froze, scared to death. Someone was breaking into our
house and tearing the front door off its hinges to get in! Just then,
Mother heard something else. With a burst of courage she ran toward
the door and jerked back the curtains that covered the half-door window. This time she really screamed, and I saw why.

She was face to face with a "burglar" who was wearing an Army
uniform with a cap that looked like a tent and colorful medals on his
chest. The soldier and my mother shouted to each other, and she punctuated her shouts with more screams. They both appeared to dance
frantically with each other side to side, separated by the large window
whose glass quivered each time the soldier shook the doorknob outside. Mother tried feverishly to unlatch the old thumb-bolt lock. The
shivering and quivering door window made its stick-on six-inch
American flag take on new life.

At the instant the front door flew open, my grandma peeked
through the door right behind me from a back room. My mother dived
into the soldier's arms and screamed, "Oh, Robert, you're home!"
Grandma screamed to me, "Bobby, your daddy is home!"

One by one the lights went on up and down our street, and neighbors began to come out of the night into our front room. Women cried
and hugged Mother and me as if we had won something or found
something that everyone wanted. Men pounded Daddy on the back and
shook his shoulders, seemingly to see if he might fall apart. All the
while they smiled and looked at his medals and thanked him for what
he and the other soldiers had done in the Big War.

What is most vivid to me is when Daddy picked me up and held
me out in front of him and exclaimed with joy, "Boy, you sure have
grown!" He then pulled Mother and me up close to him as if we were

only one person—kissing us both. Mother, through her tears, made the victory official: "Bobby, Daddy is home from the war!"

Yes, the war really was over for us, and we were home now, to live on together!

The Warrior Leader knows that this land is not his home. We look forward to the day when we will say farewell to arms and fall into the arms of Christ and those who are waiting for us, just inside the gate.

⚜ ⚜ ⚜

FAREWELL TO ARMS

His golden locks time hath to silver turned;
O time too swift, O swiftness never ceasing!
His youth 'gainst time and age have ever spurned,
But spurned in vain; youth waneth by increasing:
Beauty, strength, youth, are flowers but fading seen;
Duty, faith, love, or roots, and ever green.

His helmet now shall make a hive for bees;
And lovers' sonnets turn to holy songs,
A man-at-arms must now serve on his knees,
And feed on prayers, which are age's alms:
But though from court to cottage he depart,
His saint is sure of his unspotted heart.

And when he saddest sits in homely cell,
He'll teach his servants this carol for a song:
"Blest be the hearts that wish my sovereign well,
Cursed be the souls that thinketh her any wrong."
Goddess, allow this aged man his right,
To be your beardsman now, that was your knight.[72]

When George Peele (1558–1596) wrote this verse for Queen Elizabeth, he intended to express the humble heart of a faithful warrior knight who had come to the end of his earthly combat and who longed for "his right" to be forever a servant of his sovereign.

The Warrior Leader knows that spiritual warfare is costly in many ways. Cornelius Vanderbreggen Jr.—in an attempt to comfort and encourage soldiers in his book *Soon the War Is Ending*—amplified that fact. He reminds us that millions have laid down their lives in Christian war fighting. Such warrior leaders have been given the right by the Lord—as George Peele's warrior knight was given "his right"—to be forever a close and true servant of his sovereign Lord.

The Savior often allows Christians to die in the fulfillment of their calling. A Christian doctor may contract the disease that he is treating in others and may die prematurely himself. A Christian missionary may go far away to some strange place where Satan holds most of the people in his wicked control. This missionary may be murdered by the very people whom he came to help. That was exactly the case with the young missionary, Jim Elliott, in Ecuador. Further, a Christian soldier may respond to the call of his country and go to some place to fight and defend his homeland and family, only to be killed in combat action.

However, for every Christian warrior there is the assurance that he will never be forgotten or forsaken. His big concern must always be not how long he lives and battles on this earth but how long he has been a good and faithful servant soldier of his heavenly Commander-in-Chief.

To die young as a Warrior Leader and to see the face of Jesus in heaven sooner than expected can sometimes be easier than living a long life in a global society that is more and more under the command of Satan. Sometimes God's assignment for living can be harder than His assignment for dying. The blessing is that the Lord never gives us more than we can handle, with His help. Every person who has ever served in the military knows what his military occupational specialty (MOS) is—the job he was trained to do and the job he does best. God knows exactly what faithful soldier to select for what objective He wants to reach.

Sometimes He allows a healthy Christian father to become a cripple while his children grow up without a father being able to do much for them . . . except to be a brave, joyful, and faithful Christian soldier before them. Other times the Lord allows a healthy Christian father to stay healthy and stand by the grave of his only child and say, "Thank You, Lord. I know you do all things well, and I trust you." Other times a wonderful Christian widow warrior is called on to allow her young son to go off to war against the forces of hell.

No duty station is meant to be easy, but every assignment can be made easier by depending on the indwelling Lord Jesus for power and direction. Every assignment represents an opportunity to know Him better.

Vanderbreggen urges all believers to see all opportunities as assignments from the Commander–in–Chief "for sharing the words of God with lost souls who know Him not and for letting miserable, nervous, fretting, fear filled, dissatisfied slaves of Satan see that the life of the obedient Christian is a life of endless joy and peace and satisfaction and victory."[73]

The Lord's enemy is our enemy, and this enemy will never cease to attack believers any more than he ever ceased to attack the Lord Jesus Christ. Every step of the way, from the manger to the tomb, our Lord was hated and attacked by the devil. But in the end our Lord and leader arose from the grave, and He will return in total victory. The Warrior Leader wages spiritual warfare for the sake of souls, knowing that when he says farewell to arms in this earthly war he will share in glorious victory with Christ forever. The glorious truth is that in the Lord's army "soldiers never die." No, they *fly* into the presence of the Lord, reaching their full maturity and exercising their God-given right to serve their Sovereign forever.

But it seems that some people have to go "to hell and back" before they can find their way home.

✤ ✤ ✤

TO HELL AND BACK

I know I'm going to heaven, because I've already been to hell!"

This was my first day out in the field of a combat zone. The big Chinook helicopter had brought me in with the supplies. It was hot, dusty, and dangerous on the ground, but it was a welcome relief to be out of that chopper. It was loaded with goats and chickens, baskets of onions, and everything else imaginable. All of us had been bobbing and banging around together in a state of nausea in the back of the chopper that was running wide open just above the treetops. As soon as I got clear of the chopper, I stopped near several soldiers waiting to get on the aircraft to go back to the base camp. They had finished their time in this war and were now headed home.

One of the soldiers looked as if he had just been dragged from some nearby front-line battle. He was sitting on a C-ration box turned up long ways, and he was slumped forward with his head against the barrel of his M-16 rifle. His hands holding up the weapon looked just like the rest of him—totally worn out. His uniform was in tatters, his boots were worn thin, his face was sunken, and he had blistered skin, parched lips, and bloodshot eyes. He was caked all over with mud and dirt. He could have posed for a portrait that might have been entitled "Complete Exhaustion."

His camouflage helmet cover was worn and torn to match him. His little plastic bottle of insect repellent was jammed in behind the elastic band around his combat headgear. I wondered, *Will I soon look like this?* Just then, he moved his head, and I read his conclusion to the entire war as if it were on a lighted billboard in Times Square.

200

Somewhere in a foxhole or waiting at an ambush site or as a sentinel sitting on a hillside—somewhere—this soldier had taken a ballpoint pen, and retracing his letters again and again until they were large and dark enough not to be missed, he had inscribed his epitaph on his helmet: "I know I'm going to heaven because I've already been to hell!"

He believed he had been to hell and back. We all know that an eternity in hell is worse than any war. Nevertheless I, like most frontline combat war fighters, was now heading straight to a war that would give me a strong dose of its own hell.

The blood was gushing—I mean gushing—out of my mouth. I forced my mouth open wider, but the blood gushed even more. *I am hit in the heart!* was my immediate thought. It was gushing out like water from a water hose. You know when you have your thumb over the opening of a hose and then remove it, how it gushes out? Every time I tried to breathe in, the blood just shot out of my mouth and seemed to go two or three feet in front of me.

Days before, an enemy soldier had tried to do this to me, but instead I had got him. Now my leather jungle boots had long since faded from black to almost a white buff from the incessant sloshing around in water and tearing through jungle vines and underbrush. As I stood straddled over the chest of the lifeless body of my would-be killer, a thought flashed in my mind about how the color of my boot color differed from the black on his tattered "pajama" clothing. The contrast of the boots caught my eye because I was looking down as I rifled through a tiny worn-out bag he used for a billfold.

This was my job. My men and I had been assigned the mission to go out into the jungle areas to "find, fix, and finish" the enemy and collect all meaningful, intelligent information possible. We were to be the "eyes and ears" out front of a larger combat battalion. They put their lives on the line based on the information we sent back to them.

As I searched through the dead man's pitiful little pouch, a few coins fell out and landed on his chest. I instinctively looked at his face again. Looking again had become a force of habit. We soldiers in

Vietnam learned that everyone who lies still is not always dead. He was dead, though. I had learned early to make double sure of that.

At that instant my eyes focused on a small picture all mashed up in the bottom of the pouch. It was damp, cracked, and crumpled. When I unfolded it I felt the sting in my gut and eyes both at the same time. It was a picture of this young man and his wife on their wedding day, both with big happy smiles. I was also a young, recently married soldier with a picture of my dear wife in my pocket.

Suddenly the reality of war hit me harder than ever before. This could be me on the ground dead. This unknown enemy could be standing over my body with my wife's picture. But I was extremely glad it was this way—him dead and me alive. Now I knew why warriors of old often stood over the bodies of their foe and shouted victoriously. They were glad they were still alive. Right there I renewed my vow to live—*This is not going to happen to me! Never ever!*

TOUGH GUYS

But it had! My own blood was now gushing out of me. Was the enemy on their way to put a knife to my throat or a bullet in my brain to make sure I was dead? I was now helplessly trapped. *Helplessly trapped* are words that tough guys don't like to hear and certainly don't want to experience. These guys I served with were tough. I was tough, and I knew it. We all knew it. The Army had trained me tough, but even before combat platoon leader's school, paratrooper's school, ranger school, jungle expert school, and all the rest . . . my growing up had made me tough.

I grew up in a mill village. If you don't know what a mill village is, you probably should just thank God, count your blessings, and go on with your life. The "Big Mill"—W. B. Davison Hosiery Mill—was the lifeline to everyone in Fort Payne, Alabama, whether they worked there or not. It took a huge manpower force to work around the clock in order to turn out enough socks to keep a whole town alive. People came from all around to work at the mill, but most of them lived within walking distance of the Big Mill.

The houses were close to each other, and some were owned by the mill. The cadence of life in that section of town was sounded by the mill's whistle. Lots of kids lived in that corner section on the other side of the Great Southern railroad tracks. Those two tracks divided the town both literally and figuratively. Most of the boys who grew up over there, as my grandma declared, "were as mean as a snake and full of devil-ment." It was our survival technique, and it made you tough.

My mother and father loved me and my brother, and there was never a day we did not know that. My dad was a good provider but not because of the mill. He had worked at the mill once. Everybody seemed to have worked at the mill at least once. But he worked mostly in highway construction that kept him away from home until the weekends.

Talk about tough—he was. He had been kicked around as a kid and had spent his time in World War II overseas. He was a two-fisted, drinking, smoking, pool-shooting, guitar-playing, gambling, cussing construction worker who killed himself at work five or six days a week and lived for some relief on the weekend. He never took a vacation in the fifty-one years of his life that I knew of. He was the nicest and kindest man in the world until he started drinking. Did I tell you he was also part American Indian?

My mother did not drink, shoot pool, or play an instrument, but she smoked, could cuss, and would mix it up with my dad when he was "three sheets to the wind and on his high horse."

When I was a little boy I heard Daddy and Mother fussing and cussing as they were coming to the room I was in. It sounded as if they were about to fight. I had one half of a peanut butter and jelly sandwich in my right hand when I dove underneath a bed that had a high cast iron bed frame ("bedstead"). Peering from underneath the bed, I could see their feet shuffling around as if they were pushing and shoving each other.

Then I began to hear things I had never heard before as they threatened each other's life. My heart was in my throat. Just then in the midst of more pushing and shoving, a butcher's knife fell to the floor only inches away from my face. Then they fussed some more and finally went in different directions.

With my mouth open and my heart pounding, I slowly slid out from under that bed, but I was too weak to stand up immediately. Lying there scared to death, I felt something running down my forearm. I opened my hand. That half of a peanut butter and jelly sandwich had been squeezed out of existence. All that remained was its mush and juice, which were running down my arm and dripping off my elbow.

That kind of stuff will make you tough early in your life. It was even tougher on a lot of boys in that area of town. Today, it is very chilling to me, even after these many years, to look back and name so many of those kids who died a violent death or went to prison. Some died violent deaths in prison, some are still in prison today, and some will die in prison in the years ahead.

I once visited in prison one of the boys I had grown up with. After weeks of processing, I finally received permission to visit him at the Missouri State Prison. He was in the twentieth year of a life sentence, with no possibility of parole. After passing through several electrified banging doors, being searched over and over, with accompanying instructions, questions, rules, and regulations, I finally stood face-to-face with a no-nonsense jailhouse guard, who pointed me to a table with two chairs and one sign. The sign warned, "Only one person will stand at a time—all others *will* remain seated."

What a hard and crass command. I was just here to visit an old buddy from the mill village neighborhood back home, where we both grew up. He and I had spent the night at each other's house, slept in the same bed, played ball and went squirrel hunting together, and had been in countless fights and marble games together.

Two other of those mill village guys who lived up the road past the mill had already been in prison. We were told that one was killed in a knife fight. The other boy got out on parole, only to meet another violent fate.

I remember going into the embalming room of the funeral home where the mortician reached into a black bag. It was on top of a glistening white porcelain table, which was tilted to drain toward a big sink. Out of that large bag he pulled a man's hand, attached to a forearm, and an upper arm that had been torn off the body, just below the shoulder. "We believe this guy was murdered and then put on the railroad tracks so as to grind him up beyond recognition. Bobby, do you know who this is?" There was no doubt about it, because the prison tattoo on his forearm had his initials inside a crudely shaped heart. "We agree," the mortician said.

Another boy hanged himself with a clothesline wire around his neck, intentionally stepping off his mother's back porch. Another was found shot to death and left in a ditch, after being robbed of his gambling winnings, and still others were lost to equally bad things.

No, everybody didn't go that way. Some did really well, in spite of it all, but everyone came out of that environment having grown up quickly. Playing sports was one of the escape routes some used to break out into an open field with more possibilities. Coaches had an eye out for boys in that part of town. The coaches could scream and cuss at us, and we would work harder instead of going home and telling our mothers. Some of the mothers were capable of out-screaming and cussing our coaches! Also the mill could hire a dad from some other town, and the dad would bring his hot-shot boy with him and try to take our position on the team.

We hated that, and those boys got a double dose of tough stuff. Baseball was my starting place. A bat in the face knocked out three teeth and gave me 132 stitches inside my mouth and a distinctive scar in the upper left corner of my mouth. A matching scar came later, in the lower corner of my mouth, after losing another tooth in a fist fight in the high school homeroom. This wasn't my last bloody face smash. Two front teeth were next to be involuntarily extracted, but I had to get to college before that happened.

The only way I had a dog's chance of getting to college was on a football scholarship. I did pretty well in high school. I wasn't smart, big, or very talented, but I wanted to try college. I had fallen in love with a girl who was a big influence on me and a strong encouragement in my life, including going to college.

When I pulled on to the north Alabama campus of Jacksonville State College (now University), my car died on the spot. The sixty-five dollars I had with me was gone before I could turn around, but I had made it to the coach's office. He seemed to pronounce a warning: "So you're a walk-on."

"No, sir!" I replied, "I can run!"

He blasted back, "I mean you are here for a try-out!"

Playing college football ended up being far harder than I thought it would be. What made it worse was that I was a linebacker—a small linebacker. The only hope I had was that I had come up tough. I was getting tougher—and as Grandma pronounced and prophesied, "Those boys are mean as a snake!" I was what defensive coaches call a "head-hunter" with "killer instincts."

The scholarship came, I played a lot of football—and yes, I got my two front teeth kicked out, which made a bloody mess. Blood coming out of my mouth was not a new experience to me when I got wounded in Vietnam—but not gushing blood. Not so much that I couldn't open my mouth wide enough to get air. Not with my head and ears ringing and the pains of what felt like red-hot molten steel being poured into my upper left chest cavity—no, never anything like this.

A BAD OMEN

When the bullet tore into my chest, it was fired from point-blank range. I came face-to-face with my enemy shooter. If I were superstitious I would say the "omen" of all this blood, guts, and killing we were now in the middle of had been presented days before. No doubt there were indications and signs that this was coming.

A reconnaissance unit like ours would always try to link up with larger groups of soldiers at night, if at all possible. If we stayed out in enemy territory at night by ourselves, this meant we had no light, no fire, cold food, a cold night, and we had to sleep on the bare ground with at least one boot on. Just about everyone had to pull guard duty on our small security circle. What little sleep we got was nothing but a series of nervous jerks punctuated by kicks and tugs by other soldiers who were trying to stop someone from snoring or talking and yelling in their sleep.

The benefits of bedding down with a larger crowd were just the reverse. My unit linked up about sundown with a larger group, and some of my men began to pick up complaints from the men of the larger unit. Complaints—what's new in the Army! But these complaints had to do with what these soldiers felt was a risk that could be avoided. When soldiers get nervous and shaky in combat, it adds even more danger, regardless of their reasons, whether real or imaginary.

The next morning before sunup the larger unit launched a patrol. They slipped the men out beyond our perimeter into the dense vegetation. There they formed a single line, with a few feet of space between each man, waiting until first light and the order to move out on the patrol. One of the men moved off the trail a little distance to relieve himself. When he started to return, one of his buddies thought he was the enemy and shot him. At breakfast one of the soldiers sitting on the ground beside me foolishly and accidentally fired his M-16 rifle. The bullet passed in front of me and struck a fellow soldier standing in the chow line. The way he looked it probably killed him.

The guys in my unit began to come to me expressing what I had already decided: "Let's get out of here as soon as possible!" We did.

Now in a new area of operation, Sergeant Al Watts, my platoon sergeant, and I split up. This allowed us to conduct two recon patrols. My earlier helicopter flight over this terrain had assured me we would make enemy contact. In fact, I had the pilot to fly at treetop level in one area. I dropped a fragmentation grenade from the helicopter. It was timed to go off just above a few elephants in a clearing, near what appeared to be a number of burned-off tree stumps. When the grenades went off the elephants panicked and ran. So did those "tree stumps!"

That was a Viet Cong trick. If they got caught in the open by a chopper, they would halt, put their weapons between their legs, discard their hats, bend at the waist, and pretend not to be people. They were hoping for an opportunity to run for cover.

Watts and I had been on the ground for hours, and he and I agreed to rejoin at a stream near a bombed-out bridge. He said there was a dead Viet Cong in the stream near the bridge. We had captured several VC and had them tied together by their necks. We were waiting to interrogate them for intelligence to assist our larger unit's deployment.

But we were very aware and concerned about what was developing some miles away. Our radio operator came running to me, indicating it was the commanding colonel in that area—our big boss. The simplest way to describe the dilemma of him and his men is to say that about 100 to 120 American soldiers had been caught in a bad situation. A number of them were trapped in an open area, and they were being killed off by the enemy. How they ever got into that predicament was a mystery and a tragedy. Was this just another accident in a series?

There was no time to speculate on that now. The "old man" told us to get over there as soon as possible and to do our best to get them disengaged from the enemy and out of there. His last words were that they had to be out before nightfall. Apparently, he believed when dark came the VC would come out of their bunkers and try to finish them off.

As I turned and looked at those VC prisoners we had captured, it was obvious from their eyes they were aware of what I was deciding. *What am I going to do with these guys? We can't run cross-country dragging them by their necks.* Only two choices, and I had to make one. I chose to cut them loose and let them go rather than the deadly alternative. They instantly disappeared. If they are living today—or for as long as they lived—those men had an indelible imprint of that moment burned into their hearts and minds.

Run! Run! Watts and I and the others kept reminding ourselves. Running through the jungle and in combat is dangerous and exhausting, but we did our best. We made good time over the estimated three miles, and we hit our designated rendezvous point. In order to link up with the company commander for some details and update before pushing into the hot spot and going to work, it was essential that we hit the designated rendezvous point. Remember the soldier who was killed because he wandered off on the way back to his patrol? The same fate can befall an entire group of soldiers who cannot find their way.

The battle-seasoned buck sergeant back at Fort Benning's Ranger School had straightened me out on that subject. "Sarge," I mused, "we'll never be able to cross all this rugged terrain day and night and come out at the right place without more help than just a map."

"Well then," he replied, "you'll die!"

I became a believer. By now there had been days when we hardly saw the sun because of the thick jungle canopy, and I had the responsibility to lead my men across miles and miles of terrain and arrive at a predetermined point. You learn to constantly check and recheck all indicators to make certain you are staying on course. You would die if you didn't. Others would die, too.

LOSS OF DIRECTION

Before the gushing blood coming out of my mouth and chest would stop, I would come to a deeper regret—that I had not given enough attention to the direction of my spiritual life. I had allowed it to just wander off course and consequently die out.

There was a time when I was on the right course. That high school girl I fell in love with not only urged me toward college; she also led me to Christ. She and her friends were different than most all the friends I had in the past. I could see that contrast. She went to church every time the doors opened. In fact, she was there so much I wondered if she didn't open the doors.

You have concluded by now that my parents were not Christians. They were fine, hardworking people, but they did not know the Lord. My mother did once buy me a blue-backed children's Bible story book with colored pictures from a door-to-door salesman. However, only a few people in our neighborhood went to church. "Stay away from those money grabbing hypocrites at that church," was the advice I remembered.

While I could not resist following the girl I loved to church, I would not go inside. I waited for her outside. At night I noticed that the church lights were turned off during the service, and it appeared dark inside. Actually, they were dimming the lights to baptize people. No matter, I was tired of being outside, and I saw the lights go down. All the biological juices that run through the body of a sixteen-year-old, unsaved boy in love were percolating at full force. Who knows, I might get in a little hand-holding or no telling what. I was going in!

Putting what little money I had down in my sock, just in case any money-grabbing hypocrites got desperate, I slid in the side door at the back of the church. When I sat down beside her, Maudellen smiled as if she had known I would eventually accept her kindness and come inside the church. I was not interested in anything the preacher said, but he spoke loudly over a sound system while reading and quoting from the Bible. Without trying or even knowing it, I was experiencing the truth of God's Word: "Faith comes by hearing . . . the word of God" (Rom. 10:17 NKJV).

One Thursday afternoon, after several services of hearing the Word of God and after football practice, I went to the office in back of the church. Reverend Bob Mowrey was the pastor I had been listening to, and he took time to talk with me. Not knowing the church jargon, I struggled a bit to know how to tell him why I had come. Then I questioned him, "Do you think my life could become like that girl's—Maudellen?"

Immediately, he knew exactly how to translate what I was trying to say. "Oh yes," he assured me, nodding his head and smiling and producing a small red Gideon New Testament. He read the verse, "All have sinned, and come short of the glory of God" (Rom. 3:23). I knew I had sinned. I expected the pastor had, too, but I was not certain that verse applied to Maudellen. Lord knows, I sure had tried my hardest to get her to—but with no success.

Pastor Mowrey went on reading, "The wages of sin is death; but the gift of God is eternal life through Jesus Christ our Lord." Finally, he quoted Revelation 3:20, "Behold, I stand at the door and knock. If anyone hears My voice and opens the door, I will come in to him and dine with him, and he with Me" (NKJV).

We knelt on our knees, and he led me to pray what's affectionately called "the Sinner's Prayer": "Dear Jesus, I believe that You died on the cross for my sins and that You arose from the grave. I now ask You to forgive me of my sins, come into my heart, and save my soul."

It was the first time I think I had ever prayed out loud, maybe the first time I had ever really prayed. Most of the things I was praying about I did not understand very well. But the Lord understood. He understood I needed and wanted my life to change, that I trusted His Word, that I believed the testimony of these Christians whom I had been watching and hearing, including this pastor who was helping me.

When I asked Christ to come into my heart and life, I wondered why He wanted to go into a bloody place like the heart. It seemed to me He would prefer a lung or some spot clean and clear. At sixteen years of age, He could have come into my brain because at that time there was absolutely nothing there! *How can He get into my heart,* I thought. *Go in my ear or up my nose?* You might think that's a joke, but I had never heard all those church expressions. The truth is most people have to figure out what church people mean before they can figure out what they are saying.

The reality is that Jesus did come into me, and He changed me and my life. If such an experience has never happened in your spiritual life—if you are not certain you would go to heaven when you die, let me urge you to sincerely pray that simple "sinner's prayer" as your own heartfelt commitment to Jesus.

In the years that followed, I grew spiritually as a new Christian. Then I left for college. For the next four or five years I got off course. I lost my way in following Christ. It was just like soldiers in combat. Getting off course can be deadly. I was so far off the right path that if you had seen me you would have exclaimed, "If that's a Christian, forget it. I don't want to be one!" While I did not do a lot of things most people associate with being away from the Lord, I still was way off course. It makes me ashamed and sorry to think of those wasted, wandering years. Why hadn't I been as focused on my spiritual life as I had been on military map reading? Why hadn't I learned to follow Christ as well as an army compass?

FINDING THE FIGHT

Don't get me wrong: My men and I were certainly glad we could navigate the land, especially that day when we connected with the company commander in a clump of palm trees just outside the area where the fighting was going on. My men fanned out, taking up defensive security positions facing toward the enemy. This left me, Watts, and the captain behind them to pow-wow. Bullets were flying, and red dirt was kicking up from the ground. The unmistakable "zip" of passing death was all around, and we stayed low on the ground as the captain briefed us.

He used a short stick to draw what he called a "horseshoe." It looked more like an open C—a semicircle. "This is how the VC are laid out," he said. Then he ground the point of his stick, like trying to put out a cigar, into a number of points around the semicircle. "They're in bunkers, down in the ground, covered, and it looks like they're connected by underground tunnels," he lamented. "They can give each other mutual supporting fire if needed."

My hearing perked up at that. "Mutual supporting fire" meant that if we attacked one bunker the VC in other bunkers could see well enough from their position to fire on us and help their buddies. Such a situation was a definite tactical advantage to them. I mentally logged that fact in with bold bright letters. *Must not forget that!*

The point of the captain's cigar-looking stick was then made to swirl quickly around inside the semicircle. He stabbed the ground randomly in several places before he flung it aside with disgust as hard as he could, saying, "That's where our guys are."

Nothing else had to be said. Watts and I strategized together for a minute or two before we called the men together. We were all soaking wet with sweat from the cross-country run. Their faces were still red from the run, but they had caught their breath. These absolutely superb war fighters knew how critical it was to pull themselves together quickly at every pause—to reload their weapons, get water, eat a bite of something, and then push on—always push on. They were lean, mobile, agile—some of the very best at this work.

At the signal all the men pulled back in toward Watts and me. Two of them were exchanging bites from a tomato and a raw onion they had picked up two days earlier in a Vietnamese village and which they kept inside a GI sock that dangled from the rear of a VC backpack. Several of us had discarded our U.S. issued rucksacks in favor of VC packs we had taken from the killed or captured enemy. Our VC packs were more like "beanbags" with shoulder straps. They did not snag or catch on vines or bushes easily, plus you could pile stuff into them quickly.

How could the mood and expression on men's faces get more serious than theirs? But they do! As they came toward us it was written all over their faces and in their eyes, which were looking for direct contact with ours in order to get the plan and hear the commands. At the same time their hands, like ours, were searching through packs and feeling for items that we wanted to keep with us. Inevitably, the maneuvering and fighting will strip everyone down to the bare essentials. They rapidly patted themselves all over—the way a desperate smoker hunts for his cigarettes or lighter. They were confirming that they had their ammunition, grenades, and personal weapons, usually a large hunting-type knife, or in my case a meat cleaver.

I had bought the undersized meat cleaver at a trade-day sale in Collinsville, Alabama, just before leaving the States for the war zone. Keith's Shoe Store in Fort Payne made me a holster for it. This allowed me to attach it to my belt so it would ride in the center of my back, away from the snagging jungle vegetation.

Mr. Keith had known me all my life. He had fixed our shoes and repaired my first baseball glove. "No charge," he had told me. This was his small-town, friendly, patriotic gesture that concluded with, "We're praying for you all—and be careful."

Watts and I now did our own strategic artwork on the ground. We were not speaking in lamenting and frustrated tones but in an emphatic, assertive manner, in matter-of-fact, do-or-die terms.

Our unit would span the open side of the "C," which then converted it to a backward "D" with the trapped soldiers in the middle area generally between us and the enemy. After taking up those fighting positions, we would make a determined effort to put intense firepower and pressure on those bunkers until we could disengage the enemy from the American soldiers who were pinned down. Hopefully, this would allow us to get to our men and bring them out or cover them with fire until they could fight their way back to us. Afterwards we would revise our estimate of the situation and take on the VC in their bunkers.

Everyone understood where they were to go and what they were to do. So far this was somewhat routine, except each man knew something was different about this. They were combat-seasoned enough to realize there was a strong possibility some of us could die in a mess like this. That awareness could be detected in the way they patted one another on the back, shoulders, or helmet as they crawled away toward their designated fighting positions. Watts and I separated, each taking a radio operator with us. This gave us more command presence and more information. But most importantly, it cut down the odds that we could both be hit and taken out at the same time.

Sergeant Watts was gone on "R and R" (rest and relaxation) when I became the platoon leader. My linking up with this platoon came by hopping off the strut of a Huey helicopter with rucksack and weapon into a battalion command base camp of the famous First Air Mobile Cavalry, best known as the "First Cav" and later to be dramatized in the movie *We Were Soldiers.* This division always lived up to its combat reputation. My reporting to the battalion commander was inauspicious. The colonel was hunkered down over a campfire in front of his tent, pouring himself coffee from a pot on the open fire into his metal cup. I reported, and he never looked up as he gave me my duty assignment.

"Welch, we've been expecting you. With your background (undoubtedly referring to my training because I had not yet been in combat), we have just the spot for you. You'll lead our battalion recon outfit." The battalion intelligence officer, a major who was standing nearby at a large map, added, "And they are very important to us here." It seemed to me like the major was saying, "And don't mess this up."

BULLET HOLE IN THE FOREHEAD

Now the commander was on his feet looking me over with no encouraging expressions but fully engaged in troubling thoughts, plans, hopes, horrors, and nightmares. His was the same kind of look that you see years and years later in the mirror of your own safe and secure, lily-white bathroom while changing a soaked-with-sweat T-shirt after crawling around at 2:00 A.M. in your bed on your hands and knees screaming "Where's my weapon! Where's my weapon!"

This warrior had already been where I was headed. Maybe he did not want to look at me. Maybe he knew I would last no longer than my predecessor or successor as the leader of this unit. We had a short life expectancy in this job. Maybe I reminded him of his son headed this way or all those others soldiers who had arrived in Vietnam. No one knew the turns our battle or war would take, but this old soldier knew the odds of survival in such a place.

With his head he pointed in the direction behind me, "Most of your men are over in that area. Go and see if they will have you. Welcome aboard." As he turned away he saluted me before I could raise a salute to him. Nevertheless, I returned my best exchange.

Nobody but God could have known on that day that the back of the man whom I saluted would be one of the set of shoulders that my bloody body would hang on, one day, as he helped me in my distress.

The sides of a can of Spam had been split four ways and bent downward to form shiny petals of what resembled a metallic flower that was floating on a puddle of red-hot coals from their small fire. Each petal served as the cooking surface for a slice of Spam. "Don't get up," I said as I approached the four weather-beaten troops huddling at the fire. "I'm the new platoon leader." Sergeant Gibbs did jump to his feet. He was the acting platoon sergeant during Watts's absence.

We saluted, and I went to my knees at the fire and shook hands with these men. They offered me a slice of Spam. I had already counted the slices and matched them to the number of soldiers and tried to refuse. But this seemed to be their act of extending themselves toward me, and I accepted. It was great, especially with the Tabasco hot sauce that was guarded by everyone like the platoon's crown jewel.

Even though I had not been in combat, these men showed appreciation for and some confidence in my preparation for war. They understood that the insignias on my uniform were for leadership in small-unit tactics, front-line fighting, patrolling, ambushes, and survival while living and moving among the enemy in their own territory. This is what they did, and they seemed pleased that I at least understood their (now our) mission.

Gibbs had a poncho lean-to set up to keep off some of the rain that was again coming down. He invited me to share his spot for the night before we would be dropped into enemy territory early the next morning. Now out of earshot of the others, I made my best effort to become their leader before we faced the enemy in a few hours.

"Gibbs," I told him, "I know and you know I'm now the leader of this platoon."

He quickly replied in the affirmative.

"Further, I've got all the background and training for this job other than actual combat. I don't ever want you to put me on the spot or embarrass me in front of these men. But Gibbs, for God's sake, don't let me get us killed!"

Gibbs remained silent, waiting to see where I was going with this.

"What I mean is, I'm not going to make a move in these early weeks until you and I have connected on what the move needs to be. And if you see I'm about to do something out of order or foolish, call me aside and tell me. My goal is to kick and defeat this enemy and keep everyone in our unit alive to go home."

Now Gibbs became animated. "Sir, thank you—thank you for saying that. The trouble with so many new officers is they think listening to us means they're not in charge. Sir, you'll see, all these men will love you for this and will give you their best. You'll see!"

No doubt, all the men had been worried and wondering about this very thing. Soon it was apparent among the men that Gibbs had given me his stamp of approval.

That first night Gibbs and I pulled up against each other back to back, trying to stay out of the rain, and went to sleep. That was the first time this boy from Alabama had ever slept up against a black man. But Gibbs was only one—among a number of them—upon whom my life would later depend.

After that first night, operations seemed to be in the fast-forward mode—patrols, fire fights, ambushes, search and destroy, and so much more that had led us to this present danger as we attempted to help get these American soldiers out of their entanglement.

Sergeant Watts was back now from R and R and had been back for a while doing his outstanding job as our platoon sergeant. This made him second in command since I was the only officer. With both of us present, our unit should deliver maximum force and firepower to help these men who were pinned down. Duck-walking and crawling, all of us were now in motion toward the enemy to deliver exactly that.

Urgently we tried to push toward the enemy. With my head down, I crawled some yards forward and then slowly I raised my head slightly to peer out toward the front. My mouth fell open, then I bit my lower lip and cussed but refused to blink or unlock my stare ahead. Lying dead on his side directly facing me was a soldier with a bullet hole in his forehead, almost between the eyes. I had recently met him and really liked him. He was a staff sergeant, an American Indian from out west, who had been decorated for combat. He was scheduled to go home in just two more weeks. He wasn't far in front of me. I wanted to do something for him, but there was nothing I could do.

Realizing we were trying to move in toward them, some of the other trapped soldiers called out to us. Calling for help between what could have been sobs, one officer who recognized me sounded as if he had called my first name and then pleaded, "You've got to help me— I'm bleeding to death!" But the enemy fire was too strong. We could not get to him, and neither could the others.

Why were these VC fighting with such unusual determination? Later I was informed they had a North Vietnamese army intelligence colonel with them and could not allow him to be captured. By then, they didn't have to worry about that possibility with me. I was not in a "capturing" mood.

In the hours that followed we tried everything available to shake the VC up and gain an opportunity to move against them. Nothing worked. Some choppers dropped in CS gas (a type of tear gas), but the drop was not precise. Some of us got the gas and had to move to another position.

More ineffective struggling brought us to a decision time. Men were dying, time was running out, dark was coming, and we had to act.

WE WILL ATTACK

We would attack! Was that crazy? Yes, exactly! But that was the only way left, and it could be the best way. Three things made me favor the assault. One, the VC would not be expecting a head-on attack. Two, they could not help one another with mutual supporting fire if their own position was being assaulted at the same time. Three, I doubted these VC had ever hit head-on with what our guys were about to cram down their gun barrels, bunkers, and throats.

You may have heard some stories about an isolated case somewhere, where American soldiers were unwilling to fight or timid in fighting. I never saw any of that. American soldiers are beyond comparison in training, patriotism, courage, and old-fashioned guts. Little wonder it's hard to settle them back down sometimes after all that is within them has been activated and pushed to the max. It's mother, dad, family, wife, children, hometown, God, country, American flag, the Pledge of Allegiance, freedom, forefathers, and a million other things all pumping and dumping in a do-or-die situation. We need to thank God for people like that who will lay it all on the line for us.

There was never one moment when I needed to urge my men forward. They were, as I often said, "Lean, mean, mobile, agile, and hostile." They never did anything out of line, but war is not a Sunday School picnic. These men and I had already forged a clear understanding backed by experience. They knew Watts and I would do what we said we would do, and he and I knew they would do the same. Our lives every day, in dozens of ways, depended upon the simple law of integrity. Each of these men was a Warrior Leader in his own right.

Watts was now working his way to the right, and I was working my way to the left. We were grouping the men into three- and four-man assault teams and making certain they knew their target bunker. We found two of our men who had been wounded, one in the neck and the other in the wrist. Because of the need for us to have maximum flexibility and mobility, we were lightly armed. We had one M-60 machine gun. All the other men had M-16 rifles, and a couple of M-79 grenade launchers had been brought along.

I ordered one M-79 grenade launcher to be fired—not at the bunker my team and I were preparing to attack but at the jungle behind the bunker. Twice as I watched our target to determine my approach, the bushes behind it moved in an unnatural manner. Fearing an enemy "stay-behind," I hoped to get some return fire or confirmed movement. A "stay-behind" is a soldier whom the enemy hides away out of the immediate area of action. Then when you least expect it, he becomes a one-man ambush, killing and wounding as many as possible and then running away. We Americans did that, and the VC knew how to do it, too.

In this case, neither movement nor returned fire ocurred. But this was another of those things that I had to mentally log in with bold, bright letters. Little did I know this would be the last one of those combat things I would need to mentally log in. All teams had reported. We were ready to launch the attack.

Within the next sixty to ninety seconds, it would take volumes of books to describe the feelings that became clear inside each of us. What was about to take place is the last thing in the world a soldier wants to happen to him. Soldiers who have never been to war and soldiers who have been in the worst of wars have awakened screaming and stabbing the air with nightmares about what was about to happen. We were only heartbeats away from entering an inescapable roaring ring of certain death for someone.

When I gave the signal, only one thing mattered to each man. It was kill or be killed. My goal was to live through the next minutes, and my aim was to kill anyone who had the slightest chance of denying me that goal. Each man, enemy or American, in a matter of moments, was forced to lose all consciousness of everything in existence—family, love, home, children, and even God and eternity. Our total being was obsessed by the motivation to live by killing. If we could not do this, we would be killed and the enemy would live. It was that simple.

Final-phase fighting is the war fighter's description of this dynamic phenomenon. This phase of fighting was certain to be final for one of the combatants. After the next few minutes it would be settled for some of us—perhaps most of us. The news then would begin to move toward a mate, a child, a mother, a father, a sister, a brother, a grandparent, a neighbor, a friend. Sooner or later the news would go out that somewhere in this hellhole, we had thought our last thought and breathed our last breath, and we were gone—never to return in this life.

Not me, I thought. *I've been down this road before. I made a vow to live. I'm alive now, and I will kill to live!* Those words describe what was trying to force every other emotion out of each soldier's mind and heart.

Our last few fumbling actions reinforced our obsession. From team to team the distinct metallic clicks of our bayonets became the sounds of our countdown clock. Ammunition clips were checked. Fingers kept pushing the full automatic switch into position on the rifles. We were finding our personal side arms—our knives—my meat cleaver. Our objective was clear: "At the signal everyone is to charge at full speed directly toward their assigned bunkers! Surprise, speed, and firepower will save our lives! Get on the bunkers! Get into the bunkers! Clean the bunkers out!"

My radio operator was handing me the phone, indicating he had the medi-vac chopper's commander on the horn. "We are attacking now!" was my immediate response. Not far away, with their engines revved up, the bravest men in the world were waiting to launch and swarm down upon this scene to bring out the wounded, dying, and dead troops. "When you hear and see the fire fight crank up," I told the chopper commander, "get in as quickly as possible, because I don't know how long this is going to last or how it will turn out. So get in here!" Above the unmistakable "pop, pop" background noise of his chopper he acknowledged, "Roger, out!"

THE CHARGE

One last thing: The M-60 machine gun had been put on our right flank. I passed the word down to the gunner: "When we go you're all the supporting fire we have, so burn the barrel off that M-60 for us!" I was looking for somebody to confirm that the machine gunner was ready. He was. Then I took one last glance at as many men as I could spot. They were twitching, adjusting, pulling, jerking, checking. Nothing on them was still, and nothing could duplicate the expression on their faces. These were men who would stand firm among passing bullets, charge full speed forward, screaming in the face of death.

Still looking toward the men nearest me and rising to one knee, I cried out with all that was in me, "Go, go, go!" Instantly their confirming echoes came down the line. Like foreshadows of the rapture, they rose suddenly from the ground as if they were resurrected and possessed by all the front-line infantry warriors of the past. We were now on automatic pilot. We drove hard forward on instinct. We were now up and into the charge. Soldiers were preoccupied with only what was ahead of them, and there was no looking around. Everything had become so much louder, but in it all there was some sort of small space of sanity that allowed you to make instantaneous adjustments.

How did this happen? was the thought that flashed through my mind. I realized that my team and I now had this enemy bunker up against our chest. *How did we get here this fast?* But there was no time to deal with any of these thoughts because I was now within eighteen inches of the face of one of the VC whom I had to kill in order to live.

Our team hit our bunker perfectly, and we were pressing against the red dirt that had been piled up around the enemy's hole in the ground. Then they had covered the hole with logs and covered those with more dirt. Some of the top dirt had been knocked away. Face down, peering between two of the logs, just eighteen inches away, was the head of one of the VC. He was fighting for all he was worth to keep our rifle barrels out of his opening. My guys were after the enemy soldiers in a ferocious way. Seeing that, I slid my face away, fearing a bullet from somewhere might come up through the roof of the bunker into me. At the same time, I grabbed a hand grenade, intending to put it in the bunker and end this stand-off.

Just as I signaled the soldier on my left what I was about to do, I pulled the pin on the grenade. At the same instant the thin metal handle on the grenade broke off. This meant it was ready to blow, and I didn't have time to get it into the opening of the bunker. Like handling a red-hot horseshoe, I threw it away from us as far as I could, hoping none of our troops got hit by its fragmentation. Just then something favorable happened. I don't know what it was—but we were able to get into the bunker. Now our mission and the objective could be carried out against the enemy.

Other units of our soldiers were doing the same thing at about the same pace. I tried to make sure that I stayed low. I looked and began to evaluate what was happening at the other bunkers nearby. I could see a couple of our men who appeared to be exiting their bunker—and of all things they were starting to stand up. Have you ever been held by force underneath the water too long? Once you get free you explode to the surface gasping for air. There are some similarities to that when

222

a soldier is down in a hole against his enemy in do-or-die final-phase fighting.

It is hard to imagine what it is like to be face to face in close quarters with another madman who is trying—just like you—to kill to live. There is no room for rifles—just bare hands, teeth, knives, or whatever weapon is handy. In just a minute it is all over. But the person who killed to live is now smothering and drowning, surrounded by the smell of gun powder, spit, sweat, blood, and body fluids. He wants out of that situation as quickly as possible. He's gasping for fresh air to confirm that he is still alive.

"Stay down, stay down!" I called. They got down and passed the word to others. I still had on my mind the movement in the bushes behind our target bunker that I saw before we made this assault—the spot at which we fired our M-79 grenade launcher. We had to make certain that no enemy was staying behind to cut us down like fish in a barrel. Sending two men around to the left, I went to the right with a soldier named Mayberry. We headed back into the underbrush where I had seen the movement earlier.

BLEEDING TO DEATH

Coming to a trail where villagers had been moving through the area, I stopped to look for a booby trap or something on the trail. Instinctively, I thought of what I would do if I were an enemy stay-behind at this location. I would be set up on the trail at some vantage point. If I saw soldiers on this trail, I would open fire on them and run. As soon as I thought those things I turned my head to the right to look down the trail. That's when everything seemed to explode. Right in front of my face—it seemed only a few yards away—a blast came right at me. The flame I saw was the blast of his weapon as he fired a bullet into my chest.

Because he fired before my upper body turned broadside toward him, his bullet entered my body at an angle. It tore into me at the middle of my chest and made its trajectory through my left upper chest cavity. At this close range the high-velocity shot jerked me off the ground, turned me 360 degrees in the air, and sent my helmet and M-16 rifle flying. The first thing that hit the ground was the back of my head.

Sergeant Watts was already crawling in my direction searching for me even though I was out of his sight. Somehow I was able to call to him, and he found me. He tore open my blood-soaked jungle fatigue shirt, leaning forward to see my chest. He moved his head from side to side in a disparaging way and folded my shirt back over the wound. Then he began to drag me back toward the open area where the bunkers were.

A long, skinny, black finger felt through the blood and down into my mouth and pulled out my two false front teeth that had replaced the ones I got kicked out while playing college football. Rivers was our platoon medic. He packed the wounds with all he could find, but the blood continued to run out. He put me on my left side so the wound would continue to drain away. My face was just inches away from that puddle of my own blood that was getting larger and larger.

"Don't go to sleep! Don't go to sleep!" yelled one of my men. They were now rallying to my side to help me. I was getting cold, and some of the men were rubbing my right arm and my legs. Someone slapped me gently a couple of times and urged again, "Don't go to sleep!" Whether they knew it or not, I was not going to sleep. I was bleeding to death and fighting to stay conscious. But I was losing my fight to stay alive.

Twice the men by my side had shouted to the radio operator, "Get a medi-vac chopper in here. Welch is in bad shape!" Both times he had shouted back, "None available—they're all in the air—they are all gone!" I was just about gone, too. It seemed to be getting darker and darker, probably because I was losing so much blood and slowly losing consciousness. Sergeant Watts had stayed by my side, and he could see I wanted to tell him something. He leaned closer to my face. With the last energy I could muster, I told Watts the last thing I wanted my wife to hear me say to her before I died. He leaned closer and replied, "Yes sir, if I get out of here I'll tell her."

By the way, I eventually married that girl whom I had followed to church as a teenager. But it now seemed certain I would never see her again.

The tables had turned. Now some soldier would stand over my body, go through my billfold, find my wife's picture, and make this foolish vow as I had done: "This will never happen to me!" But it *had* happened to me—and it happens to everyone eventually.

As the bullet tore through my chest, diagonally right to left, it followed a path along the inside of one of my ribs. "Soldier, it's a good thing you have large ribs!" my army doctor exclaimed as he produced a mechanical lead pencil from his shirt pocket. Sitting on the end of my small mosquito-netted hospital bed at the 85th medi-vac hospital in Qui-Nhon, he caused the lead of his pencil to stick up more than usual and continued, "See the width of this lead in my pencil? That's about how far away from your heart the bullet passed.

"Most of the time the bullet shatters the rib and a piece of the rib then punctures the heart. That's the miracle of this. The projectile cut your pectoral muscle in two and it just rolled up and down like a window shade. The bullet also went through your lung before exiting your body on the left side of your upper-chest area where it tore out a piece of flesh about the size of a baseball. No doubt about it . . . you're lucky to be alive, soldier."

As a result of that wound I would lie there on the battlefield dying. For me there was no out-of-body experience, no brightly lit tunnel, nor did all of my life flash before me. None of those things happened, but what did occur was just as miraculous.

Everything became silent and there was nothing before me except two forms, side by side, that were shaped like men. The one on the left was a little taller. They were like shadows, and I could make out no details. They appeared to be touching against each other as if they were one. It seemed that we were slowly moving toward one another. My sense was that these figures were God and Christ. I thought they had come for me and as soon as I recognized them they would take me away to be with them forever. I experienced absolutely no fear of

225

dying at that moment but had assurance that I was going to heaven because of my commitment to Christ as a teenager.

Then I remembered I had gotten away from the Lord in college days and had drifted further and further away from Him. I had become a foul-mouthed, hard-charging, rear-end kicking, combat platoon leader on his way up through the ranks. I was doing well at it, and my superiors were giving me high marks. The Lord was nothing more to me at that time than the little Gideon New Testament that I had in my backpack—the one the preacher read from the day I gave my life to Christ—the same one that lay unopened in my sock drawer at college. Even though that New Testament seemed to be a good-luck reminder, I had long since stopped thinking about reading God's Word or meeting with God.

I did not get up that morning planning to meet with God and Christ. But like it or not, God and Christ were now coming to meet me. And yes, I remembered that I had abandoned Him, left Him, stopped living for Him, and consequently had led others away from Him.

Never had I been unfaithful to my wife. I did not drink or take drugs. But still I was a backslidden, mediocre, compromising, good-for-nothing "church member" Christian. And now I was about to face God Almighty with this empty life I had been living. I remembered—and I was ashamed, embarrassed, horrified. I had wasted my opportunity to use my life for Christ, and now I would die and stand before God and Christ in my shame. It was all over, and there was nothing I could do.

I had no hope that I would live. Everyone else had given up hope as well. If there was any grain of hope left, it was that the Lord would be merciful to me—not save my life. I knew I was a dead man, but perhaps He would have mercy and forgive and cleanse me before I met Him. Face down, only a few inches away from that ever-expanding puddle of my own blood that seemed to be sucking the life from me right into the ground, I breathed this three-word prayer, "God, help me."

I was able to say those three words one more time: "God, help me." That was it . . . that was all I had. Nothing else was left. It was all gone in this last prayer. These are the last words of a dying soldier: "God, help me! God, help me!"

THEN THE MIRACLE HAPPENED

That is when the miracle happened. Suddenly a light began to move across my body. Although I was on my left side, face down, I saw the light. At first the light was small, but it grew larger. The wind rustled through some small bushes as well as the leaves and the grass. Although my body would not move, I strained to roll my eyes in every direction to see what was happening. The soldiers around me now seemed distant, and they sounded frantic.

Someone once asked me when they heard me tell this story, "Bobby, what was it, an angel coming?"

"Yes!" I declared. "And it was dressed in an Army camouflage green outfit!" But when you desperately need an angel, its fashion statement is not an issue. You just want it to get there and get there on time. It was an angel in the form of a U.S. Army helicopter. Its landing light was searching the ground for a spot to set down. It was not a medi-vac chopper but the command chopper of our battalion commander.

Three dead soldiers were piled on top of one another on what most people would call the back floorboard of the chopper. Now people were moving me toward that same pile of bodies. Watts heard the Colonel say he believed I would die. The Colonel and Watts, one under each of my arms, were dragging me. For Sergant Watts's heroic actions that day, he received our nation's second highest decoration for a soldier—the Distinguished Service Cross. The only decoration higher is the Medal of Honor. Other men also received decorations for heroism on that day.

For the first time in my life I could not stand on my own two feet. The toes of my boots dragged helplessly along the ground. My head would not stay up; it flopped as if my neck were broken. When a light came around to the front of my body, I saw that I was covered with blood as far down as I could see.

The soldiers kept trying to stuff me into the chopper on top of the dead bodies. Again, I lay on my left side facing forward, half of me on the back seat and half on top of the dead soldiers. The door slammed. Then the chopper quivered and lifted off. My right hand located a small box of something, and I wedged it behind my head. If I passed out I hoped my head would stay forward so the blood wouldn't drown me. Now it was just me and the dead warriors underneath me. No one was there to help. No one except God and Jesus, who had come to meet with me.

The chopper quivered again and touched down. The door opened, and two men began to pull on the bodies of the dead men underneath me. The two men started pulling at my ankles and one of them said to the other, "Hey, this one is still alive!" They placed me on a canvas stretcher and rushed me to a small medical tent.

The next thing I knew I was on the table with my shirt gone, and the Army doctors were working on me. I wanted to sit up enough to see my stomach because I wanted to take a look at how badly I was wounded. That idea vanished when I saw a piece of flesh about the size of the end of my finger stuck in a small pool of congealed blood in my belly button. It was sickening, and I did not want to see any more.

By this time those trying to help me had given up on finding a blood vein for transfusions. They were now working on my right upper arm. They cut a gash into the arm, and the doctor dug into the hole and pulled up a vein that looked like a fat rubber band. Practically in that same motion he punctured that vein and began a blood transfusion that also introduced morphine throughout my system. That stuff is powerful! In a few minutes, I began to sing out as loudly as I could an old military running cadence: "I want to be an airborne ranger—live on blood and guts and danger! All the way—every day!"

A few more minutes passed. They called the chaplain in because it appeared I was about to die. Just then the doctor said, "We can't do any more; we have to move him." Another helicopter ride into the night

landed me at the end of a long line of freshly wounded combat soldiers. Like waiting in line to buy tickets for a movie, they waited their
turn to go in for help. They were in every imaginable condition. Some
were walking, a few were in wheelchairs, and others were being helped
because they were too wounded to help themselves. Believing I was
about to die, the medical personnel went past everyone standing in line
and pushed me on top of a rolling table straight into the surgery ward.

Taking my boots off, someone said in a surprising tone, "He
doesn't have any socks." A more seasoned soldier explained, "Some of
these guys who stay out in the wet and damp areas a lot don't wear
socks, T-shirts, etc. That keeps down fungus and the like." They were
about to discover, as they continued to cut my jungle fatigue pants off,
that some soldiers didn't wear any underwear!

An extension had been pulled out from the operating table on my
left side, and my left arm was outstretched and taped to the extension
in a position where the surgeons could get into my left side and chest.
I was lying there naked except for a cloth across my midsection. I felt
someone pulling at the fingers on my left hand. Realizing they were
trying to get my wedding ring off, I protested and pleaded, "Please
don't take it off. That's all I have left of home." They were kind
enough to leave it alone, and they wrapped the ring with adhesive tape
instead.

Just then another person was over my chest with what looked like
an ordinary razor. He was there to shave my chest for the surgical
work. At the very moment the razor touched my chest, it felt like ice
was going through me. My entire body went wild—I mean wild! I was
not able to obey any of their commands to lie still. My entire body was
rebelling about something. I flailed around like I was being electro-
cuted. Two nurses came up with a mask to render me unconscious.
"Don't be afraid; this won't hurt," was their response to the terror I'm
sure they saw in my face. As soon as they got within reach, my free
right hand jerked the mask to my face and I took the deepest breath
I could. Then I slipped into unconsciousness. Peace had now come for
a while to my own private hellhole.

Some time after the surgery, I regained consciousness, but I was still battling for my life. Medical attendants plunged a needle through my back into my lungs to draw off the blood and fluid that were suffocating me. I slipped into unconsciousness again, and the days passed. Then I regained consciousness. *Am I completely paralyzed from that bullet?* was the horror of my first thought. Nothing on my body responded. The only things that moved were my eyelids and my eyes—nothing else, not even a toe or the tip of my finger—and I could not speak. It felt as if I were a person locked inside a body of stone.

For several days, about a week as best as I could determine, my condition did not change. Late one night I watched the soldier across the aisle from my bed struggling, gasping, and fighting to call for help—but he couldn't. He died right there in front of my eyes, and I couldn't help him.

The climactic moment came on the morning when I awoke and discovered that I was not paralyzed and that I could speak again. My first words to the nurse were, "Can I have some water and a Bible?" He brought me both at the same time. After taking a drink of the water I held the little New Testament to my chest and made a commitment to the Lord: *Dear Lord, I do not know if I will live through this. I may die here like the soldier who died the other night. But, Lord, if and when that time comes, I want to promise You that you will not find me in the spiritual shape I was in before. Lord, I intend to live for You from this day on.*

WHY TELL THIS STORY?

The last words of a dying soldier had now led to the first words of a life surrendering to the Savior. I was not playing "let's make a deal" with the Lord. There were no strings attached to my prayer. I did not say, "Lord, You get me out of this and I'll be a preacher." No, this was a sincere and earnest commitment to Jesus Christ by a soldier of this country to become a soldier of His cross, until promoted to everlasting service for all eternity.

What should be our response to such a powerful, loving act of God as I have just shared? Our response to this account should not be "Wow, what a story!" but "Wow, what a Savior, what a Lord, what a God!"

Catch this and hang on to it: The Lord Jesus who had the love and power to reach down to an ungodly, dying soldier on a lonely jungle trail, halfway around the world from home; a soldier given up for dead and face down in a puddle of his own blood—that same Lord Jesus who worked a miracle to save a soldier's life, change him, and use him—is the same Lord Jesus who can do that for anyone! Don't you feel the thrill of that truth? "Wow, what a Savior, Lord, God!"

This same Savior is now calling you to be a Warrior Leader so He can accomplish His Great Mission through you. Your family, friends, and acquaintances need the miracle of His love and power. You are "chosen . . . to be a soldier" and a Warrior Leader for the cause of His kingdom. This mission is worth the best of the rest of your life until our Commander-in-Chief promotes you to your full reward.

Will you now say, "God, in Jesus' name, help me. Help me be the Christian You died for me to be. Help me allow You to fill and control me. Help me yield my life to You so others may be saved and follow You. Help me be the Warrior Leader You want me to be—in my home, in my world, and for the sake of souls. Help me be found as a good, faithful, servant soldier when You come to take me home."

❖ ❖ ❖

DYING WORDS OF A WARRIOR LEADER

"For I am now ready to be offered, and the time of my departure is at hand. I have fought a good fight, I have finished my course, I have kept the faith: henceforth there is laid up for

*me a crown of righteousness, which the Lord, the righteous
judge, shall give me at that day: and not to me only, but
unto all them also that love his appearing."*
2 TIMOTHY 4:6–8

Son Tay Raid

Minutes after 2:00 A.M. on November 21, 1970, more than one hundred U.S. war planes shattered the dark calm of the skies over Hanoi, North Vietnam. Their mission was to rescue sixty-one American POWs from Son Tay prison twenty-three miles west of Hanoi. Fifty-six men actually went in at the Son Tay prison raid, some violently crashing their helicopter inside the prison compound.

Benjamin F. Schemmer hailed this operation as "the most daring operation of the Vietnam war" in his classic book entitled *The Raid: The Son Tay Prison Rescue Mission.*[74] This extraordinary raid has become the pattern and guide for any such heroic undertakings by the U.S. military. These warrior rescuers concluded that prisoners taken by the enemy had every right to expect that their fellow soldiers would die trying to liberate them from their captors.

All the raiders of Son Tay were awarded for their bravery. All but a few were decorated by the U. S. secretary of defense at Fort Bragg, North Carolina. However, the remaining few were decorated by President Richard M. Nixon at the White House.

I had an intimate conversation with one of those decorated by President Nixon for bravery in this rescue operation. Our exchange took place late on a cold, rainy night. We were in a guerilla base camp where Green Berets were preparing for Special Operations combat in different parts of the world.

Hunkered over a Coleman lantern underneath some discarded camouflage parachute silk, which was being upheld by assorted poles, he shared several gripping things about the Son Tay raid, but two of those things I will never forget.

One of those "unforgettables" came when we talked about dying. I asked him, "How do you want to die?" His reply was explicit: "With honor!" This decorated warrior spent years in combat. I don't mean years in the military but years in actual combat. Through many heart-stopping, near-death escapades he had already come to a definite determination. Wherever and however he died, he wanted it to be with honor. This warrior made it clear that honor to him meant faithfulness to his duty and mission.

That brings me to the next unforgettable that came after he had humbly lauded many of the brave soldiers whom he had served with in the wars, battles, and operations of the past. There was one defining decision that those of the Son Tay raid made that demonstrated self-denial, sacrifice, suffering, honor, and faithfulness in an extraordinary way. This one decision he soberly recalled: "If there are more rescued POWs than we had seats available for on the choppers, then we would give them our own seats and we would stay behind." Even though years had passed since that band of soldiers had joined in such a heroic pact, you could see he was still touched by the bravery, commitment, sacrifice, and honor of such warriors.

He continued, "This decision required us to develop a strategy for what we would do when we did stay behind. Our map showed that the Red River, near the prison, had a bend in it that afforded us a fighting position. We then agreed that those who stayed behind would meet at that point on the riverbank. With the river to our backs to defend our rear, we would form a line for our fighting position to the front." He paused and then declared, "Backed up to the Red River, we committed that we would then fight until one of two things happened—someone came back to get us, or we died."

Does that sort of unrelenting faithfulness and commitment not touch your heart and soul? I repeated those words in my head: "With the Red River at our backs, we would fight until someone came for us, or we died!" Then I prayed, "Dear Lord Jesus, make me and millions of others that type of Warrior Leader for You—one who will have the 'gospel guts' to back up to the Red River that flows from the cross of Calvary and band together with my brothers in Christ and faithfully fight the enemy of souls—until you come for us, or we die and meet You."

North America and the world, like never before, need an army of millions of such Warrior Leaders like that. But it will require ordinary folks like us to make a decision and to take the risk of being Warrior Leaders.

Napoleon said, "If the art of war consisted in not taking risks, then glory would be at the mercy of very mediocre talent." The Warrior Leaders who give themselves to fulfilling the cause of Christ and His kingdom on this earthly battlefield are all but mediocre. They are soldiers of meritorious service and valor who are destined for the presence of the King of glory. We have such monumental figures who line the corridors of Christian history. They call us to give the best of the rest of our lives for souls. There are also warriors of recent days who call us as well.

John Brady, International Mission Board (IMB) worker in the Middle East region, survived a terrorist attack by a lone gunman that resulted in the murder of three Southern Baptist workers. He challenges us, "God has tested our souls these past few days, asking if we are willing to be people who willingly give our lives so that others might know His love." Avery Willis, speaking about the same slaying, added, "They gave their lives as they could, when they could, so the grace of God would be poured on those people. But many Christians don't do that, and many of us have walked away for a safer day or a more convenient time."[75]

Bill Bright, through Campus Crusade for Christ, likely impacted more people for Christ and salvation in the twentieth century than any other person. Bright did so because he had determined what his life would count for. He said on one occasion, "If I'm going to suffer at all and one day die, why not suffer and die for the highest and best—for the Lord Jesus and His gospel."[76]

Anyone who knew Bill Bright knew he was referring to soul-winning evangelism. This quote was not only what he lived by, but it was also what he died by . . . the dying words of a Warrior Leader.

This is our place and time, and this is our call to reach the lost. Many Christians today may remember B. R. Lakin, a great pastor and evangelist seen many times in his later years on Jerry Falwell's television services. When Lakin was eighty-five years old he was in a central Florida hospital because of failing health, which included extreme forgetfulness.

A pastor visited him when he heard that Lakin had just a few days to live. As the pastor entered the room, there stood old Lakin facing toward the window, with an IV in his arm. He was leaning on a crutch with tears streaming down his cheeks and preaching to the world he saw through his window. This old warrior leader saw all those cars in the parking lot as a sea of souls, and he was pleading with them to come to Jesus as their Savior. The old soldier for one last time was extending one last plea to give his world one last chance. Those are the dying words of a Warrior Leader.

As she lay dying, Betty Smith, missionary to Ecuador, asked her husband to give her the shoes she had worn to the hospital.

Knowing of her terminal diagnosis and impending death, he said, "Honey, you are not quite ready to leave the hospital and go home."

Again, Betty asked for her shoes, and he gently placed them in her hands. "Honey," he reminded her, "you can't go home yet."

At that she said, "I know. I know I'm going to die." Reaching to place her shoes back into her husband's hands, this Warrior Leader charged, "Please find someone to fill these shoes for the Lord." Then she died. Hundreds of men and women are on the front lines of ministry today because of those dying words of a Warrior Leader and her shoes. I am one of those hundreds called by God through the echoing words of this precious soldier of the cross, the Warrior Leader.

Two years ago I heard Rick Warren at a convention give a testimony about his father's dying words that are now in print in his book *The Purpose-Driven Life*. Hear Rick's account of the dying words of a Warrior Leader—his father's.

> My father was a minister for over fifty years, serving
> mostly in small rural churches. He was a simple preacher but

he was a man with a mission. His favorite activity was taking teams of volunteers overseas to build church buildings for small congregations. In his lifetime Dad built over 160 churches around the world.

In 1999, my father died of cancer. In the final week of his life the disease kept him awake in a semi-conscious state nearly 24 hours a day. As he dreamed, he'd talk out loud about what he was dreaming. Sitting by his bedside, I learned a lot about my dad by just listening to his dreams. He relived one church building project after another.

One night near the end, while my wife, my niece, and I were by his side, Dad suddenly became very active and tried to get out of bed. Of course, he was too weak and my wife insisted he lay back down. But he persisted in trying to get out of bed so my wife finally asked, "Jimmy, what are you trying to do?" He replied, "Got to save one more for Jesus! Got to save one more for Jesus! Got to save one more for Jesus!" He began to repeat that phrase over and over.

During the next hour he said the phrase probably a hundred times. "Got to save one more for Jesus!" As I sat by his bed, with tears flowing down my cheeks, I bowed my head to thank God for my Dad's faith. At that moment Dad reached out and placed his frail hand on my head and said, as if commissioning me, "Save one more for Jesus! Save one more for Jesus."

These dying words of Rick Warren's father have made an extraordinary impact on his life's work, as he goes on to indicate:

I intend for that to be the theme of the rest of my life. I invite you to consider it as a focus for your life too, because *nothing* will make a greater difference for eternity. If you want to be used by God, you must care about what God cares about, and what He cares about most is the redemption of the people He made. He wants His lost children found! Nothing matters more to God; the cross proves that. I pray that you

will always be on the outlook to reach "one more for Jesus"
so that when you stand before God one day, you can say,
"Mission accomplished!"[77]

As surely as Rick's father reached out his hand to place on his
son's head to commission him to "win one more for Jesus," our heavenly Father is reaching out H7is hand to place on our heart to commission us, as His children, "to win one more for Jesus."

One morning recently I drove to the home of a dear elderly lady
who was a member of our church. She was a wonderful Christian, and
I was thinking about this very subject, "the dying words of a Warrior
Leader." Hazel Smith was dying. That was why I was being led
through the home by her daughter to Hazel's bedroom. We were alone
for a while, and we exchanged warm and loving memories of our years
together serving Christ through First Baptist Church, Daytona, Florida.
She was tiny and frail and could only whisper on this day, which would
be her last day on this earth.

I brushed her hair back a time or two and asked her if she had any
medicine to relieve her of the obvious pain. Almost in alarm her eyes
opened wider and she attempted to rise up as she whispered as loudly
as she could, "No, no! No drugs!" Then she added, "I must stay alert
because it is likely that I can win one more for the Lord when people
come to visit me."

When I was leaving the room, she mouthed toward me—with a
faint smile and her bony little index finger pointing upward—"One
more." Those were the dying words of a Warrior Leader. Hazel had
never heard of Rick Warren or the testimony of Rick's dad, but she was
a Warrior Leader in the same army under the same Commander with
the same mission.

General George Patton reminisced, "There is a wide disparity
between generals and private soldiers out on the battlefield, but it is
military tradition that in death all soldiers are equal. Thus the same
simple, dignified white cross marks the grave of every soldier buried
in an American military cemetery."[78]

Likewise, there is a commonality among Warrior Leaders found in all walks of life. The Warrior Leader may be found living out life as a mother, a dad, a son, or a daughter. They may be serving in a hundred places and a multitude of duty stations, but they will be on the Great Mission that Christ gave His life for—lost souls—yes, *one more soul.*

The Warrior Leader will stay at his post and stay at his mission, come what may. Regardless of how terrible the attacks of the foe or how fierce the fight, the offensive must continue without fail, whether waged from a well-to-do position or from a Christian's unjust prison cell. The Warrior Leader presses the war fighting beyond the gates of hell with unwavering faithfulness and determination. He is filled with vibrant, victorious anticipation because of the worth of one soul rescued from hell and the fact that the war for him will soon be ended.

Soon the War Is Ending

He is coming! We shall meet Him in the sky!
Ransomed sinners shall behold Him, even I.
Blessed sunset on the strife of life always!
Blessed sunrise of the bright, eternal day!
All who've known Him will adore their risen Lord;
All who've suffered for Him will receive their due reward
When He gathers in the realms of outer space
All who trusted Him to save them by His grace.
Soon the war is ending! Onward in the fight.
God-sent, blood-bought Christian soldier, day and night!
Shame on him who when earth's battles brief shall end
Never bore a wound for Him, the sinner's Friend!
Yes, the war is ending! Oh, what joy divine!
Jesus Christ is coming soon, and He is mine!"[79]

THE SECRET HANDSHAKE

*H*is eyes become misty, his lips will usually either quiver a little or tighten a bit. Sometimes speechlessly, if only for a moment, in order to cover what he is afraid his face is about to reveal, he will look down or stare blankly across the room. He will always refocus on my face and usually at that same time his other hand will come up to sandwich my one hand between his two with a grip that is only understood by a certain band of brothers.

He then will repeat almost exactly what he has just heard me say to him. Perhaps this is the first time he has heard this from anyone in more than thirty-five years. He is now hearing what he so longed and waited for: "Welcome home! Thank you for what you did."

It never fails, and I've been a part of that thrilling, humbling moment a hundred times—including last Saturday in the grocery store checkout line, last month in an airport, and two weeks ago in a hotel lobby. Almost every place you can think of, either I or the other man has initiated that "secret handshake" which exposes deep emotions, hurts, affection, honor, and respect. All of those things caused by this stranger's handshake and greeting come rushing unexpectedly like hot water from behind your eyes and nose.

This secret handshake belongs to those soldiers who have never met before but who fought, suffered, gave limbs, and lay beside buddies while they lost their lives in the fighting—all in a war that was misunderstood and unappreciated. When they returned home from Vietnam, there was no band to play, no crowd or victors' headlines to greet them. In fact, some were cursed by the very people they went off to defend. They were spat upon and given the worst societal beating any group of U.S. soldiers has ever received upon returning from war to their homeland.

Such mistreatment was puzzling, hurting, confusing, and killing to their hearts. Even the most outspoken of such soldiers still have buried emotions about that experience that no one can evoke. It takes the handshake of a fellow soldier to get to him. It takes one who has been there and who knows the longing of their heart and soul—one who knows those assuring and confirming words they have yearned to hear for so long—"Welcome home! Thanks for what you did."

This exchange between two "unknown soldiers" takes place somewhere every day. Of course, these soldiers do not actually have a "secret handshake." But when they embrace each other in this way, it opens a door of love, comfort, authentication, care, appreciation, and endearment that is beyond words. (It is the same even if one of the two has never been in the military or in a war.) Try that greeting on a soldier at the next Fourth of July celebration, Veteran's Day, Memorial Day, or any other day for that matter. It is possible that the veteran combat war fighter will reply, "Thank you. You are the first person in all these years who has stopped and taken the time to say those words to me."

How glorious it is for the warrior who left home and laid his life on the line for the cause to finally hear, "Welcome home!"

There is a wonderful story about a missionary returning home after an entire life serving Christ on one of the most difficult mission battlefields for souls. As his ship docked, a band played, the crowd cheered, banners waved, and a warm welcome was extended. This welcome was not for this missionary but for a wealthy, famous, and ungodly man of the world. Not a person was there to meet the missionary as he arrived back home. Just then a chilling thought came to his heart: *All this life of sacrifice, self-denial, and suffering for Christ—and no one cares enough to be here to say, "Welcome home."*

At that instant God sent to his soul the most sublime message: "Child of God—you are not home yet. Your home is not here; it's heaven!" No matter how hard your battle or how hurt, puzzled, confused, disillusioned, and unappreciated you feel, don't worry or give up. There is a handshake and a hug waiting for you from Jesus that you will remember for all eternity. Our dear Commander-in-Chief will step back to behold you face-to-face and put your sweet hands between His hands. You will feel those nail scars and hear Him say, "Welcome home. Thank you for what you did for Me, for souls, and for the kingdom." What a day that will be! You will see that it really is true: His soldiers "never die; they fly." And they land in His hands.

The Warrior Leader realizes that in that moment of meeting Jesus, one of the most joyful rewards will be to know you have helped others come to know Him as their personal Lord and Savior. Dr. Lee Scarbrough, great evangelist and professor at Southwestern Seminary in years gone by, emphasized the great joys and rewards of reaching lost souls.

> A star-filled crown is promised in the Word of God to none other than soul winners in life's earthly pilgrimage— not to the salesman, not to the philosopher, not to the great preacher as such, but to the soul winner. God seems to save His stars for the crowns of soul winners. These rewards are not all reserved for the crown after a while. God gives them along the way as we go in the successful soul winning battle. Heaven is not the only place that has joy in it. Soul winning gives a foretaste of heaven to the heart of the soul winner here on earth.

Scarbrough continued his emphasis:

> I was on a train, near the end of a long journey. I had spoken two and three times a day for forty days. I had had the rest of nearly every night broken by the change of trains and the change of beds. I was tired of body, depressed of soul, discouraged in spirit.

> A Christian mother sat by my side on the flying train, and said, "I know you, though I have never seen you before. I recognize you from your picture which I saw in the paper. I have long wanted to know you. Our boy, Charlie, was wild, wayward, and worldly. Our patience in trying to lead him right and give him an education had been tried for years beyond measure. Finally we got him to college. We feared he

would not stay. As he went away he bore our love and prayers for the salvation of his soul and the right use of his life. He was not doing well in college. His studies were hard. All the life about him was new and strange.

"You were in the college holding a revival meeting," this mother continued. "He heard you preach. The Spirit of God got hold of him. You talked to him and found him under conviction. After the service you followed him to his room. Eleven o'clock passed, and twelve, and one and two came. You persisted, and he held out against Christ. Finally, early, before the dawn of day, you, faithfully, persistently pushing Christ to his soul, won him to Christ. He joined the church, attended Sunday School and the young people's meetings, he graduated at college, he is now married and has a beautiful family. He is a deacon in our church, superintendent of our Sunday School, a generous, consecrated, Christ-honoring, successful Christian businessman."

By this time tears were running down her cheeks and down mine. Something seemed to rest my body, give me strength to my mind, and put leaping, bounding joy into every part of my soul, when this mother with tear-stained face, glowing, grateful heart, said, "I wish to bring to you, the winner of my son to Christ, the deepest expressions of a mother's gratitude and thanksgiving, and to let you know that, through your persistence, tactful and helpful ministry to my son you have blessed our home and helped to give to the world a consecrated Christian layman who himself is winning souls." I cannot describe the joy that fills my heart. I know that renewed my life like the eagle's, and with wings I mounted up into the holy places of spiritual joy. This same joy, more or less, waits for everyone—preacher, teacher, gospel singer, faithful mother, or any other witness who, for Christ's sake, will go out in the search for souls and seek to develop themselves in the finest of the fine arts, soul winning.[80]

The Warrior Leader is committed to the very end of his earthly service, as Scarbrough termed it, to "the successful soul winning battle." That is why he is, in fact, the Warrior Leader.

SPEAKING OF ETERNITY

The little man with white hair in Sydney, Australia, should urge every one of us on as Warrior Leaders to remain faithful at our duty station, no matter how remote and unsuccessful it may seem. The Warrior Leader will not abandon his post, no matter what, because he remembers that the Lord Jesus' soldiers "never die; they fly." Yes, they fly home one day to the Lord. There is no place like home.

My stretcher on wheels was about six inches above the hot tarmac, and my limp body had no influence on the stretcher's movement as someone pushed me toward the aircraft that was to take me from Vietnam back to the States. It was sickening hot, and they kept stopping the line on the runway while others ahead were loaded on the huge air hospital.

All of us were in such poor physical condition that it required two stops and one overnight before we finally touched down at Oakland Air Force Base in California. Another overnight and I was on to Brook Army Hospital, San Antonio, Texas. Several more days and procedures went by. After talking the sergeant in charge of the hospital morgue out of a used uniform, I manipulated my way on to another flight.

Yes, I was in the States, but I was not home yet. Home was where the person I loved most in the world was waiting. My plane landed in Birmingham, Alabama, and taxied toward the terminal where my wife was waiting. Months before I had left as a young fire-breathing Airborne Ranger, college football linebacker, a jungle expert full of vim, vigor, and vitality, and weighing in at about 180 pounds. Now, still hurting, slightly bent over and finding it hard to move without some pain, and weighing maybe 140 pounds, I slowly made my way down the steps and toward the glass doors.

Then I saw the one I loved! Somehow all the pain left, and the heartaches of the war went away. I was overcome with joy as the door opened and then I was inside—in the embrace of all that mattered to me in the entire universe. Yes, I was home! Really and truly home. Home away from the war and with family and loved ones. Home in the presence of my beloved.

Max Lucado expresses the same sense of arriving home:

> I'll be home soon. I can feel the nose of the jet dipping downward. I can see the flight attendants getting ready. Denalyn is somewhere in the parking lot, parking the car and hustling the girls toward the terminal. I'll be home soon. The plane will land. I'll walk down the ramp and hear my name and see their faces. I'll be home soon.
>
> You'll be home soon, too. You may not have noticed it, but you are closer to home than ever before. Each moment is a step taken, each breath is a page turned, each day is a mile marked, a mountain climbed. You are closer to home than you've ever been before. You know it. Your appointed arrival time will come; you'll descend the ramp and enter the city, you'll see faces that are waiting for you. You'll hear your name spoken by those who love you.[81]

In that moment, your greatest joy will be for your beloved Lord and Leader and Commander-in-Chief to reach out with His nail-scarred hands and embrace you and say, "Welcome home! Thank you for what you did. Well done, good and faithful servant. Enter into the joy of your Lord." Oh yes, you, the Warrior Leader, are closer to home than you have ever been before. Soon and very soon you'll be home, but for now keep your focus on your Mission-Vision:

- To develop victorious spiritual war fighters
- who form a force-multiplying army
- that accomplishes the Great Commission.

IN THE ARENA

It is not the critic who counts, not the man who points out how the strong man stumbles, or where the doer of deeds could have done them better. The credit belongs to the man who is actually in the arena . . . who strives . . . who spends himself . . . who, at the worst, if he fails, at least he fails while daring, so that his place shall never be with those cold and timid souls who know neither victory or defeat.

—Teddy Roosevelt

Come away from those cold and timid souls in the shadows so we may strive and spend ourselves for souls. "In the arena" is the only place for the victorious spiritual war fighter of the twenty-first century to be—those like . . .

You, the Warrior Leader.

See You There!
Bobby

"Chosen . . . to be a soldier."

NOTES

[1] Jerry Vines, *Basic Bible Sermons* (Nashville: Broadman Press, 1995), 65.

[2] James I. Wilson, *The Principles of War* (The Continental Press, 1964), 2.

[3] Edward C. Meyer, the Chief of Staff, U.S. Army, *On Leaders and the Profession of Arms* (Washington, D.C.: The Pentagon, March 24, 1997).

[4] Field Manual 22–100 (Army Leadership, Department of Army, 1999).

[5] The words of General MacArthur, from MacArthur's speeches at Memorial Library, MacArthur Square, Norfolk, VA.

[6] Special Forces are the elite, highly cross-trained, Army soldiers who are often called "Green Berets," although they prefer to be known as "The Silent Professionals." They are warriors capable of winning the hearts and minds of a group and then multiplying them into an effective force for victory.

[7] Tom Clancy and John Gresham, *Special Forces* (N.Y.: Berkley Publishing, 2001), 69.

[8] Mark Bowden, *Black Hawk Down* (N.Y.: Signet Books, 2001), 421.

[9] David Watson, *Called and Committed* (Wheaton, Ill.: Harold Shaw Publishers, 1982), 1.

[10] Greg Zoroya, *USA Today,* October 20, 2003.

[11] Malcolm McDow and Alvin L. Reid, *Firefall: How God Has Shaped History Through Revivals* (Nashville: Broadman & Holman, 1997), vii.

[12] Guy H. King, *Brought In* (Fort Washington, Pa.: Christian Literature Crusade, 1966).

[13] Carlos D'Este, *Patton: A Genius for War* (Harper Collins Publishers, 1995), 645.

[14] King, *Brought In,* 102.

[15] *Citizen Soldier* (N.Y.: Simon & Schuster, 1994).

[16] Margaret Chase Smith, in a speech at Naval Station, Newport, Rhode Island, 1952.

[17] Richard Wheeler, ed., *Sergeant York and the Great War* (Bulverde, Tex.: Mantle Ministries, 1998), 158.

[18] *The Diary of Alvin York*, 18 October 2001 at http://acacia.pair.com/Acacia.Vignettes/The.Diary.of.Alvin.York.html.

[19] *The Diary of SGT York,* 18 October 2001 at http://volweb.utk.edu/ school/York/diary.html.

[20] Interview with Colonel Gerald York, grandson of Alvin York, in April 1996 at the Presidio of Monterey.

[21] Wheeler, *Sergeant York and the Great War,* 58–60.

[22] Ibid., 72.

[23] http://volweb.utk.edu/Schools/York/biography.html. From *Alvin C. York* by Gladys Williams.

[24] Wheeler, *Sergeant York and the Great War,* 81–82.

[25] *COMMAND* Magazine, June 2002, pp. 3–5. Used by permission.

[26] Paul D. Harkins, *War As I Know It: George S. Patton, Jr.* (Boston: Houghton Miffin Co., 1947).

[27] "Leadership & Command," Field Manual 22–103 (Department of the Army, 1987).

[28] Adrian Rodgers, *Kingdom Authority* (Nashville: Broadman & Holman, 2002), 211.

[29] Sun Tzu Wu, *The Art of War: The Oldest Military Treatise in the World,* translated by Lionel Giles (Oxford University Press, 1971).

[30] *Soldier's Handbook* (Department of the Army, April 1, 2001), 2–22.

[31] Paul B. Malone III, *Abuse 'Em and Lose 'Em* (Annandale, Va.: Syneray Press, 1990), 3.

[32] Malone, *Abuse 'Em and Lose 'Em,* 3.

[33] FAITH is a highly effective and comprehensive ministry approach that identifies ministry needs and then mobilizes the church to meet those needs through Sunday School small groups, with an emphasis on evangelism.

[34] Malone, *Abuse 'Em and Lose 'Em,* 37.

[35] Force means group, class, team, or organization.

[36] Dan Carrison and Rod Walsh, *Semper Fi* (N.Y.: Amacom Publisher, 1999), 109–110.

[37] Alan Axelrod, *Patton on Leadership* (Prentice Hall, 1999), 106.

[38] *COMMAND* Magazine, June 2002, pp. 6–8. Used by permission.

[39] *The Noncom's Guide,* FM 22–100 (Army Leadership, Department of the Army, 1962), 210.

[40] Peter Smith, *Men Against Fire* (Peter Smith Publishing, 1978), 200.

[41] Douglas Southall Freeman, *Lee's Lieutenants: A Study in Command* (Charles Scribner's Sons, 1942).

[42] John A. Wickham, Jr., *Collected Works of the Thirtieth Chief of Staff* (Washington, D.C.: Department of the Army, 1988), 200.

[43] *Manual for Noncommissioned Officers of the U.S.A.* (West Point, N.Y.), 12.

[44] *Soldier's Handbook* (Department of the Army, April 1, 2001), 2–12.

[45] Robert Debs Heinl, *Dictionary of Military and Naval Quotations* (Annapolis: U.S. Naval Institute Press, 1988), 151.

[46] Axelrod, *Patton on Leadership,* 255.

[47] Long, *Memoirs of Robert E. Lee* (Nashville: Thomas Nelson, 2001), 464.

[48] *Small Unit Leadership: A Common Sense Approach* (Novato, Calif.: Presidio Press, 1983), 29.

[49] Jerry Adler, "Jessica's Liberation," *Newsweek,* April 14, 2003, 42–43.

[50] Axelrod, *Patton on Leadership,* p. 145.

[51] Ibid., 143.

[52] Ibid., 68–69.

[53] Amy W. Carmichael, "Things as They Are" (London, England: Dohnavu Fellowship).

[54] Gordon Sullivan and Michael Harper, *Hope Is Not a Method* (N.Y.: Broadway Books, 1997).

[55] James Clavell, *The Art of War* (N.Y: Dell Publishing, 1983).

[56] Carlvon Clause Witz, *On War,* translated by Michael Howard and Peter Paret (Princeton, N.J.: Princeton University Press, 1976).

[57] Axelrod, *Patton on Leadership,* 67.

[58] James I. Wilson, *The Principles of War* (Continental Press, 1964), 14.

[59] Ibid., 13.

[60] Axelrod, *Patton on Leadership,* 65.

[61] Clavell, *The Art of War,* 77.

[62] Ibid.

[63] Wilson, *The Principles of War,* 15.

[64] American Tract Society, Garland, Texas.

[65] Guy H. King, *To My Son* (Fort Washington, Pa.: Christian Literature Crusade, 1976), 127.

[66] *Our Daily Bread,* October 1979 (Grand Rapids, Mich.: Radio Bible Class).

[67] Vorin E. Whan, Jr., *Douglas MacArthur: A Soldier Speaks* (N.Y.: Frederick A. Praeger Publishers, 1965), 354–56.

[68] J. Lawton Collins, *The Infantry School Quarterly,* April 1953, 3.

[69] James Clavell, *The Art of War* (Clearbridge Publishing, 1997), 61.

[70] Mick Walsh, *Ledger Inquirer,* Columbus, Georgia, November 12, 2003, p. 1.

[71] *Reminiscences by Douglas MacArthur* (N.Y.: McGraw-Hill Book Company, 1965), 460.

[72] John Keegan, *The Book of War* (N.Y.: Penguin Books, 1999), 90.

[73] Cornelius Vanderbreggen, *Soon the War Is Ending* (Hiawassee, Ga.: The Reaper's Fellowship, 1968), 183.

[74] Benjamin F. Schemmer, *The Raid: The Son Tay Prison Rescue Mission* (N.Y.: Ballantine Books, 2002), cover page.

[75] *Florida Baptist Witness,* January 23, 2003, p. 7.

[76] *Amazing Grace* (Colorado Springs: Waterbrook Press, 2000), 238.

[77] Rick Warren, *The Purpose-Driven Life* (Grand Rapids: Zondervan, 2002), 287–88.

[78] Carlo De'Este, *Patton: A Genius for War* (N.Y.: Harper Perennial, 1996), 804.

[79] Vandebreggen, *Soon the War Is Ending*, 193.

[80] Lee Scarbrough, *A Search for Souls* (Nashville: Sunday School Board of the Southern Baptist Convention, 1925), 139–41.

[81] Max Lucado, *The Applause of Heaven* (Dallas: Word Publishing, 1990), 188–89.